JUNG AND MORENO

To many, Jung and Moreno seem to be on opposite sides in their theories and their practices of psychotherapy. Jung defines self as emerging inwardly in an intrapsychic process of individuation; Moreno defines self as enacted outwardly in psychosocial networks of relationships. *Jung and Moreno: Essays on the theatre of human nature* shows how Jung and Moreno can be creatively combined to understand better and facilitate therapeutic work.

Craig E. Stephenson and contributors write about how and why they put together Jung and Moreno. They describe and discuss psychodrama sessions grounded in the fundamentals of Jung's analytical psychology, as well as dream and fairy tale enactments and individual psychoanalytical sessions in which they employ psychodramatic techniques. The essays retheorize Jungian concepts of transference and complexes in the light of Moreno's insights. They reframe and deepen traditional psychodramatic techniques by securing them within Jung's archetypal context.

Jung and Moreno challenges our understanding of healing practices and the integration of spontaneous unconscious processes, bringing these two ground breaking practitioners to meet collaboratively in the theatre of human nature. The contributions are original and insightful arguments by nine important thinkers. This book will be of interest to psychotherapists, analytical psychologists, psychoanalysts, psychodrama practitioners, drama therapists and students.

Craig E. Stephenson is a Jungian analyst and psychodrama practitioner. He is a graduate of the C. G. Jung Institut Zürich, the Institut für Psychodrama auf der Grundlage der Jungschen Psychologie, Zumikon, and the Centre for Psychoanalytic Studies, University of Essex. His books include *Possession: Jung's Comparative Anatomy of the Psyche* (Routledge, 2009) and *Anteros: A Forgotten Myth* (Routledge, 2011).

Contributors: Ellynor Barz, Christopher Beach, Doreen Madden Elefthery, Mariolina Graziosi, John Hill, Emilija Kiehl, Barbara Helen Miller, Siri Ness, Wilma Scategni

JUNG AND MORENO

Essays on the theatre
of human nature

Edited by
Craig E. Stephenson

Саши и Маши,

с любовью,

мил мисзя

Лондон, септембар 2016

Routledge
Taylor & Francis Group

LONDON AND NEW YORK

First published 2014
by Routledge
27 Church Road, Hove, East Sussex BN3 2FA

Simultaneously published in the USA and Canada
by Routledge
711 Third Avenue, New York, NY 10017

*Routledge is an imprint of the Taylor & Francis Group, an
informa business*

British Library Cataloguing in Publication Data
A catalogue record for this book is available from the British
Library

Library of Congress Cataloging in Publication Data
Jung and Moreno : essays on the theatre of human nature /
edited by Craig E. Stephenson.
     pages cm
   Includes index.
   1. Psychotherapy.   2. Moreno, J. L. (Jacob Levy), 1889–
   1974.   3. Jung, C. G. (Carl Gustav), 1875–1961.
   I. Stephenson, Craig E., 1955—editor of compilation.
   RC480.J86 2013
   616.89'14—dc23   2012048809

ISBN: 978-0-415-69644-9 (hbk)
ISBN: 978-0-415-69645-6 (pbk)
ISBN: 978-0-203-79483-8 (ebk)

Typeset in Garamond
by RefineCatch Limited, Bungay, Suffolk, UK

MIX
Paper from
responsible sources
FSC   FSC® C013056
www.fsc.org

Printed and bound in Great Britain by
TJ International Ltd, Padstow, Cornwall

This book is dedicated to Dean Elefthery and Doreen Madden Elefthery, and to Helmut Barz and Ellynor Barz-Hoffmann.

CONTENTS

CONTENTS

ACKNOWLEDGEMENTS

First of all, thanks to the contributors for their enthusiasm and intelligence.

Thanks also to the analysands, psychodrama participants, dreamers and performers who gave permission for their personal material to be shared in these essays.

A special thank you to Lucie Pabel for translating Ellynor Barz's essay from the German and to Ellynor and Dr Ute Jarmer for responding generously under difficult circumstances to editorial queries.

Thanks to the Jungian psychodrama colleagues with whom I participated in sessions at the Institut für Psychodrama in Zumikon and, subsequently, to psychodrama training colleagues from the International Foundation for Human Relations, including Leata van Amesfoort, Merete Hansen, Lieven d'Hauwers, Dermot Kelly, Fons Koper, Pierre de Laat, Geir Nybo, Camilla Tamargo, Moira Verhofstadt, Hanne Weitjens and Bertil Wolff. Thanks also to psychodrama director Johannes Barz for his friendship.

Thanks to Pierre Fontaine, Pierre de Laat, Frits Van Hest and Leni Verhofstadt-Denève, organizers of the conference, 'Psychodrama, Studies and Applications: In Honour of Dean and Doreen Eleftery for their 40 years psychodrama training in Europe', May 2008, where I first lectured about Jung and Moreno, and to Chantal Nève-Hanquet, whom I met there, for her supportive interest in this book. Thanks to Tom Kelly for taking my paper on Jung and Moreno to The Fourth IAAP Conference on Analytical Psychology and Chinese Culture, at Fudan University, April 2009, when I was unable to attend. Thanks also to Pramila Bennett who meticulously edited for publication the version of that paper presented at the IAAP Congress, Montreal, August 2010.

Thanks to Doreen Madden Eleftery, Suzanne Eleftery, Ann Marie Eleftery and Angelico for their hospitality.

Thanks to Kate Hawes, Kirsten Buchanan and Kristin Susser at Routledge, and to Klara King and everyone who worked on the production of the book.

Image permission: Thanks to Marcel Bauer, Mayor of Sélestat and Laurent Naas, Head Librarian at la Bibliothèque Humaniste de Sélestat, for their generous permission to reproduce on the cover of this book an engraving from the library's special collections: 'Térence, *Comoedia*. Strasbourg: Johannes Grüninger, 1496. Bibliothèque Humaniste de Sélestat (F. – Bas-Rhin), K617, page de titre'.

Text permissions: Thanks to Terence Nemeth, Theater Communications Group, for permission to quote from *The Presence of the Actor* by Joseph Chaikin. Thanks to Jennifer Reis, Executive Director, and John Rasberry, Chairperson of the Library of the American Society for Group Psychotherapy and Psychodrama, for permission to quote from 'Motto' by J. L. Moreno. Excerpts from *Wild* by Ben Okri, published by Rider, reprinted by permission of The Random House Group Limited and by permission of The Marsh Agency Ltd on behalf of Ben Okri.

Finally, once again and even more so, thanks to Alberto.

CONTRIBUTORS

Ellynor Barz (†2012) was a Jungian analyst and psychodrama director. She studied pedagogy and theology in Hamburg and Tübingen. She was a training analyst, first at the C.G. Jung Institut Zürich in Küsnacht and later at the International School for Analytical Psychology (ISAP), Zürich. She was co-founder (with her husband Dr Helmut Barz) of the Institut für Psychodrama auf der Grundlage der Jungschen Psychologie, Zumikon. Her books include *Selbstbegegnung im Spiel: Einführung in das Psychodrama* (Kreuz Verlag, 1988) and *Gods and Planets: The Archetypes of Astrology* (Chiron, 1993).

Christopher Beach is a Jungian analyst who practises in Portland, Maine. He studied Jungian psychodrama with Helmut and Ellynor Barz while training to become an analyst. A graduate of the C.G. Jung Institute Zürich in Küsnacht, Chris works with both individuals and groups, serves on the IAAP Ethics Committee, and enjoys teaching courses on difficult ethical dilemmas, psychological type from a depth perspective, and dream work. When younger, he served first as a secondary school headmaster in Kenya and later as an assistant attorney general in Maine.

Doreen Madden Elefthery is a member of the American Board of Examiners in Psychodrama, Sociometry and Group Psychotherapy, and a Fellow of the American Society of Group Psychotherapy and Psychodrama. She is co-founder (with her husband Dr Dean Elefthery) of the International Foundation for Human Relations. She began her career as a member of the Irish National Theatre, Abbey Theatre, in Dublin, Ireland. After moving to the United States, she trained as a psychodramatist with J. L. Moreno at Beacon, New York. She has a degree in Theatre, with postgraduate studies in both Jungian Psychology and Spirituality. She resides in Miami, Florida, where she continues to work with groups.

Mariolina Graziosi is tenured Associate Professor of Sociology at the University of Milan, Italy. She earned her PhD in Sociology from the University of Wisconsin–Madison and her post-doctoral degree from the C.G. Jung Institute, Zürich. She is an author and editor of books, articles and essays in the field of sociology and psychoanalysis, the most recent including 'Sradicamento e ricerca di significato: Il dilemma dell'uomo contemporaneo' in 'L'individuo e la contemporaneità', edited by Mariolina Graziosi and 'Etty Hillesum: Individuation and the gift of bringing new meaning' (Harvest). She was a visiting scholar for several years at the University of Wisconsin and has offered lectures at the Jung Club of London. Her new book is entitled At the Roots of Morality (Liguori, forthcoming).

John Hill has practised as a Jungian analyst since 1973 and is a training analyst of ISAP Zürich. He received his degrees in philosophy in Dublin and the United States and is a graduate of the C.G. Jung Institute Zürich. He completed an intensive training programme in Psychodrama under Doreen Elefthery in 1990. He has written on Jung's Word Association Experiment, Celtic myth, James Joyce, dreams and Christian mysticism, and he is the author of At Home in the World: Sounds and Symmetries of Belonging (Spring Journal Books).

Emilija Kiehl is a Jungian analyst trained at the BAP in London. She received trainings in Psychodrama and Systemic Family Therapy and works with individual patients and couples. She has translated a number of books and articles and has contributed to cultural and informative publications of the former Yugoslavia with book reviews and interviews. She is the publications editor for the International Association for Analytical Psychology (IAAP) and the newly appointed book review section editor of Spring Journal. She works in private practice and at the St. Marylebone Healing and Counselling Centre in London.

Barbara Helen Miller, born in the United States, has had a varied career. She was the second solo cellist with the Radio Philharmonic Orchestra of the Netherlands for thirteen years. She returned to academia receiving her Master of Arts in Psychology of Religion. She received her PhD in Anthropology from Leiden University (the Netherlands) having authored Connecting and Correcting, A Case Study of Sami Healers in Porsanger (CNWS, 2007). A graduate of the C.G. Jung Institute Zürich (Küsnacht, Switzerland), she is in private practice. She works in co-operation with the Research Group Circumpolar Cultures, and is the author of a variety of publications.

Siri Ness is a graduate of the C.G. Jung Institute Zürich and is a training analyst at the International School of Analytical Psychology (ISAP) in Zürich. She has a private practice in Oslo, Norway. Previous to her training she was a freelance translator and reader of fiction for various publishing houses; the translator's 'ear' is still central to her work as an analyst, as is her life-long interest in stories, from myths to picture books. She has published articles on symbols and on symbolic understanding and gives seminars in Norway, Sweden and Switzerland.

Wilma Scategni is a psychiatrist and individual and group Jungian psycho-analyst (AGAP/CIPA/IAAP) in private practice in Turin, Italy. She is a founding member of the European Federation of Psychodrama Training Organizations (FEPTO), a staff member of the Granada Summer Academy, Andalusia (supported by IAGP and UNESCO), and has conducted group training in Austria, Bulgaria, Germany, Great Britain, Greece, Lithuania, Portugal, Romania, Spain, Switzerland and Argentina. She edits the journal *Anamorphosis* and has written many books and essays, including *Psychodrama, Group Processes and Dreams* (Brunner-Routledge, 2002).

Craig E. Stephenson is a Jungian analyst with touchstones in Canada and Europe. A Canadian by birth, he currently lives in France. He is a gradu-ate of the C.G. Jung Institut Zürich, the Institut für Psychodrama auf der Grundlage der Jungschen Psychologie, Zumikon, and the Centre for Psychoanalytic Studies, University of Essex. His books include *Possession: Jung's Comparative Anatomy of the Psyche* (Routledge, 2009), *Anteros: A Forgotten Myth* (Routledge, 2011), and a translation from the French of Luigi Aurigemma's *Jungian Perspectives* (University of Scranton Press, 2007). He contributed essays to *Psyche and the City* (Spring Journal Books, 2010), *Ancient Greece, Modern Psyche* (Spring Journal Books, 2011), and *How and Why We Still Read Jung* (Routledge, 2013). He has lectured for the Philemon Foundation at the Bodmer Foundation, Geneva, at the Warburg Institute, University of London, and at the Taiwan Institute of Psychotherapy, Taipei.

1

INTRODUCTION

Craig E. Stephenson

Whom do you see when you look at me?
Whom do you think you see when I look at you?
Who or what is it that you think cannot be seen by anyone – is
it still you? . . .
Would you say that there are parts of yourself which have not lived
yet?
What would bring forth the life of those parts?

'Questions of Character', from Joseph Chaikin,
The Presence of the Actor, 1987, pp. 16–17

On 3 March 1907, at Bergstrasse No. 19 in Vienna, Freud and Jung famously
met for the first time. The afternoon dinner conversation continued for
thirteen hours, well into the night. How that exchange ended six years later
with a curt typed postcard and subsequent silence is also common knowledge.
Since then, it has taken Freudian and Jungian thinkers and practitioners
almost a century to find effective ways to speak to each other about their
differences within the larger circumference of their shared assumptions and
values.

Perhaps less known is the only meeting of Freud and Moreno. It was in
a lecture hall in Vienna, five years after his encounter with Jung. After
delivering a lecture on dreams, Freud casually asked a young audience member
what he did. In his autobiography, Moreno reported himself as having
answered, 'You analyze people's dreams. I give them the courage to dream
again. You analyze and tear them apart. I let them act out their conflicting
roles and help them put the parts back together again' (Moreno 1985). Moreno
may have enjoyed telling this story in order to emphasize the extent to
which he regarded his work as opposing the Freudian bias in mid-twentieth-
century American psychotherapy, thereby compensating for the loss of
spontaneous creativity in the cultural conserves of Western psychologies
(see Feasey 2001).

Jung and Moreno never met. Certainly, their psychotherapeutic practices theoretically opposed each other in fundamental ways. Would they have found common ground on which to stand and speak to each other? For instance, what would Moreno have said about Jung's statement:

> the theatre is the place of unreal life; it is life in the form of images, a psychotherapeutic institute where complexes are staged; one can see there how these things work ... So in inviting him to the theatre, [one] invites him to the staging of his complexes – where all the images are symbols or unconscious representations of his own complexes.
>
> (Jung 1984, p. 12)

Or how would Jung have responded to Moreno's voiced conviction that he felt inspired, not by Freud's psychological materialism, nor by Marx's economic materialism and the technological advances of modern industrialism, but, rather, by the tenets of the world's great religions (Moreno 1947)? Would they have discussed the extent to which they both regarded the performativity of 'healing' in psychotherapeutic practices as inherently 'religious' in the etymological sense of the word, denoting, as it does in Latin, both 'bond' and 'reverence'? Jung defined his Eros principle as a psychological concept sitting on top of a human mystery which he could not fathom. Moreno employed the Greek word *'tele'* to define the connection 'coming as if from a distance' that binds human beings together, a fundamental and primary concern to which 'transference' bears only a faint resemblance.

But this is my editorial spirit wanting to jump to the promise implicit in the title of this book, to the cumulative force of the arguments in these essays. Better first to delineate some of the fundamental differences between Jung and Moreno and to hold that theoretical and practical opposition, before introducing the contributors who will be speaking creatively from that contradictory space.

Consider first the etymology of the word 'complex'. The word, in English, French and German, derives from the Latin *complexus*, meaning 'embrace' or 'sexual intercourse', and from *complecti*, meaning 'to entwine', made up of the prefix *com*, meaning 'together', and *plectere*, meaning 'to braid'.[1] In the natural and social sciences, the word 'complex' denotes a system composed of related parts that, coming together as a whole, manifest properties not evident in the individual parts themselves (see, for example, the work of the French philosopher Edgar Morin, *On Complexity*, 2008). In mathematics, a complex number consists of a real and an imaginary part, either of which can be zero. In psychology, complexes are organized groups of ideas and memories that exist, for the most part, outside awareness but that carry enormous affective power when activated. Here, embedded in the denotation of the word 'complex', is an image that surely interested Jung: something Other, which significantly entwines and alters the psychic system as a braided whole.

Freud regarded Jung's empirical investigations of complexes as an important experimental corroboration of his theoretical concept of the unconscious. But Freud increasingly shunned the term 'complex' after Jung and Adler placed complexes at the centre of their theories as natural phenomena. Orthodox Freudian psychoanalysis regards complexes, including Freud's Oedipus complex, as symptoms resulting from failed acts of repression, whereas Jung does not theorize complexes as synonymous with neurosis: in other words, for Jung, the experience of being 'complexed' may be painful, but it is not necessarily pathological. A feeling-toned complex is an image to which a highly charged affect is attached, and which is incompatible with the habitual attitude of the ego. Often attributable either to a trauma that splits off a fragment of the psyche or to a moral conflict in which it appears impossible to affirm the whole of one's being, a complex is a splinter psyche that behaves with a remarkable degree of autonomy and coherence, overriding will and blocking memory.

Jung argues that the technique of personifying provides a psychotherapeutic means by which the ego can free itself from being possessed by an unconscious complex. To 'personify' means 'to attribute a personal nature to an abstraction by giving it human shape', 'to embody an abstract quality', 'to provide a spirit with bodily form'. Jung observes that if, rather than simply suffering the complex's often difficult affect, we deliberately permit the complex to manifest spontaneously to our conscious awareness as a personified image, then we depotentiate its power over our ego consciousness and make interpretation possible. Going one step further, if we employ 'personifying a complex' as active imagination, we can consciously direct psychic energy towards incarnating an unconscious complex; we compensate for a possibly one-sided power position maintained by ego-consciousness and momentarily privilege an unconscious potentiality.

Personifying unconscious contents can provide an effective way to claim the personified aspect as one's own and, at the same time, to experience its autonomy and distinctness from ego consciousness. Personifying demands a dramatically engaged response to the unconscious as Other, in contrast to intellectualizing and conceptualizing it. As Jung explains, the more that possessing unconscious contents are lived and engaged with through personifying, the less intensely are they experienced as real (Jung 1929, para. 54–5). Splinter psyches are ontologically 'unreal', in the sense that they are not only disowned by the ego but often are disembodied, projected interpersonally onto an external Other. At the same time, ironically, unconscious complexes acquire an ontological status that is 'more real than real', since they insistently overwhelm ego consciousness with their reality and unseat the personality:

> The characteristic feature of a pathological reaction is, above all, identification with the archetype. This produces a sort of inflation

CRAIG E. STEPHENSON

and possession by the emergent contents, so that they pour out in a torrent which no therapy can stop. Identification can, in favourable cases, sometimes pass off as a more or less harmless inflation. But in all cases identification with the unconscious brings a weakening of consciousness, and herein lies the danger. You do not 'make' an identification, you do not 'identify yourself', but you experience your identity with the archetype in an unconscious way and so are possessed by it.

(Jung 1934, para. 621)

Becoming conscious is, then, synonymous with reversing this process, with making real and integrating as much as possible what has been rendered 'unreal' – in other words, with incarnating what Jung would express in personified form as 'disembodied spirit'. Jung employs his deliberately equivocal language of unconscious 'complexes', which he also calls 'spirits' or 'gods', in order to honour their ontological claim as unlived potentialities of the personality:

The essential thing is to differentiate oneself from these unconscious contents by personifying them, and at the same time to bring them into relationship with consciousness. That is the technique for stripping them of their power. It is not too difficult to personify them, as they always possess a certain degree of autonomy, a separate identity of their own. Their autonomy is a most uncomfortable thing to reconcile oneself to, and yet the very fact that the unconscious presents itself in that way gives us the best means of handling it.

(Jung 1962, p. 187)

In this way, Jung pictures complexes forcefully, kinetically pushing the individual psyche towards a more genuine entwining of its parts.

An important component in Jung's psychotherapeutic practice focuses on supporting the ego of the analysand up to the point that it can experience the autonomy of the unconscious complex and eventually reconcile itself to that psychic reality through a personified meeting. Andrew Samuels, Bani Shorter and Fred Plaut (1986) state this emphatically: 'A patient who cannot personify tends merely to personalize everything. Analysis can be seen as an exploration of the patient's relationship to his or her personifications' (p. 108).

By contrast, Moreno's psychotherapy addresses the psychosociological problem of the individual. According to Moreno, the self emerges through the roles one plays in relation to others, rather than the roles emerging from the self. In other words, Moreno locates the experience of selfhood in an external field of interpersonal relatedness. He draws maps and defines laws of social forces from the patterns that emerge when individuals interact spontaneously,

4

and he proposes a triad of psychotherapeutic practices – group psychotherapy, sociometry, and psychodrama – to address the loss of spontaneity in what should be a naturally ongoing emergence of self.

Moreno addresses the suffering of the individual self within problems of role. He evaluates the effectiveness of a particular role in terms of the degree of spontaneity and creativity operating in the interpersonal relation: 'Role-playing is an act, a spontaneous playing; role-taking is a finished product, a role conserve' (Moreno 1960, p. 84). So, for Moreno, 'role-taking' signifies confining oneself to a finished, fully conserved, scripted interaction that does not permit the individual any degree of spontaneity or creativity, while 'role-playing' permits some degree of both, and 'creating a role' permits them to the highest degree. When we are possessed by or trapped in a role conserve, we are no longer able to interact spontaneously and creatively within that role, and we suffer from a loss of self. Moreno sees that the continually emerging self is threatened when a role is so 'conserved' that it eliminates possibilities for spontaneous and creative interaction.

To interact spontaneously and creatively requires that we constantly confront the unknown in ourselves and in others. The notion of self as a finished, perfected product is a comforting illusion, which the cultural conserves of groups and societies reinforce:

> There is a shrewd motive in this procedure . . . because if only one
> stage of a creative process is a really good one, and all the others are
> bad, then this chosen stage substituting for the entire process can be
> memorized, conserved, eternalized, and can give comfort to the soul
> of the creator and order to the civilization of which he is a part.
>
> (Moreno 1934, p. 363)

Moreno introduces his three-dimensional practice of psychotherapy as an intervention that compensates for this inclination to create conserves by working to make accessible once more the spontaneity of the individual self and the spontaneity of the society within which individual selves locate their selfhood.

In the first of Moreno's three practices – group psychotherapy – individuals experience self in terms of their ability to participate spontaneously and creatively within a field of interpersonal relations. In the encounter with others, the individual learns to distinguish between experiences of projection and experiences of what Moreno calls '*tele*'. He differentiates between 'projection' (from the Latin meaning 'to throw in front of one') and '*tele*'. Projections throw in front of individuals a set of conserved roles, fixed vocabularies and familiar scripts, to which they are then confined. The effective practice of group psychotherapy provides a safe container within which the individual can witness and work to withdraw, as much as possible, these projections. But Moreno emphasizes that group psychotherapy should also provide experiences of role-play and of 'flow' between people as authentic here-and-now exchanges of attraction and repulsion. With his notion of *tele*, Moreno emphasizes an irrational non-verbal (as if 'from afar') processing of interpersonal relationships and the bonds which hold groups together:

> Group cohesiveness, reciprocity of relationships, communication, and shared experiences are functions of *tele*. *Tele* is the constant frame of reference for all forms and methods of psychotherapy . . . Neither transference nor empathy could explain in a satisfactory way the emergent cohesion of a social configuration.
>
> (Moreno 1960, p. 17)

Moreno emphasizes that the effective practice of group psychotherapy provides opportunities both for minimizing projections and optimizing the authentic communication of *tele*.

Moreno's second element – sociometry – maps and evaluates networks of existing and preferred relationships. Sociometry is a phenomenological study of an individual's or a group's interpersonal choices. The emerging self is momentarily observed in time and space as it manifests in all its roles. Group psychotherapists also employ sociometry in order to track psychological mechanisms such as scapegoating within the group dynamic. They chart the group's need to reinforce cohesion by creating a star and expelling an isolate. At the same time, they anticipate which individuals have in their repertoire of roles a collusive desire to carry the conserved role of scapegoat for the group. In the case of scapegoating, Moreno would argue that the effective practice of group psychotherapy depends on the capacity to measure the collective desire to isolate an individual member of the group as this sparks, and to re-integrate potential isolates back into the natural cohesiveness of the *tele* of the group. Sociometry is used to try to ensure that no individual fuses with the role of sacrificial Other, and that no group succeeds in banishing its own integral Otherness from its midst.

Moreno's third component is the most familiar: psychodrama, in which all the guided mimetic activities are used to examine problems, to explore new role possibilities and to revitalize stale role-conserves. Psychodrama is ritualistic in the sense that psychodrama sessions are highly structured, moving through clearly demarcated phases both in time and space. It begins by identifying an individual as protagonist in whose service the group agrees to work, and then moves into a phase of incarnating the protagonist's problem through dramatic action. It ends with observation and shared reflection, hoping to make possible a synthesis of the spontaneous insights experienced verbally and non-verbally during the action phase.

One important psychodrama tool is mirroring. In the most basic terms, mirroring entails a protagonist who enacts a moment. He or she then chooses someone from the group to play himself or herself, to re-enact the same

6

moment as precisely as possible, while he or she steps out of the action in order to observe it. For Moreno, the elements of both enacting and observing are crucial for the possibility of psychotherapeutic synthesis. Individual insight resides potentially in the spontaneity and creativity of psychodramatic action, but the structure of a psychodrama session ritualistically contains the participants as they each move back and forth between acting and observing, between insight in action and insight in reflection.

Because he locates the self externally, Moreno is critical of Jung for defining the self in terms of the individual psyche. He considers Jung's concept of the collective unconscious flawed, as leaping from a personal context to a universal context without sufficiently taking into account the psychology of groups and the positive phenomenon of *tele* (Moreno 1960, pp. 116–17). In Moreno's psychotherapeutic practice, the individual self re-emerges within the paradox of acting and observing. This paradoxical play heals the individual who suffers from being trapped in a petrified role conserve, and it also challenges power-motivated cultural conserves with the spontaneity and the genuine social cohesiveness of *tele*.

For Moreno, projecting a power-driven role conserve causes a loss of self: 'What conserved creativity truly represents, at best, is power, a means of expressing superiority when actual superiority has ceased to be available' (Moreno 1960, p. 13). A role conserve skews negatively any new encounter by throwing in front of it the old story. Likewise, it skews negatively any analysis. The psychodramatic action of mirroring provides an opening and an insight: by stepping into and out of roles, the protagonist experiences in a spontaneous creative moment the possibility that someone is looking at him differently and wanting to speak from another place, with another vocabulary. He intuits in spontaneous creative action the possibility that he can access a wider repertoire of roles and narratives.

For Jung, a possessed ego suffers in a fused state with autonomous unconscious contents, and selfhood is unseated. A complex occupies tyrannically the seat of the self. At the same time, whenever the archetype at the core of the complex is constellated, Jung would say that it 'suffers' from the ego's wilful resistance to change, almost as if a defended ego preferred the predictability of a world filtered through the complex rather than opening up to the unknown in the psyche and in the world. When the analysand personifies the complex, narrates dreams, and reflects on the transference, then the ego defences diminish, opening up to the possibility of re-imagining the analysis as an intrapsychic dialogue. The analysand can then personify rather than personalize.

It might seem misleading to insist on the similarities between these two theoretical frameworks. Moreno sees his psychosociological theory as critiquing psychodynamic concepts such as Jung's, which locate individual selfhood intrapsychically. For his part, Jung privileges the intrapsychic over the interpersonal. He argues that what is not integrated intrapsychically is only then experienced externally as fate. And Jung suggests that 'group therapy is only capable of educating the *social* human being' (Jung 1973, p. 219; see also Boyd 1991). For Jung, 'group therapy' addresses only the problems of the 'persona' as a social role within which an individual self meets an external Other.

Moreno and Jung may be mapping a similar problematic, but each does so on his own exclusive terms, from the opposing perspectives of the extravert and introvert, Moreno privileging an interpersonal map of the self, Jung an intrapsychic one. For example, they both write about projection, but either from outside or from inside. Moreno sees projection as creating obstacles for the spontaneity of genuine *tele* between people; Jung sees projection as avoiding an intrapsychic encounter with an unconscious Other by throwing it outside the ego's role definition of 'that which I am' and then experiencing it outside in someone who is definitely 'not like me'. At the same time, Jung regards projection as a natural psychological process, in which we project outwards the unconscious as Other in order to meet it and integrate it on a more human scale back into consciousness:

> Now when one is possessed by the unconscious to a certain extent, he has of course a very difficult time in dealing with it, so as a rule people simply cannot do it alone. One cannot isolate oneself on a high mountain and deal with the unconscious; one always needs a strong link with humanity, a human relation that will hold one down to one's human reality. Therefore, most people can only realize the unconscious inasmuch as they are in analysis, inasmuch as they have a relation to a human being who has a certain amount of understanding and tries to keep the individual down to the human size, for no sooner does one touch the unconscious that one loses one's size.
>
> (Jung 1998, p. 331)

In other words, for Jung, an unconscious content is too large, too collective, too archetypal, and it is only when we meet it in a human encounter face to face that we can take in its reality, its meaning and its purpose. Perhaps here would have been the seed-moment of a dialogue between Jung and Moreno: in the notion of the therapeutic value of mimesis, in the possibility for inner transformation, actively imagining and embodying the otherness of the Self found in a 'You'.

But even if there exists no historical meeting between Jung and Moreno to recount, there is the subsequent history of the people who have sat in the tension between their two methods and who have worked in that place, finding new essential insights. The essays in this book contribute, I believe, to the telling of that history. The opening essay is by Doreen Madden Elefthery who, with her husband Dean Elefthery, trained with Moreno in New York. In the early 1960s, they brought Moreno's work from the United States to Europe. The Eleftherys emphasized Moreno's psychotherapeutic triad of interventions. Their way of working was informed by and grounded both in Doreen Elefthery's experiences as a Dublin Abbey Theatre actress and Dean Elefthery's training as a psychiatrist. In her essay, Doreen Elefthery writes from the perspective of her professional experience as a stage actress, explaining how it helps her to differentiate theatre from therapy – a differentiation often overlooked by psychodrama practitioners, to the detriment of their work. Doreen Elefthery describes how actors work to create catharsis in the theatre audience, and how Moreno worked to facilitate not only catharsis but insight in psychodramatic action, and how she often works to contain defensive 'acting out' and create moments for 'acting in', employing drama as both a mode of inquiry and a practice of restraint.

With regard to this notion of restraint in the context of Moreno's psychotherapeutic triad, Dean Elefthery insisted that psychodrama should be understood and employed as an *extension* of group psychotherapy rather than as a practice in itself. In some contemporary psychodramatic groups, dramatic action can take precedence over group psychotherapy and sociometry to the extent that not to perform psychodrama within a session means failure to meet the criteria of the group (Kate Bradshaw-Tauvon 1998, p. 293). Dean Elefthery emphasized that moving from group psychotherapy to the spontaneous and potentially volatile action phase of a psychodramatic session is justifiable only in terms of the need of an individual who functions as protagonist and never in terms of the director's or the group's needs. For this reason, he employed sociometry to assess the group dynamic in psychodrama – for example, measuring the degree to which a director or a group is inclined, often unawares, to produce a protagonist and a psychodrama in order to avoid individual and collective processing of the attractions, repulsions, and conflicts engendered within the group itself. Doreen Elefthery uses sociometry precisely in this way: to evaluate the extent to which the group dynamic has been sufficiently processed, to ascertain that the spontaneity and creativity of the group have been made available to serve a protagonist rather than to satisfy the group's need to cohere – to say nothing of the therapist's needs manifested in the countertransference. If the unconscious group dynamic or the therapist's needs predominate, then it is not safe to do psychodrama. The Eleftherys emphasized this so much in their training sessions that it has come to be considered *their* method; but the point they made is that it was Moreno's, and that two essential components of his psychotherapeutic triad are often being left out and ought not to be left out (see Elefthery and Elefthery 1966; Moreno and Elefthery 1975).

Jungian analysts Helmut Barz (see Barz 1990) and Ellynor Barz (see Barz 1988) studied with the Eleftherys and eventually created their own Institute for Psychodrama grounded in the principles of Jungian psychology, in Zumikon, Switzerland. Ellynor Barz's essay in this book describes in detail how they worked to situate Moreno's psychodramatic techniques in a Jungian framework. For example, she explains their rationale for following the Eleftherys' example of employing, for a psychodramatic session, not one but two facilitators or directors: one as director of the session, its symbols and its frame, and the other as psychotherapeutic companion to the protagonist. For the Barzs, the director of the session carries the symbolic manifestations of the Self both for the protagonist and the group, while the second director accompanies the protagonist and the group members so that insights constellated in the action can be incorporated into ego consciousness through reflecting and sharing. From their Jungian perspective, psychodrama as a psychotherapeutic practice must support the protagonist's ego in the encounter with the Other so that it can endure the truth about itself while making space for that very Otherness. At the same time, the work must support all the group members (who are, psychologically speaking, all protagonists during the session) as they acquire the agility and spontaneity to enter into play in support of a process in which the protagonist, the group and the Self are all engaged together.

The essay by Jungian analyst Christopher Beach recounts and examines with great precision and acuity a single psychodramatic session conducted by Helmut and Ellynor Barz in which a participant named 'George' asks to investigate his early childhood asthma attacks. Jungian analyst Siri Ness's essay offers a longer-term perspective, describing with candour and overarching insight her participation in an on-going group with the Barzs and her own psychological process in response to a series of psychodrama sessions. Beach and Ness bear witness to the skilfulness and passion with which the Barzs worked in their psychodramatic sessions to make space for movement in what appeared to be closed conserves, and for spontaneous manifestations of archetypal energies in what seemed to be stereotypic dilemmas. Their essays also demonstrate their own very distinctive and strong ways of working analytically, creatively combining insights from both psychodramatic and Jungian perspectives.

For many Jungians, the invitation to enact a dream might seem objection-able, rendering an inner process public and subject to psychic infection from without. Dreams are considered a private theatre, and, no doubt, a private consultation with an analyst is the ideal setting in which to attempt to re-enter that psychic space. At the same time, for Jungian analyst and psychodramatist Wilma Scategni, to enact a dream in a psychodrama session is to honour the archetypes, to incarnate their energies in a ritualized psychological container and, by embodying them, render them more real ontologically (precisely in the way Jung describes in the passage quoted earlier). Much has been written about the importance of the analytic frame: weekly sessions at the same time, objects in the therapist's office that anchor the analysand in constancy, the familiar repetition of opening greetings and closing gestures – all these help to create a safe environment in which to confront difficult emotions and questions (Gray 1994). In the same way, Moreno deliberately structured psychodramatic sessions to function ritualistically to support the participants as they move in and out of the psychodramatic space, from the initial warming up to the entry into the action phase, to the exit towards the different layers of sharing, and finally to the return to the here and now. Scategni has recorded and analysed hundreds of dreams in which psychodrama group members dream about the group itself and bring these to enhance further the group's ritual process, the dreams functioning sociometrically to define the personality of a particular group and the correspondences and differences between individuals' themes and those of the group. In her essay, Scategni describes the challenges and therapeutic possibilities in enacting, in particular, dreams, emphasizing the special care with which a director and a group can create a container to hold the work responsibly so that insights during the dream enactment can be integrated and the unfathomable aspects of the dream, as evidence of the Otherness of the psyche, can remain protected.

Similarly, in his essay Jungian analyst John Hill describes his work with groups enacting fairy tales. Hill carefully outlines his rationale and his method, emphasizing in particular the therapeutic potentialities of inviting protagonists to step in and out of archetypal narratives. Fairy tale enactments provide participants with a dense living vocabulary of symbols with which to better differentiate their experiences. From a Jungian perspective, in choosing a tale, a group investigates and enacts a particular collective problem, as well as the spontaneous attempt by both a specific culture and the objective psyche to ameliorate and amend the situation. From a psychodramatic perspective, participants experience the subtle difference between role-taking, role-playing and creating a role, between the moments when a fairy tale confines them within a role conserve and other moments when the narrative liberates them with an equivocal symbol.

In his second essay for this book, Beach extrapolates from Jungian psychodrama sessions to explain how he has used Moreno's techniques in one-to-one psychotherapeutic work. Beach recounts a few brief moments in a specific case when, after inviting his analysand to move out of the analytical chair and to 'double' from behind a psychodramatic chair, the quality of the analysis shifted remarkably. Beach characterizes these moments as volatile and difficult, but his essay attests to their value and draws inferences that he has carried forward into his work as analyst.

Beach's chapter emphasizes the potential risks for therapy when the Jungian psychodramatic technique of personifying complexes is practised without the therapist keeping in mind the danger for power to be acted out in the transference and countertransference. Jung argues that psychotherapeutic healing depends on the care with which the therapist considers all the implications of the religious function when the Otherness of the unconscious manifests in the *temenos* of the therapeutic encounter. At many points in these practices, the therapeutic process can slip back negatively into unconsciousness. When this happens, then Moreno's *tele* or Jung's Eros or relatedness

11

slips into power. In this regard, Jungian analyst Mariolina Graziosi takes up the difficult task of comparing the theoretical concepts of transference in Freud, Jung and Moreno. First she contrasts Freud's concept of transference with Jung's, then she presents an intriguing affinity between Jung's under-standing of transference as a shared psychological process imaged in medieval alchemy, and Moreno's concept of *tele*.

Jungian analyst, anthropologist and cellist Barbara Helen Miller describes how in musical performances she employs Jung's active imagination and Moreno's principles of spontaneity and creativity in order to play with more integrity. Based on her experiences playing cello, Miller conducted before an audience two workshop experiments with members of the Shanghai Conservatory during the Fourth International Conference of Analytical Psychology and Chinese Culture at Fudan University in 2009. In her daringly original discussion, she explores anthropological literature on the performativity of healing, early infant–mother observations on attunement, and theories of entrainment, in order to unlock the implications of what she herself and the Shanghai musicians experienced when, rather than suffering a failure to concentrate because consciousness is interrupted by a complex, they allowed a space for it in their music-making.

Active imagination and psychodrama can tip into placing the unconscious element in service of ego development or a regressive restoration of the persona, or they can degenerate into the acting-out of shadow aspects of the personality with no possibility for moral reflection. Jung describes the images and affects associated with a complex as clustering around an archetype that is both ambiguous and numinous, so that the archetypal aspect of a constellated complex may cause the analytical container to feel tinged with numinosity, power and fear. The predicament and the paradox that active imagination and psychodrama present can resemble psychosis. Therapists like Beach and Miller describe moments when they employ a psychodramatic technique or use active imagination, and grapple with the ontological paradox of allowing analysands both to act and to feel themselves being acted upon; for precisely this reason, they exercise caution. Nevertheless, they do take up consciously the natural braiding or entwining quality of the complex and use that quality in support of the self's inclusiveness.

In the final chapter, playful in tone but profound in the breadth of its references, Jungian analyst Emilija Kiehl traces a life-path from Belgrade to London and beyond, in which her early interests in Jungian psychology and Moreno's Theatre of Spontaneity constantly meet in ways that continue to delight, challenge and surprise her. Kiehl's essay mentions, in passing, a moment of reunion when she attended a lecture I gave about Jung and Moreno at the 2010 IAAP congress in Montreal. Kiehl's essay fittingly closes this collection because it was that occasion of honouring the work of the Eleftherys and the Barzs and re-connecting with her and so many Jungians who know and use Moreno's work that sparked the inspiration for this collection of essays.

12

This book takes its title from *Theatrum Vitae Humanae* [The Theatre of Human Nature], published in 1596 by the artist Theodore de Bry, who accompanied a series of his engravings with poems and prose commentaries by Jean Jacques Boissard. Our book's cover image is taken from an even earlier publication, an edition of Terence's *Comedies*, printed in Strasbourg in 1496 by Jean Grüninger (now in the Humanist Library at Sélestat, France). In her classical study, *The Theatre of Memory*, Frances Yates (1966) links the images in de Bry's book to Jaques's speech, 'All the world's a stage', in Shakespeare's *As You Like It*. That play was first performed at the Globe Theatre, whose motto was also *'Totus mundus agit histrionem'* (see Joy Hancox 1992, pp. 106–7). According to Yates, from the ancient Greeks and Romans to the Renaissance, the art and science – that is to say, the psychology – of constructing memory as a defining feature of personal and cultural identity was linked imagistically to the architecture of theatre: emphatically, I repeat, art and science as one practice (in this regard, see Jungian analyst Mark Saban on theatre and psyche, 2005).

Of course, collective notions of what is art and what is science shift constantly. In our time, Moreno's word 'psychodrama' has become degraded in current usage to denote subjective 'histrionics'. The same bias in the English vernacular hears, more often than not, the word 'theatricality' in its negative connotation, meaning false or exaggerated emotions expressed in a calculated fashion. For similar reasons, the word 'hysteria' has been dropped from contemporary psychopathology's vocabulary, since psychiatry associates hysterics with passive–aggressive malingering and now positions hysteria in both its dissociative and somatoform disorders. Working to recuperate the complexity of the word 'hysteria', psychiatrist and Jungian analyst Neil Micklem (1996) traces it back etymologically to the Greek notion of the womb that walks about in the bodies of women and men, and he defines hysteria phenomenologically as 'theatricality without play'. Both Jung and Moreno would immediately appreciate Micklem's notion that one can be trapped unconsciously in theatricality, possessed at it were by mimetics and yet not able to move spontaneously and creatively.

When the training of psychotherapists falls under the increasingly powerful rubric of psychiatry and clinical psychology, in universities whose research programs are funded externally and thereby often compromised (privileging cost-effective drug treatments and short-term psychotherapeutic practices), there is very little talk about elevating the quality of training to a place outside objectivity versus subjectivity. How many psychotherapists-in-training find themselves falling victim to the multiple amputations of a role conserve in order to gain licensure? (This is to say nothing of the many patients who find themselves seduced by insurance payment schemes to conform to the definitions of the American Psychiatric Association's DSM in order to gain access to a therapist.) In this regard, in his important book, *The Drama of Everyday Life*, Karl Scheibe describes a course that he taught over thirty times

13

in the Psychology Department at Wesleyan University, entitled 'The Dramaturgical Approach to Psychology' (Scheibe 2000). Scheibe writes that innovative courses such as his disappear because they pose too much of a challenge to academic convention, even though the best discoveries often are made in these places at the borders of disciplines (Scheibe, personal communication, 1 July 2012). D. W. Winnicott may have positioned 'play' at the centre of twentieth-century psychoanalytic theorizing, but current psychotherapeutic practice recuperates and transposes 'playing' into the banker's mode of 'performing profitably' or the sports coach's goal of 'performing optimally'. A new generation of analysts and analysands, therapists and clients are going to have to contradict current trends in order to find their way out of such zones (see Pines 1979).

Hence, framing this collection of essays with this particular title and with this particular cover-image is a political as well as an aesthetic decision. Thanks to the stereotypes and clichés that psychically infect our contemporary cultures, we are steeped in 'theatricality without play', even if the old diagnostic word to describe it has fallen from favour. The point is that, behind all these phenomena of 'theatricality', still resides the multifaceted ambiguous living archetype of the theatre, with its architecture of memory and liminality, in which are housed the epistemological opposites of acting and observing, of knowing ourselves from within and knowing our world by looking without. For this reason, this book is dedicated to the Eleftherys and the Barzs, who, like Jung and Moreno themselves, have compensated for the one-sidedness of Western psychologies by positioning themselves in the epistemological chasm between these two ways of knowing – and deliberately playing there.

Moreno and Jung mirror and personify the Other and incorporate aspects of this experience within the *temenos* into the dynamics of selfhood. Clearly, Moreno's definition of self residing in interpersonal roles opposes Jung's intrapsychic model of self. But the rich legacy of their work, as described in this book, challenges us to recognize to what extent Jung's and Moreno's practices of psychotherapy are not so much contradictory as complementary – that is to say, creatively oppositional. The writers of these essays ask us to give priority in our psychotherapeutic work to preparing over and over again the *temenos*, in which we then map out how the analysand's interpersonal self emerges in roles, record how the analysand's intrapsychic self emerges in symbols, and work to minimize the transferential projections in service of genuine *tele* and Eros. And then they ask us for more: to reserve a space for something that we cannot control, that we cannot force, so that the analytical encounter becomes itself a personifying and a mirroring of the mystery in the patient and in ourselves: acting and observing, embodying and reflecting the emerging self and its Otherness.

Note

1 All definitions are taken from *The Concise Oxford Dictionary of Current English* (Fowler, Fowler and Thompson 1995).

References

Barz, E. (1988) *Selbstbegegnung im Spiel: Einführung in das Psychodrama*, Zurich: Kreuz Verlag.

Barz, H. (1990) 'Dream and Psychodrama', in R. Papadopoulos (ed.), *Carl Gustav Jung: Critical Assessments*, London: Routledge, 3, pp. 425–40.

Boyd, R. (1991) *Personal Transformation in Small Groups: A Jungian Perspective*, London: Routledge.

Bradshaw-Tauvon, K. (1998) 'Principles of Psychodrama', in M. Karp et al. (eds), *The Handbook of Psychodrama*, London: Routledge, pp. 29–46.

Chaikin, J. (1987) *The Presence of the Actor: Notes on the Open Theatre, Disguises, Acting and Repression*, New York: Atheneum/Theater Communications Group, 1993.

Elefthery, D. and Elefthery, D. Madden (1966) 'Our Psychodrama Demonstration in the Permanent Theater of Psychodrama', *Group Psychotherapy*, 19, pp. 17–21.

Feasey, D. (2001) *Good Practice in Psychodrama: An Analytic Perspective*. London: Wiley.

Fowler, H. W., Fowler, F. G. and Thompson, D. (1995) *The Concise Oxford Dictionary of Current English*, Oxford: Oxford University Press.

Gray, A. (1994) *An Introduction to the Therapeutic Frame*, London: Routledge.

Hancox, J. (1992) *The Byrom Collection: Renaissance Thought, the Royal Society and the Building of the Globe Theatre*, London: Jonathan Cape.

Jung, C. G. (1929) 'Commentary on The Secret of the Golden Flower', in *Alchemical Studies, Collected Works 13*, Princeton, NJ: Princeton University Press, 1967, pp. 1–56.

Jung, C. G. (1934) 'A Study in the Process of Individuation', in *The Archetypes and the Collective Unconscious, Collected Works 9i*, Princeton, NJ: Princeton University Press, 1959, pp. 290–354.

Jung, C. G. (1962) *Memories, Dreams, Reflections*, New York: Random House.

Jung, C. G. (1973) *Letters, Volumes 1 & 2*, Princeton, NJ: Princeton University Press.

Jung, C. G. (1984) *Dream Analysis: Notes of the Seminar Given in 1928–1930*, Princeton, NJ: Princeton University Press.

Jung, C. G. (1998) *Seminar on Nietzsche's Zarathustra*, ed. J. Jarrett, Princeton, NJ: Princeton University Press.

Micklem, N. (1996) *The Nature of Hysteria*, London: Routledge.

Moreno, J. L. (1934) *Who Shall Survive? A New Approach to the Problem of Human Interrelations*, Washington, DC: Nervous and Mental Disease Publishing.

Moreno, J. L. (1947) *The Future of Man's World*, Psychodrama Monographs, New York: Beacon House.

Moreno, J. L. (1960) *The Sociometry Reader*, Glencoe, IL: Free Press.

Moreno, J. L. (1985) *The Autobiography of J. L. Moreno, M.D.* (abridged), Moreno Archives, Cambridge, MA: Harvard University.

Moreno, J. L. and Elefthery, D. G. (1975) 'An Introduction to Group Psychodrama', in *Basic Approaches to Group Psychotherapy and Group Counseling*, ed. G. Gazda, Springfield, IL: Charles C Thomas.

Morin, E. (2008) *On Complexity*, Denver, CO: Hampden Press.

Pines, M. (1979) 'Group Psychotherapy: Frame of Reference for Training', Paper given at the International Congress for Medical Psychotherapy, Amsterdam, August.

Saban, M. (2005) 'Theatre and Psyche', *Harvest*, 51, 1.

Samuels, A., Shorter, B. and Plaut, F. (1986) *A Critical Dictionary of Jungian Analysis*, London: Routledge and Kegan Paul.

Scheibe, K. (2000) *The Drama of Everyday Life*, Cambridge, MA: Harvard University Press.

Yates, F. (1966) *The Art of Memory*, London: Penguin.

2

THEATRE OR THERAPY
A historical account

Doreen Madden Elefthery

There is a lot of confusion about psychodrama, about how it should be used, where it belongs in therapy – if, as some say, it belongs at all. This is not surprising because, when we look at the history of psychodrama, we see that it started in the legitimate theatre and emerged from its theatrical setting, and that there are historically many different types of psychodrama. No wonder the confusion.

The German philosopher Gottfried Wilhelm Leibniz said that everything exists, not primarily for the sake of things, not as an instrument for the ulterior good, but because its essence, like every essence, has its own underivative right to exist.

We play many roles in our lives. The role of the actor is symbolic of the human search for self and for freedom of expression. The actor has come full circle, from being an instrument in classical Greek theatre, to being the voice of the playwright, and then to being the voice itself in twentieth-century experiments such as Grotowski's in Poland or the Eugenio Barba Theatre in Copenhagen. In our time, actors, performing their art and in communion with fellow human beings, can finally, as Leibniz said, exist not primarily for the sake of other things, not as an instrument but because of their own right to exist. The right to be, and not as an object of need. There has been such a great change in the theatre in the last twenty years, a breaking down of conserve, a fragmenting of the role of the audience in experimental theatre.

Therapy has also changed drastically. We see, in some areas of psychodrama, for instance, that there is little concern for the protagonist and, often, even less for the group. The criterion of 'keeping the audience involved' takes precedence in sessions led by unskilled or unqualified psychodrama directors or therapists, in the same way that, in theatres, unskilled directors do not respect the integrity of the actor, to say nothing of their disrespect for the audience.

I recall J. L. Moreno and his search for his own spontaneity, and how he once suggested a topic for a lecture: 'Why not talk about teaching psychodrama to actors?' I could hear the two possibilities in his question: to teach actors in their 'lives in the theatre' to be free in their roles and also aware of them, and to teach people in the 'theatre of life', people who are locked and frozen in fixed roles, to discover the excitement of being.

We live with fixed perceptions of ourselves and of the significant others in our lives. Moreno, in his search for his own spontaneity, for his depth, for the source of his creativity and for his reason to exist, discovered psychodrama, sociometry and group psychotherapy.

I was introduced to Moreno's work before I met him personally in New York. I encountered him first when I was an actress at the Irish National Theatre at the Abbey Theatre in Dublin and read his book, *The Theatre of Spontaneity*. Some of my fellow actors and I questioned what this psychiatrist was doing with patients and theatre. My second encounter was in New York. It was then I asked Moreno, 'Doctor, do you disagree with Stanislavsky?' Moreno replied, 'Yes, he works from the outside. I work with feelings, from the inside. Stanislavksy would say, "Bend your leg and be old". I say, "Feel like an old man, feel the age, feel how you are, and your legs will bend by themselves." Stanislavsky is concerned with "as if", I am concerned with "is".' The Abbey Theatre, where I trained as an actress, worked with natural character building from within, so we had this first moment of sharing. I was struck by Moreno's magnetic personality, his extremely sensitive self, his softness and humour in the midst of great histrionic behaviour, his extreme vulnerability, and his keen interest in all aspects of life and literature. Indeed, there is a question as to whether he discovered his techniques for psychodrama before or after his discovery of literature: 'role reversal' from Plato's Socrates, 'mirroring' from Shakespeare's Hamlet, 'doubling' from Dostoyevsky's Yakov Petrovich Golyadkin in *The Double*. However, it is what he did with these techniques that matters most.

Later, I trained with Moreno as a psychodramatist and saw him work with patients in Beacon, New York. I saw for myself his concern for his patients. I saw the poet and the theatre director at work, but I especially saw the psychiatrist who, through the use of his psychodramatic techniques, employed psychodrama as a therapy of restraint. I understood why he left behind the Theatre of Spontaneity and entered the therapeutic theatre of psychodrama and group psychotherapy, where the insights emerge in the framed action, in the contained 'doing'. He discovered the therapeutic value of role playing, the excitement of sociometry, and the power of role reversal to change a life. Even later, as a psychotherapist, I agreed with my husband, Dr Dean Elefthery, a psychiatrist, who valued psychodrama as intervention in the therapeutic process but emphasized that the 'doing' is not as important as the 'reason for doing' – or, perhaps even, the 'reason for not doing'.

The idea of catharsis, coming from the Greek word '*katharein*', to cleanse, has had a long and controversial history. This includes the moral, ethical, religious and aesthetic interpretations of catharsis since the Renaissance to the psychological 'cathartic therapy' of Freud and Breuer in the 1890s (Brunius 1968). All of these Moreno worked to synthesize into his psychodramatic concept of catharsis. In early Greek religion, the catharsis was localized in the actor or 'doer', in the individual participating in the mystery cults at Delphi and Eleusis. The process of religious purification and realization took place in this subject, in the living person who was seeking an active catharsis. The medical concept of catharsis linked this religious notion of the spiritual purification of sins with the purging of disease. So, in the story of Oedipus, an unacknowledged sin causes a plague that infects the citizens of Thebes. Both Hippocratic medical practice and Asclepian therapy connected religious and medical concepts of catharsis. In *Ion*, Plato described how distress in the Homeric hero produces distress in the storyteller and may produce the same distress in the audience. In *Poetics*, Aristotle took this further, maintaining that tragedy excites not only pity and fear but also a cleansing in the audience. The active process of a symbolic person realizing a role on the Attic stage produced a passive catharsis in the audience, structured in such a way that the social conserve was maintained. (Much later, John Milton, in his 1671 preface to *Samson Agonistes*, described this effect as *'similia similibus curantur'*: the pain of the hero of the tragedy will purge you from pain.)

The Greek theatre was a contained means of expression and political growth for the masses. The Greek tragedy had a formal division: the prologue, an introductory monologue or dialogue; the *parados*, the entrance and first recitation of the chorus; the *episodes*, dramatic scenes performed by the actors, similar to our dramatic units of scenes or acts; the *stasimon*, a choral ode, written in intricate metres without rhyme, between the episodes or scenes. The tragedy closed, as a rule, with the chorus's finale, called the *exodus*; occasionally the *stasimon* would be replaced by a song, a *kommos*, sung by an actor alone or with the chorus. This last element functioned to provide closure for the audience. We deduce this because, the exception proving the rule, the Greek playwright Phrynichus was fined 1,000 drachmas because his play *The Capture of Miletus* left the audience in tears after Phrynichus showed the Athenians how they had failed to help an ally under attack by the Persians.

When I say Moreno synthesized the concept of catharsis, I mean that he structured the third phase of a psychodrama, the 'sharing', so that it provides many levels of closure. In this third section of a psychodrama, the protagonist (the one who emerged from the group and enacted some element of her life-space) and the 'observer–participants' (the group members) reverse roles. The protagonist becomes a 'participant–observer', that is to say, a group member, and the group members become protagonists, free to share (or not) with the protagonist and the group as a whole those aspects of their own life space that were awakened by the work of the protagonist. The protagonist has now been reintegrated into the group, and the group has made a shift. In my opinion this sharing is the most valuable part of the psychodrama. And no one is fined 1,000 drachmas!

Moreno was born in Bucharest in 1889. As a medical student and then a young psychiatrist in Vienna, he struggled with his ideas of God, self, and freedom. He felt gripped by an *idée fixe* which became the constant source of his productivity and which resonates very much with Jung: 'There is a sort of primordial nature, which is immortal and returns afresh with every generation, a first universe, which contains all beings and in which all events are sacred. Nothing was further from my mind than the stage and its trappings' (Moreno 1947). However, in this struggle of ideas, he took up an unusual approach, employing theatre as a method of inquiry, in what he called the Theatre of Spontaneity – and here psychodrama was born. Moreno wanted to bring back the self to the consciousness of mankind, to revive the spontaneous element of 'being' in human beings. In order to do this, he decided first to develop the spontaneous element in himself and then give it to others. In order to avoid the stares of men and the slur of madness, Moreno went into the theatre, the professional and conservative theatre, to explore this possibility. In this, he was not unlike Jung who, at the time, was taking up active imagination and the inner theatre as the way to the Self.

Moreno felt that theatre had moved far away from its basic therapeutic potential, so he constructed a stage for the new theatre of his vision that would give back to humans a dramatic 'religion'. The stage would be placed in the centre, rather than on the periphery. It would be round. It was neither the classical Greek theatre, nor was it Shakespeare's theatre. The model came to Moreno as he sat in the park in Vienna observing children, and as he dreamed of a newly spontaneous and creative world that was full of living people, not isolated individuals devoid of original thought.

The Theatre of Spontaneity had two periods: a spontaneity theatre for children in 1911, and a theatre for adults, the 'Stegreiftheater', in the Maysedergasse near the Vienna Opera House, from 1922 to 1925. But the Theatre of Spontaneity ran into difficulties. In the first case, the audience, who were used to the spontaneous conserve of the legitimate theatre, could not accept real spontaneity from the children with whom Moreno worked. Either they believed the children had been rehearsed, or, if the children were weak in spontaneity, they jumped to the conclusion that as theatre it did not work. In the second case, in the adult theatre, the actors discovered the extent to which they inclined towards a clichéd spontaneity: in other words, they resorted to mere tricks and gimmicks in an attempt to stay fresh. Later, many of these actors left the Theatre of Spontaneity for the legitimate theatre.

After this, in 1925 Moreno immigrated to the United States and took up the practice of a therapeutic theatre that would allow for greater freedom, without the expectations of the legitimate theatre. His first demonstrations of psychodrama came in 1927 and in the role-playing situations enacted in the Impromptu Theatre at Carnegie Hall in 1931. In 1937, he worked at Beacon, New York, with the Theatre of Catharsis in which, for example, couples enacted their marital struggles on a stage, professionally contained and under medical supervision.

Psychodrama can be defined as 'psyche', meaning the soul or mind, and 'drama', meaning an action or a thing done. It is a science of the mind that searches for the truth by means of action methods. Moreno defined it as one part of a triad of therapeutic practices: group psychotherapy, sociometry, and psychodrama. What's more, he regarded psychodrama as an extension of group therapy, and not as a practice in and of itself.

There are many levels of psychodrama, from cold role-playing to deep therapeutic psychodrama with patients in acute psychiatric hospital settings. The five principal instruments of psychodrama are: the protagonist, the director, the group, the auxiliary ego, and the stage. The three main portions of the psychodramatic session are: the warm-up, the action, and the sharing with the protagonist by the group members. As with any therapy, psychodrama is used at the discretion of the therapist.

We must remember that the psychodramatic stage is not the ancient Greek or Renaissance stage. Instead, it is a life space that is given to the protagonist to explore his own life experience, which he chooses to share with the group. The stage is circular, with three levels, demarcated physically and symbolically.

The function of the group is different from that of the theatre audience. The conserve of the theatre audience is no longer present. The group may play roles pertaining to the life of the protagonist, at the discretion of the director, and at the end of the session the group members share their personal involvement with the protagonist. In the legitimate theatre, applause and curtain calls are forms of closure for the audience. In psychodrama, there is the responsible act of sharing.

To the extent that there is no 'pretend' in the protagonist, there is no 'performance' in psychodrama. He is sharing his life-space, his problems, his ideals with the people around him. The members of the group or audience hear his words (as in the ancient Greek catharsis), see reflected in his actions their own problems and ideals, and are encouraged to share these with the protagonist in the third portion of the psychodrama. Since no two protagonists are alike, one must be careful using techniques that could betray that individuality. Psychodrama is concerned with the private personality of the protagonist and his catharsis. It is not concerned with the role represented and its artistic value or the effect of the role on the audience. For all these reasons, psychodrama is a method of restraint as much as a method of expression.

This is not to say that the therapeutic theatre and the artistic theatre do not have definite interrelationships. The spontaneous element of psychodrama may make it almost impossible to keep the private ego out of the role playing. In theatre, we rehearse to 'control the emotion', to fine-tune it and project it, so that the audience, not the actor, weeps. The skill of acting is to have the audience react. If the private ego of the actor is overwhelmed by the emotion of the role, she cannot deliver the lines of the playwright, nor can she control the timing.

The Italian performer Tommaso Salvini once described actors as split into two parts when they act (Hewitt 1958): an actor lives, weeps, and laughs on stage, but as he weeps and laughs, he observes his own tears and mirth. This double existence, this balancing between life and acting, makes for Art. This division does not harm his inspiration; one encourages the other. In this sense, the theatre actor holds two parallel perspectives when acting: the perspective of the role and the perspective of the actor on the stage, remembering moves, pauses, entrances and exits. These parallel perspectives also inform the work in psychodrama of the therapeutic auxiliary ego or co-director, who functions as an extension of the director and an extension of the protagonist, facilitating the process by which the protagonist gains insight through the enactment.

In the course of history, then, we have used the theatre as a mirror to project our thoughts and personal growth, our unconscious and our individual fragment of the collective unconscious of our society, onto the stage. Down through the centuries, the presentation has changed from the ancient Greek passive cathartic participation, through the Medieval control of the audience by the influence of the Church, to the Renaissance when listening 'audiences' became more 'spectators', watching pictures that moved before their eyes (Gassner 1954). From the modern influence of playwrights such as Strindberg and Ibsen, the individual has become more involved in the happenings onstage. Today, some theatres function responsibly, aware that if one opens an individual in the group and breaks through the conserve, one takes risks. Other theatres, not aware of the psyche, strive only for effect. If we are moving towards the breaking of the conserve of the legitimate theatre, we must be concerned for the quality of the closure of the audience. They may leave the shared space of their role as 'audience' and return to their own awakened problems with no possible opportunity to share these with anyone in the theatre. Ironically, this form of theatre invades and infects the personal freedom of the individual in the name of freedom and spontaneity.

Here I feel Moreno would speak of the spontaneity cliché in the theatre and in psychodrama. This is not pure spontaneity that evokes responsibility, the two springing from the same source. If I believe in my freedom, then I must respect your freedom, too.

Moreno, the psychiatrist, intended psychodrama to be part of a psychotherapeutic triad with group psychotherapy and sociometry. In the United States, in the 1960s psychodrama moved away from group work and sociometry, as many people were carried away by the action of the drama. However, a psychodrama director is not a theatre director, and the group is not an audience. Psychodrama has been misused by people who confuse the role of director with theatre directing, rather than the role of therapist who facilitates a process, placing as much emphasis on the working-through as on the catharsis.

Moreno stated again and again that psychodrama is as much a method of restraint as of expression and should only be in the hands of qualified therapists. The techniques of psychodrama are therapeutic interventions used at the discretion of the therapist. A misused technique may do a lot of harm. He further emphasized that psychodrama should always be used with respect for the freedom and dignity of each individual member of the group. Freedom begets responsibility.

Dean Elefthery always cautioned therapists to take their time, to ask themselves whose need it is to move from discussion into action; and to give ample time to the sharing phase when the protagonist returns to the group, time for the role players to share out of their roles as extensions of the protagonist's work, and time also to share out of themselves, time for the group members to share, if they wish, aspects of their own life space that were touched by the work of the protagonist. Closure is so important!

A knowledge of sociometry and group dynamics allows therapists to read the depth dimension of the group and helps to protect them from being unconsciously manipulated by the group dynamics and their own unconscious into inadvertently repositioning themselves from the role of therapist/'isolate' to theatre director/'star' – indeed, into 'acting out' as co-protagonists. That is to say, psychodrama directors who stumble unawares in a session into directing theatre have unconsciously co-opted the therapeutic intervention for themselves and have sacrificed their protagonist to their own need.

The concept of encounter is at the centre of the group process. In 1914 Moreno defined encounter as:

> A meeting of two: eye to eye, face to face.
> And when you are near I will tear out your eyes
> and place them instead of mine,
> and you will tear out my eyes
> and place them instead of yours,
> then I will look at you with your eyes
> and you will look at me with mine.
> (Moreno 1914/1964, ix)

This is role reversal, a way to really meet oneself and the other person, a way to touch the heart within the role. It offers an opportunity to become and remain alive in societies where, more and more, we relate to each other not as human beings but as object to object, and often without respect for the dignity and freedom of the other. We are in danger of becoming friendly users in a user-friendly society. Role reversal can help to keep what Martin Buber called the I–Thou relationship alive.

Moreno may have had a flamboyant personality, but his heart was always with his patient's heart, and his knowledge as a clinician was obvious. He dared to struggle with concepts of God, self, and freedom, he found a way to each, and he devoted his life to sharing that way with his fellow human beings.

References

Brunius, T. (1968) 'Catharsis', in *Dictionary of the History of Ideas, Volume 1*, P. Wiener (ed.), New York: Charles Scribner's Sons, 1973, pp. 264–70.

Gassner, J. (1954) *Masters of the Drama*, New York: Dover.

Hewitt, B. (ed.) (1958) *The Renaissance Stage: Documents of Serlio, Sabbattini and Furtenbach*. Coral Gables, Florida, University of Miami Press.

Moreno, J. L. (1914) 'Motto', translated from *'Einladung zu einer Begegnung'*, in *Psychodrama, Vol. 1*, New York: Beacon House, 1964.

Moreno, J. L. (1947) *The Theatre of Spontaneity*, New York: Beacon House Inc.

3

PSYCHODRAMA GROUNDED IN THE PERSPECTIVE OF ANALYTICAL PSYCHOLOGY[1]

Ellynor Barz

Grounding psychodrama in Jung's analytical psychology – as my husband Helmut Barz and I did – is not to be understood as a modification that distances us from Moreno but is, rather, meant to clarify and deepen the psychological processes in psychodrama.

Something like a more abstract form of psychodrama is created by decreasing somewhat the emphasis on external events for the benefit of clarifying inner psychic processes. This simplification of the exterior elements leads to a greater transparency of internal processes. Moreno himself proposed such a simplification with reference to Shakespearean drama.

Moreno's five 'media' – the stage, the protagonist, the players, the director, and the group – still remain, but they have been considerably restructured. The role of the single leader who, according to Moreno, should act in three functions is divided between two people: a pair of directors – in other words, a co-therapist is added as the auxiliary ego of the protagonist. As a result, the experienced role players whom Moreno employed to function as several 'auxiliary egos' are no longer needed. (Also role players from the group are no longer considered in this sense as 'auxiliary egos'.)

The 'stage' is shifted to the centre. The group does not sit opposite it; neither do they surround it in a semicircle. The stage is actually created within the circle formed by the group. There is no specific auditorium – this has become common practice nowadays. Psychodrama can take place in any room that is large enough to accommodate the group of a maximum twelve to fourteen people, including the leaders, leaving them enough room to play.

After the group has gathered in a circle, the first phase takes place: the 'warm-up'. It serves the purpose of contact, relaxation, and a brief exchange of occurrences since the last psychodrama session. Above all, it is in this phase that the person who wishes to be the protagonist and to work this time identifies him- or herself.

The leader now changes seats in order to sit next to this group member, to hear one-to-one which problem or subject the protagonist wants to address, what he or she wants to work on. We can locate this exchange on the first step of Moreno's original psychodrama stage: a single person meeting with the director, uncertain about the further course of events.

It may also happen that a participant merely has a general desire to 'play' or 'work' out of some indefinite tension, without being able to specify a particular problem. In this case one would attempt in dialogue to describe the still rather vague concern and finally perhaps identify it.

Now the group moves back to form a larger, looser circle. The leader and the protagonist get up together; they step into the second stage, so to speak – walking together within the circle and trying to approach the subject mentally. The group has not only moved away externally; the protagonist, now circling around the centre of his problem, may already have forgotten the presence of the group. It sinks behind his awareness of the images and feelings that are welling up from inside.

It is possible that a key scene to the problem will emerge by itself or through memory, and it can now be played. It is also possible that the director, who has in the meantime been collecting various facts while in conversation, suggests a scene. This could be based on a real incident or be purely imaginative. In every case, however, the director will try not only to venture towards the causal basis of the problem, but still more to seek to find a most 'typical' scene that may constitute a prototype for many other possible experiences: that is, an archetypal scene that proved or still proves formative for further experiences. This will then represent – despite all the 'personal' details – such a fundamental possibility of experience that not only will the protagonist find a deeper access to his problem, but also every member of the group may see himself shown in one of his collective syndromes and will therefore be affected (as Moreno proposed).

The scene is then built up. The third phase – the action level – is now reached. The protagonist prepares by giving a very detailed description of the space into which he intends to enter. Here a chair, perhaps there a table, is placed to indicate the situation. At the end of this preparation every member of the group is able to picture the imagined space: a carpet, the wallpaper, the view outside from the window. One knows where one enters and where it leads out to. One feels the atmosphere of the space as it is and how it will be for the protagonist once he has entered it. The setting could also be a landscape or a dreamed place, for example, with a specific street, a row of houses, the front door of a parental home.

Unless the psychodrama is to remain a pure monologue on the part of the protagonist, players are now sought out and found among the group members. The protagonist chooses who is to play the mother, the daughter, the father, the brother, the teacher, the boss, the dog, and so on. This choice is a matter of importance and often only happens after long consideration, because the person chosen must embody qualities that the protagonist wishes to confront. Anyone can be chosen for any role: a woman for a man, an old man for a baby.

It is quite astonishing how significant this selecting process can be, particularly in important roles, and how often afterwards a player says to the protagonist, 'How could you know my brother also died young', or 'my mother was also divorced', or 'I also was put in foster care'. These moments are possible because for the psyche, space and time are relative.

As soon as a player has been selected, she is 'introduced' into the role. One could also say: she is warmed up to the role or charged with the qualities and energies of the role. This process did not exist in Moreno's method, because the professional role players or 'auxiliary egos' intuitively slipped into the roles supplied with the information the protagonist had provided during the warming-up. They met the roles from outside. However, our procedure for introducing the player to the role happens differently.

The player sits on a chair, and the protagonist stands behind, laying hands on shoulders, while trying to empathize completely with the person he wants to introduce. He then presents him from within, as if he himself were the father, the mother, the brother: 'I'm Lisa, I'm 45 years old . . .' The role is not portrayed as a counterpart – for instance, as the always restraining, never-letting-go mother, the person that the protagonist has to experience day after day. Instead, the character is presented in a conscious identification from inside, as he or she might experience his or her own self: 'I'm only 45 years old, but I feel very lonely, side-lined, particularly by my husband . . .'

The protagonist requires a readiness for empathy and an openness to be able to present another person as that person 'really' is. At the same time it becomes obvious over and over again that each role character introduced is the product of the imagination of the protagonist and also depicts an aspect of the protagonist's own self. Despite the goal of objectivity, introducing a role is only possible through the projections of subjective imagination and feelings onto the role player.

During the introducing of a role, the protagonist can also be addressed and challenged. For instance, the director can ask the protagonist who is speaking out of the father: 'Tell me, Mr X, how do you find your daughter lately?' From the identification with the father, the protagonist can be led to express statements that she might otherwise not make about her own self: 'My daughter disappoints me. At least she really could have been a bit nice, she could be glad when she comes home. She could like me as her father, at least a tiny bit, anyway.' Or, for instance, in reply to the director's question, 'What did you actually hope for your life?' the protagonist can answer from out of the father and say something completely different from what she might say herself when facing him: 'What I've been hoping for? What every man wants: work that pleases – that's sort of alright. A woman who stands by her man. She could at least enjoy life a bit, be a little cheerful. Have fun together. Then a family could be something wonderful, but no, not with us.'

After the protagonist has introduced the player to his role, the player can still ask questions in case he misses important information: 'What do I look like? How do I address my daughter?' As a result, the player is so modelled into the role and charged with energy by the protagonist that he actually comes to represent the father or mother completely. At the same time, every member of the group knows and feels now exactly who it is that the protagonist will confront, which aspects she will face.

This extension of Moreno's method adds to the quality of external reality and to the experience of the object, an expansion or consolidation at the so-called 'subjective level' – that is to say, the personal aspects in the seemingly objective character. All people acting roles can be considered partial aspects of the protagonist. This is what Moreno probably meant when speaking of the 'auxiliary egos' of the protagonist.

In this form of psychodrama the function of the protagonist's auxiliary ego is different. The auxiliary ego does not take on roles, but is there solely for the sake of the protagonist, to assist or reinforce, to be always close to him. The complete psychodrama session – as well as the cooperation of all participants – is in service of the protagonist only. This, however, does not mean that he is treated only gently, that everyone is always 'nice' to him. In psychodrama, he will find the opportunity to come across unconscious aspects of the self, and these will sometimes be quite unpleasant experiences. Actually, because these aspects have been relegated to the unconscious, they are often of an archaic or inferior quality. It is for this reason that the auxiliary ego is a reinforcement or support who accompanies the protagonist at all times. The auxiliary ego speaks like the protagonist, in the first person, as his 'other self' or as his 'Number Two'. It is as though the protagonist can hear himself soliloquizing, as if something slipped out of his mouth that he actually hadn't intended or dared to say. The auxiliary ego is not experienced by the protagonist as a second person, as a You, but as an inner voice from behind which he can usually accept better than someone confronting him head-on. In the event that something the auxiliary ego says does not match his basic pattern of processing, the protagonist will reject it almost reflexively, and it will be as if he has not heard it at all.

Even visually, the function of the auxiliary ego becomes clear in this regard. He or she stands behind the protagonist. He is close, but not visible to him. Thus, the auxiliary articulates things that are close to being conscious but of which he is not completely aware, things that the protagonist refuses to face or with which he doesn't voluntarily wish to be confronted.

When Moreno says that the protagonist should not play a role, but be himself as he really is, this means that the protagonist can only find his true self by relinquishing his mask before himself and the group, no matter how useful or necessary that mask may be in life. So the auxiliary ego will, above all, question the protagonist's 'persona' (the Latin word for mask). For example: 'Why do I constantly emphasize that I am a good mother?' Or: 'Is it perhaps much too important to me what others think of me? I act so extremely emancipated. . . .'

Functioning like the shadow of the protagonist, the auxiliary ego can compensate and express what the protagonist does not name or realize, whether these be negative or positive emotions and feelings. He can repeat phrases to point out feelings, especially when the protagonist becomes 'top-heavy' with tensions, helplessness, fear, and inner needs. ('I feel uncomfortable. I'm shivering cold. I feel rejected. I need help, I need protection.') But the auxiliary will also disturb the protagonist when he surrenders to self-deceptions or shuts himself away from feasible insights. ('I do not want my husband simply to do what he likes. Then he surpasses my influence, then he's not mine.') The auxiliary ego attempts to break through the boundaries between consciousness and unconscious attitudes. He 'transcends' these boundaries in as much as he leads from 'one side' to the other, building necessary bridges between them.

But when the protagonist is strongly challenged by the director, or even attacked by role players or other group members, the auxiliary ego will consolidate his conscious ego, perhaps encouraging him in a confrontation or even – and quite literally – backing him up. (A protagonist once said to her auxiliary ego after psychodrama: 'You were like a guardian angel. I was able to go much farther than usual, because I felt strong. I must preserve this feeling. And the things you said were what I knew already anyhow . . .')

By introducing a co-director as the protagonist's 'auxiliary ego' in psychodrama, the role of the director or leader becomes clearer. He no longer operates in three and more functions. He is the director standing outside the play even though, as the analytical therapist, he is internally involved. The auxiliary ego and role players are the ones who act with the protagonist, and the group is also involved, as we shall see. The leader sets the course, so to speak: he chooses the scenes and the scene changes, proposes roles and the exchange of roles. He has a certain therapeutic aim that he wishes to implement, one step closer with each psychodrama. It is impossible to solve a life problem within one single psychodrama. But every psychodrama targets one specific goal.

The protagonist always faces the director. The director does not stand protectively beside or behind him at certain times and then challenges him at other times, as Moreno did. The protagonist is always clearly guided and demanded or confronted by him. The auxiliary ego, however, accompanies, complements and literally holds the protagonist: he lays his hands on the protagonist's shoulders when talking for him, in the same way that the protagonist lays his hands on the shoulders of the players when he introduces their roles. In this way, the mutual identity is expressed and the voice from

29

behind doesn't strike him as unexpected. The auxiliary ego remains in constant contact with the protagonist.

Between the director and the co-director there must be a basic agreement concerning the theory of psychodrama, the distribution of roles, the division of tasks, and the theoretical conception that is fundamental to everything. They must know each other so well that even non-verbal understanding is possible, as they must agree – without words – which of the protagonist's signals or hints should be taken up as a guideline for the psychodrama and its therapeutic goal. Moreover, the conducting couple must have consciously worked out their own relationship in order to make sure that unconscious tensions that concern only the two of them do not contaminate the protagonist's psychodrama and the play within the group.

Dividing the leader into two persons might seem somewhat abstract and, indeed, for an outsider joining in unexpectedly, it could seem quite strange, even grotesque, to see a protagonist being followed about by a second person who adapts to his attitudes and gestures. And he would be even more startled watching and witnessing further seemingly bizarre techniques such role reversal, mirroring, and doubling. The 'alienation' inherent in this method may already point to the underlying meaning. One could consider the method as clarifying the fact that the self-conscious ego never represents the whole of a personality and that essential parts of the personality exist autonomously beyond consciousness, in the unconscious.

The directing couple might seem like two concerned and devoted parents, especially if they are man and woman and also of a suitable age. And they certainly can be experienced as parental figures by many participants over and over again. But the clearly defined division of roles between the two parties will sooner or later lead everyone involved to reflect on the different functions. If they stand for fathering and mothering or male and female – one demanding and confronting, the other supporting and complementing – these are also implied in the tension and supplementation of logos and eros, of thinking and feeling, of conscious and unconscious and the call for a synthesis of opposites.

Thus, already in the outer structure of the psychodrama everything is constructed so that it can be understood as a symbol that points beyond itself. The aim of every play, every role, and all the components in the psycho-drama is to point beyond the very concrete, viewable and tangible appearances and to make the forms and contents transparent for the conscious proces-sing of deeper associations. It is up to each individual and his capacity for insight or intuition to determine at what level the concrete realizations that he experiences in the psychodrama will be put in order and understood. Theoretical insights are not verbalized.

Finally, the fifth element of psychodrama is the group itself. And it is, indeed, of particular importance. On the one hand, it is important that a psychodrama group is not too large, so that each participant may act, that each can be a protagonist often enough. On the other hand, it should not be too small, in order that there should be a sufficient number of players as well as others who will support the acting through collaboration and participation. Generally, there should be eight to twelve participants.

In the protagonist-centred psychodrama, the group forms the framework for the play. In the centre stands the individual, the protagonist. Certain tasks are entrusted to the group: everyone should not only be a co-supporter, but also a co-actor. This is clear for those who are chosen by the protagonist to play a role. But everyone else can act also by 'doubling'. Everyone witnesses the realization and the inner construction of the psychodrama, as well as the introduction of the roles and the scope of the work. Everyone is fully involved and can now join in spontaneously. By identifying with the protagonist or with a role, everyone at any time can offer to step behind the protagonist or behind a role player and 'double'. That is to say, one can act like the auxiliary ego behind the protagonist, even temporarily replacing the auxiliary. A person 'doubling' lays his hands on the player's shoulders – doing so, he announces himself and also makes his identity clear – and can now bring in what he considers to have been lacking, be it emotions, a restrained anger, some hidden disappointment that he clearly pronounces ('You don't look at me when you speak. You don't mean me at all!' Or: 'I get the shivers when I see your look. You indeed must hate me'). Or one can propose new ideas, new views of the problem, which suddenly arise from identifying with the player ('You mustn't let me down now. You must stay, because I need you exactly now . . .').

It is not only the protagonist who is 'representative of all in action' (as Moreno suggests), but any other role can also be experienced as representative for our own experiences. It is possible to play actively, to 'double' out of feeling involved, consciously identifying in an act of shared responsibility. However, egoistic purposes are not allowed to be served – for example, if a group member attempts to act out his aggression indirectly. All doubling must integrate into the basic structures the protagonist outlined for his psychodrama. This way every member of the group can become a 'therapeutical agent' for everyone else.

Since each psychodrama is about archetypal patterns, about primary structures of general human behaviour and experience, each participant will discover personal elements and familiar aspects and will thereby become personally affected. By doubling his experience, he can set his own experiences next to those of others and contribute to a greater variety of expression and a larger perspective.

There is no risk of suggestion or paternalism here, because everyone can re-act and respond. A doubling can lead to an 'aha' experience, but it can also be rejected by the protagonist: 'My mother could never do such a thing . . . my father would never say that . . .' And if a doubling is completely inappropriate, it will often be completely ignored. The drama will continue, as if the double hadn't intervened. The protagonist is being encouraged, not imposed upon. The more all group members participate actively in this manner, the more they will be stirred up in themselves. In the seemingly personal psychodrama of the protagonist, basic patterns that are a part of each individual will increasingly become apparent. Due to this general validity – and not because of the perhaps sometimes personal explosiveness – every psychodrama is gripping for each and every individual. Even quite unspectacular psychodramas can become utterly fascinating because they are moving in the depths of the mind, like fairy tales, myths, and legends.

At least as important as doubling is the role reversal or change of roles. In the middle of the drama or dialogue, the director may have the protagonist exchange roles with his opposite, taking that place (while the other takes the place of the protagonist) and responding from the other's role and attitude. The protagonist thus temporarily assumes the role of the opponent. In changing roles, the dynamic process between two people is particularly intense and therefore of special importance. With a father–son problem, for instance, the son is forced to put himself in the role of the apparently authoritarian father. This will be even easier for the protagonist if he has 'established' the opponent at the beginning of the drama, has already 'sensed' or felt him from his inner being. Through role reversal he can now emotionally grasp even more strongly what conflict the other experiences and how he experiences it.

Role reversal may sometimes also be necessary to correct the role player – 'My father would never speak that way!' – and so the protagonist quickly demonstrates it himself for the player. However, usually it is about a deeper understanding of the other. This sometimes leads to answers to fundamental questions that have never been formulated before. (For example, to a question like: 'Have you ever really loved me, Father?' the protagonist will – through the mouth of his father – answer himself best of all.)

In reversing roles, the protagonist learns many things about others that previously he did not know or did not wish to know, or did not see because he was incapable or unwilling to empathize. He can now become aware of his projections and – perhaps – recognize that he has despised another part of himself; or perhaps he has been loved, because he has loved himself in the role.

If the protagonist is able to recognize his projections as such, 'they not only lose their power and charm over him, but he acquires their powers for himself. His personal ego is given the opportunity to find and sort itself out again . . .' 'A catharsis of integration' happens. Unconscious parts can thus be experienced and accepted by the mind.

Although the conflict is conducted from the ego, the unconscious is also allowed to speak. The protagonist steps up to a deliberate confrontation and, in the role of the other, he faces his own unconscious parts – namely, those contents and qualities that he had previously projected onto the other. He himself must in role reversal re-act from that other side and speak to himself. This way, it is possible for unconscious contents to be connected to consciousness.

Jung wrote,

> The present day shows with appalling clarity how little able people are to let the other man's argument count, although this capacity is a fundamental and indispensable condition for any human community. Everyone who proposes to come to terms with himself must reckon with this basic problem. For, to the degree that he does not admit the validity of the other person, he denies the 'other' within himself the right to exist – and vice versa. The capacity for inner dialogue is a touchstone for outer objectivity.
>
> (Jung 1916/1958, para. 187)

By reversing roles, by having to understand and to empathize with the other and speak out of that other, it becomes possible to modify one's attitude towards the opposite and the 'other' in oneself. That is, to identify projections as such and to take them in and endure them, one comes to perceive the other as 'objectively' as possible, rather than misusing the other as a screen.

The greater the self-insight, the more objectively one can view the other, the better one will be able to reflect. With 'mirroring', Moreno offered a technique for self-examination and self-understanding. The protagonist is mirrored from the outside: he can view his beauty and charm as well as his flaws, his awkwardness and clumsiness. He can see how others see him, how he is perceived by them, and perhaps he can realize the gap between what he wants to express and what he actually has mediated. Looking at himself this way he gets to know new and maybe previously unrealized aspects of himself.

In this sense one can consider the entire psychodrama as a kind of mirroring. In each player the protagonist can see mirrored parts of his own personality. And from everyone together, he finds himself reflected as a unity, introduced to himself in various facets.

After the psychodrama session has come to a rounding off – which does not necessarily mean with a 'happy end' – all participants will sit together in the tightly closed circle again, as in the beginning, and sharing follows.

Only now does the protagonist return with all his consciousness back into this framework. A bridge is drawn between the drama and this return to reality by the protagonist who individually takes his leave of each player, dismissing each in an appropriate manner, and then by personally dismantling the stage that he had initially built up. Every chair, every detail is carefully brought back to its old place, becoming again a banal stool, chair, or table. The world of the imagination is gradually put away, step by step. The protagonist needs time to get back into the concrete room and to find his way back to the group. And the group members share the feeling of his returning from far away, the more so the more he succeeded in giving up conscious control and allowing himself to be absorbed fully in his psychodrama.

It may happen that only now does a protagonist become aware of his devotion or also the desire he felt when he was allowed to drop all bonds and let himself be seen as he is, an event that is otherwise only possible or hoped for in an intimate relationship. And now he feels embarrassed, laid bare, and he needs the care of others to take the feeling of nakedness away from him. As Moreno wrote, 'He gave love, and now they [the participants] return love back to him. . . .They share their worries as he has shared his with them' (Moreno 1959, p. 83). This is the meaning of 'sharing', of dedicating, granting. But there is also the saying of a 'fine mess' when something unexpected or disagreeable happens. This situation can also be caused by psychodrama. At the beginning of every psychodrama everyone is ready to open himself completely, to reveal or go along, which is only possible within a strong shared humanity. But what is brought to light can become bewildering for some and leave others feeling angry or helpless. This can, for instance, be the case when a protagonist dared to confront himself with an extremely unpleasant shadow aspect – for example, with a murderer in himself. In this case the group's determination, love, and courage to accept him is required, whereby they consider a possible shadow of this sort also in themselves. The group members need hardly only return their own 'concerns'; instead they might, out of personal experience, admire the protagonist's courage and honesty.

On the other hand, many a protagonist believes he is confronting the group with a unique, especially incriminating problem when he brings something forward that he has never before confessed in public – his so far concealed homosexuality, perhaps – and the coherent unpleasant experience he has made of this. And he will not only be 'consoled', but almost shamed by the revelation of others who have not only also been confronted with this, but in some cases have perhaps made even more dreadful experiences than did the protagonist himself. Thus sharing can lead a psychodrama even further or make further psychodramas necessary.

Back in the reality of the group, it is important for the protagonist to see how his inner experience relates to reality: how others respond to his experience, whether they can feel with him, whether he remains accessible. And the group tell him honestly what each one has experienced and felt – but without analysing and thus dissociating internally.

The members of the group have become witnesses of a happening, and now they must bear testimony to what they have experienced and learned. But 'to be a witness', 'to testify', includes yet another aspect, that of 'generating'.

The group has not been a party of passive participants. Now, by sharing their own experiences during the drama or relating from their lives, they help to engender insights, without interpreting or instructing.

34

During the sharing the protagonist remains silent. Until this point he has been working, now it is his turn to listen to what the others wish to communicate with him. He will 'take it in' and must carry it around with himself, thinking and feeling it over until the next psychodrama session.

There are two rounds during the sharing, each with a different way of bearing witness. In the first round each player tells what he experienced from within the role: for example, what impression the protagonist made upon him as the father, teacher, mother, sister, and what feelings were aroused in him. In the second round all participants share from their experiences during the psychodrama but, above all, their own insights that complement or reinforce the one enacted here with similar patterns or counterpoints.

The next psychodrama begins with the protagonist's feedback. He is now the first speaker and has the opportunity to report what has happened to him, what he might have realized, what he considered, experienced and perhaps dreamt of and to what insights he has come. Quite important is this period in-between, during which the protagonist can mature, nurturing what the psychodrama has touched in him. He will have had to continue to handle it alone, be this in confrontation with people, in the world, or be this with his own self, meditating, dreaming, drawing. His experiences must first become concrete, and then convergent. Only then can he report about them, reviewing and accounting at the same time for himself to the others.

Completely inadmissible in psychodrama is any form of intellectual analysis or interpretation by anyone other than by the protagonist himself. The unconscious contents were formed with great care and brought to appearance. In this form, in the images, they have symbolic character, and these symbols have an effective force. Should this be dismantled and verbalized by the group, 'translated' into words, its power would dissolve.

Each and every one will, in their own time, consciously recognize and understand a symbol, a symbolic act in the psychodrama. That is the moment when a step is taken toward the synthesis of consciousness and the unconscious. But this cannot happen for everyone at the same time if it is to be real.

Having outlined the conditions and background of psychodramatic work, I will now illustrate what I have explained with an example. I will describe in detail the various steps of a psychodrama, so that the reader can better imagine them. With this clinical example I will show how to understand the psychological processes at work, but without claiming to offer an exhaustive interpretation.

As I have already said, psychological interpretation itself is never brought into the psychodrama, but the directors must have a clear understanding of the psychological patterns against which the enacting is to be seen: that is, which archetypal structures are here formative for the personal conscious and unconscious experiences and images, as well as for the current action. This is even more essential for directors working in pairs, because they can only achieve a therapeutic goal once they agree upon this. It works itself out 'by itself' when they recognize the model or the archetype behind the concrete action, which is its cause and which lends the action its symbolic character, doing this so impressively so that everyone is affected, each in his own way.

Various members of the group will also consider one thing or another in addition for themselves as they try to understand while reflecting. But that will not be brought into the psychodrama session. Here, only spontaneous action and spontaneous word have their place.

The impulse for the psychodrama I wish to relate arose in the initial phase, in the 'warm-up', with everyone sitting loosely together in the circle that had just been formed. At that moment, one participant – from now on I will simply call her 'Mona' – felt the urge to apologize for wearing sunglasses. She was aware of the fact that she had, of course, been drawing special attention to herself with them and felt that this added 'protection', or that her very 'public presentation', did not quite fit within the group. She decided to view the subject – that is to say, she wanted to work on this in a psychodrama. Everyone agreed.

The director changed places with the group member seated next to her in order to sit with her. The first step of Moreno's stage had been made. She talked about her frequent blushing and that, as a result, she dare not encounter her neighbour any more. Whenever she caught sight of her, she would quickly withdraw into the house.

Primarily she now probably wanted to get rid of the symptom of blushing, but she also wanted to find out what made her so 'suddenly' unsure of herself.

While narrating all this, she felt increasingly uneasy – a signal that it was now time to enter the next 'phase'. At the director's signal, the group moved apart into a larger, looser circle. The director, the protagonist, and the auxiliary ego, positioned behind her, circulated, continuing their talk. It was now much easier for Mona to narrate, the group having moved out of view. Mona dipped more deeply into her world, she relaxed, and suddenly last night's dream occurred to her, and she told her dream. As a dreamer, she goes down a road towards a house, stands at the door, puts her hand on the handle, and is gripped by panic and wakes up.

So it certainly was not a coincidence that she had now volunteered to do psychodrama. Already before this day, she had been unconsciously motivated to deal with her dream or her fears in psychodrama. It could be presumed that the dream contained a key to her problem; it could at least serve as an entry point.

As Mona had no specific associations to the dream, a scene was not built yet. But the third 'phase' had already been entered: Mona had to and wanted to reconstruct the dream in the drama. The director stepped aside. Accompanied by the auxiliary ego, she felt her way forward into the dream as if into an empty space. Her eyes were almost closed, and she was feeling her way into her own self rather than looking for something outside. Spontaneously, she took off her shoes – and there it was: she could clearly feel cobblestones, and she realized that she was walking down the village street of the town in which she had spent her childhood. We already know about her halting at the door, the fear that seized her, and the need to turn back.

Of course she didn't want the play – after the brief dialogue with the director – to end here. The auxiliary ego said: 'It would be easier for me if I wouldn't have to go alone.' Mona said: 'Yes, I would be happy if my mother were with me.' Together with her, she hoped, it would be more successful.

The first time going to the house had been only a repetition of the recalled dream, with which, however, the single images became very clear and the dream within grasp. Now Mona could create the scenery, the street and the houses, describing her parents' house, as she has seen it again just now. 'Here lived a girl I used to play with sometimes. That house over there belonged to an old woman we were all scared of. Just around this corner there was the butcher's . . . and so on. (And all participants are taken inside this scene, into this environment.) She herself remembers thereby clearly how the world appeared to her then, when she used to live there – she might have been 6 years old – and it was now completely present to her again. Now Mona seems increasingly younger, even smaller, also to the others.

Now she had to select a woman out of the group for the role of the mother. This was not so easy. She was first inclined to choose an older woman, who could in fact have been her mother, but then she chose a woman the same age as herself.

During the mother's introduction to her role, a few biographical details were first mentioned. The mother had been raised in this village, and she had already spent her first years of marriage here. 'Yes, so we are still here now. But I'm not happy here. There is so much talk among the neighbours. And my family, too, also lives nearby. They poke their noses into everything. Especially my mother does. My father comes and arranges my garden, and the people have even more to talk about – as if I couldn't do it myself. But, actually, I'm glad that he does it. Instead, I have community work to do. . . .'

AUXILIARY EGO: 'I will not even mention my husband, let me not dwell on him.'

MOTHER (the protagonist as Mother): 'Exactly, he is not like he's supposed to be. Before the wedding, life was still nice. I was looking forward to the future. But now I could skip out of this place. . . . But next week there will be a bazaar, and. . . .'

AUXILIARY EGO: 'I am actually skipping away. I'm already doing community work again.'

MOTHER: 'My husband is just not as I had imagined him to be. He makes eyes at other women. But at home he always crouches behind the newspaper. He often doesn't even come home. Stays in the pub – as he says! – till late with friends. – Ha! Friends! That's more important to him.'

AUXILIARY EGO: 'To be honest, I'm unhappy. And I'm jealous.'

MOTHER: 'Maybe so, but I would never admit it.'
AUXILIARY EGO: 'Hearing "friends" I think of women.'
MOTHER: 'Well, of course, what else . . .'

Now the director suggests a second walk to her parents' house, this time holding her mother's hand. We observed that the role player had taken to the role well: she accompanied the daughter only reluctantly, reflecting the notion that they could expect nothing good at all. Then, actually entering, only the daughter saw the father sitting there on the sofa. Her inner eye saw him – but it was as if he were really sitting there.

Before taking a third walk to the house, she must now choose a player for the father, who will then physically sit in the room. But first the room is set as a scene on the inner stage. Now the protagonist remembers all the details: not only the sofa and a table but the little figurines of dancers in a display cabinet, and on the wall a picture of a very pretty woman; also, the view from the window: the white curtains, an apple tree. 'But everything is without life.'

The player's choice for the father is difficult. Mona is reluctant to pick out the father. So she first sits down to gather strength. Doing so, she soliloquizes: 'How am I supposed to choose him? Father was always the big stranger. He never cared for me. There was a huge gap between him and me. Often I was really scared of him. Mother was also afraid sometimes, it seems to me. I felt uncomfortable with him. I didn't like getting near him. He probably had a smell sometimes. My mother, I think, often found him disgusting, especially when he came back home late at night from the pub. They often quarrelled then. But he was really crude – the way he would swear then! It woke me up. They often fought. And, besides, he was simply mean!'

Saying this, the protagonist jerks and chooses, without hesitation, the biggest and heaviest man in the group. She puts a hard chair before him and has him sit down on it. Then she takes her time for a second before she, at first reluctantly, lays her hands on his shoulders. 'So, I am Walter.' Her hands are now lying heavily on him. We hear that he comes from a large farming family, but being the youngest, not very much attention had been paid to him. The parents had enough to do already with all the other children and the big farm. Later he was glad that he didn't have to join the family business but could, instead, learn to be a carpenter and move away from home.

FATHER: 'Finally, in the town, I could open my own workshop . . . But now living here in H__ with L__, life is not nice at all. In the beginning we had a fine time together. When we were engaged. With the permission of the parents we were even allowed to go out at night. Before that, we could only do it secretly, over the balcony, and down to the next village with her. In the beginning she sure was swell, in every respect. But then, soon, it all began. And when the child was finally born, the woman didn't want to have anything to do with me any more. She simply can't stand me. Only jealous, that's all she can be! And then her family! They consider themselves

to be something better. And so close by! Nowadays you feel more caught
within your own four walls than earlier as a boy at home.'
Stepping away from the father's player, Mona is thoughtful.
AUXILIARY EGO: 'I am letting my shoulders droop.'
MONA: 'Yes, I'm sad, just now I feel almost sorry for him. . . . But it really was
mean of him, always walking out on us.'
She now approaches the mother (the father goes into the room):
MONA: 'Yes, we must go to the house once again.'
She instinctively assumes a childlike stance again. Now comes the third walk
to the house. The two still lag a bit. A doubling from a group member comes
from behind Mona:
MONA: 'I wish Mother would hold me tighter. I do not feel comfortable with
her at all.'
Mona pulls the mother, takes her hand in order to open the door. Then, seeing
the father, fear, anger, and horror take hold of Mona. Running out of the house,
she cries: 'But he is a rake!' Intuitively she felt the presence of a woman, and in
her mind appears the image of a young aunt who had lived with them for a
while in earlier times and whom she now imagines being in the room next door.
She cannot calm herself and stays leaning against 'the wall of the house'. Tears
well up in her eyes.
AUXILIARY EGO: (after a pause): 'I'm unhappy – and jealous.'
MONA: 'No! – Yes! Yes! – What was he missing in us? – I hate her, that one
inside! I hate her!'
And now the tears flow – of the abandoned child, the disappointed wife, and
the daughter who is afraid of 'the witch'.

Here the play came to an end. The group moved back together into a closed
circle, and the sharing followed. From now on the protagonist remained silent
and only listened. First the father's actor expressed how lonely and abandoned
he had felt in the role and in the house, totally misunderstood and unloved.
For the mother, the disgrace in the presence of the village was the worst. The
auxiliary ego emphasized how 'small' she had felt identifying with the protagonist, helpless, merely a daughter. The feeling of also being a married
woman with her own 'lively' children had not been present at any time.

Afterwards many different contributions came up, from personal experiences
the group members had had in life. Of course there were some former 'children'
from difficult or broken marriages. A woman, intimately related to an older
man, stood up for the 'other woman' and her needs, which did not necessarily
have to be 'evil'. She had actually saved the man during a crisis. A man
experiencing a marriage crisis of his own complained about the harshness of
his 'frigid' and uncomprehending wife. And so on.

In the feedback discussion at the beginning of the following psychodrama
session Mona declared that, to her own surprise, the week between the two
sessions had been much better. She was glad that she had dared to expose

herself before the group. She was glad that she had also dared to turn her attention to her childhood. 'This problem with the witch is still breathing down my neck. There's probably still a heavy chunk behind it.' But now she was no longer afraid to have a look at it again. She had reflected further in detail about her father and had occasionally felt pity for him. 'Oddly enough, my husband and I liked each other during this week more than usual, made love to each other, and everything was just fine again.' But she had been astonished in how many situations she had suddenly experienced herself being exactly like her mother. She hadn't been aware of how many rules and restrictions she tended to make. And sometimes she had caught herself being almost jealous of the children: 'How can they still take things so easily! And be aggressive without feeling guilty about it!'

It should be added here that in her next psychodrama Mona did not select the same actor for the father but, instead, a very thin young man who embodied especially the oppressed, underdeveloped side of the father, who suffered from his wife as if under a mother who always told him what to do, even which shirt he should wear, who wanted to hinder him in everything. But then he could completely harden and turn ice-cold.

One more remark with regard to technique: In every subsequent psychodrama, each actor must be reintroduced to his role, even if the role is already well known, even if the father or the mother has appeared in previous psychodramas, and even if the same actor has played the same role. The actor must be 'charged' every time anew with the power of the role in order to be able to empathize. The protagonist will always conjure up different aspects that are important to him now and which he wants to deal with. He can never grasp the complete person all at once, neither objectively nor subjectively. He will always turn to certain aspects: to the father as an authority, for example, or as a protector, as a competitor, as an overwhelming power or as that much-too-weak person who could neither support nor be a role model.

From the perspective of analytical psychology, one can speak of the blushing and the sexual problems behind it as repressed contents of the personal unconscious. The parts purged from conscious remembering have, however, not been extinguished: instead they lead an independent existence in the unconscious, causing a noticeable disturbance.

One could also speak of 'affective complexes'. There were particular topics to which the protagonist reacted, despite her deliberate intentions and insights, with affects that she could neither understand nor control.

Despite a seemingly happy marriage, she had remained in the stage of a young girl who must keep 'immorality', 'infidelity' and other threatening aspects of life away from herself. She had only partially found her own identity as a woman. During her childhood and youth she had lacked a model of a mother who could also 'bear to look' at what was disagreeable. The mother had not been warm-hearted and receptive. She offered no emotional or mental stimulation but fled, instead, into organizational activities. She lived the more 'masculine' qualities, but only in an undifferentiated, unqualified sense. In terms of classical analytical psychology, she was biased by a 'patriarchal animus'.

Mona had fled early from the harassed daughter situation into marriage. Her husband was indeed the hero who had saved her, but he remained – as later became clear, due to a similar background – more a brother than a partner, the same way Mona had stayed a 'daughter'. She had developed only partially, but she experienced this the other way around: she saw projected onto her husband not a stimulating and exciting partner, but only a good, patient, but rather boring husband. Just at the time she enacted her psychodrama, her mother's destiny seemed to be in the course of repeating itself.

In her psychodrama, initiated by the dream, a further psychological dynamic appeared that seemed to indicate a broader context – the archetypal structures that had caused the experience. The spontaneous awareness of the presence of the witch contained a key. The archetype behind this image was that of the Great Mother in its negative aspect. Instead of being life-giving, it was life-threatening and life-prohibiting. In the witch were included those aspects of the feminine that had not been admitted either into the life of the mother or into the life of the daughter and which therefore now destructively forced themselves forward in concentrated form: as emotion and passion, lust and desire, temptation and devotion.

As long as no tribute – that is, no conscious attention – was paid to this image or this quality of experience, its power remained destructive. Whatever Mona encountered from this field, and be it only the embodiment of the neighbour, she experienced it only negatively. She fell into a psychological mechanism that, from within her conscious attitude, drove her into an increasingly skewed perspective.

To the extent to which she now focused on the 'evil', the negative, the shadow aspect of the Great Mother and the hitherto ignored principle of life, its frightening aspects could convert. And with the changing attitude towards the excluded feminine, her image of the masculine changed also – in relation to the father as well as to her husband.

What Mona experienced in psychodrama was more than a repetition of earlier experiences. It had a symbolic character, it possessed an active power that emanates from archetypal images. For this reason this experience had an effect far beyond the psychodrama itself.

She learned to recognize that these were her own internal voices, assumed views, and behavioural patterns, which she re-imposed on other people and which frightened her. And she learned over time to recognize the self and to shoulder it.

It was assumed that there had been an affair between the father and the aunt, and that these repressed memories had been uncovered here. But, no matter whether these experiences were real or imagined, for Mona they were definitely certain, an inner reality.

In psychotherapy, confronting the past is not about the criminalistic uncovering of facts. It is, rather, about the recognition and acceptance of intrapsychic facts that, for the person concerned, are of equal importance, reality, and intensity as actual occurrences. Profound knowledge becomes manifest in them and influences and shapes later experience.

The fact that, in the course of time, Mona succeeded in recognizing and accepting her own traits (feminine as well as masculine), which until then she had rejected as menacing, became not only obvious in changes in her relationship with the parental figures, including the aunt, but, for example, also in the fact that she later played tennis with great pleasure with the once feared neighbour (onto whom she had projected almost all her 'negative' female attitudes). Quite simply, she came to do many things of which she had previously not thought herself capable.

Note

1 Translated by Lucie Pabel.

References

Jung, C. G. (1916/1958) 'The Transcendent Function', in *The Structure and Dynamics of the Psyche, Collected Works 8*, Princeton, NJ: Princeton University Press, 1960, pp. 67–91.

Moreno, J. L. (1959) *Gruppenpsychotherapie und Psychodrama: Einleitung in die Theorie und Praxis*, Stuttgart: Georg Thieme Verlag, 1988.

4

JUNGIAN PSYCHODRAMA

Christopher Beach

Overview

In this chapter, I introduce Jungian psychodrama as I experienced it for three years under the guidance of Zurich-based analysts and psychodramatists Helmut and Ellynor Barz.[1] I begin by reviewing a few key aspects of this form of psychodrama. I then recount one actual psychodrama in detail, discuss some of the techniques used therein, and conclude with several general observations.

A few key aspects of Jungian psychodrama[2]

The first aspect concerns how a Jungian psychodrama group is established and how it works. A group consists of twelve to fourteen members, ideally half of them women and half men. It is led by two trained facilitators, who serve as director and auxiliary ego. They interview each prospective participant to discern whether psychodrama would be appropriate or contraindicated. Those who join the group must be either already in analysis/therapy or willing to enter into it if and when issues arise that require individual work.

A psychodrama group might meet once a week for several months (holding one psychodrama per meeting) or a few weekends during the year (holding four or five psychodramas per weekend). The former schedule permits each psychodrama to settle and ferment during the week that follows; the latter schedule gives a more intensive group experience as members work together over two days. A typical psychodrama session lasts about two-and-one-half hours, with only one participant working as the protagonist.

At the start of a session, while everyone sits in a circle in the middle of the room, announcements are made, each person briefly checks in, and the protagonist for the previous session gives feedback about her or his psychodrama. Then, the director asks who would like to be the protagonist for this session. Once that person is identified[3] the director sits next to the new protagonist, and they engage in a dialogue to gain a deeper sense of the problem, dream, possibility, or situation that concerns the protagonist.

At some point, the director asks everyone to move their chairs to the perimeter of the room, and the protagonist, director and auxiliary ego begin to circle inside that perimeter, counterclockwise, as if into the Unconscious. The protagonist and co-directors work to discern how best to bring the protagonist's concern to life. The protagonist then uses props to set the scene. Group members are asked to play key figures in the protagonist's life, those figures are introduced by the protagonist, and a drama is enacted in one or more scenes.

As the drama moves to its conclusion, any circular movement by the protagonist and auxiliary ego is clockwise, marking a return to consciousness and the outer world. Those playing roles are carefully 'de-roled', the 'set' is broken down, and everyone gathers again in a circle in the middle of the room. Each role-player shares with the protagonist what it has been like to be that figure in the protagonist's drama. Finally, each group member shares from her or his life something that has been touched by the drama – each member giving something in exchange for what the protagonist has given. Often the protagonist experiences this sharing as a healing gift. At times, during the session, group members are encouraged to participate and help the protagonist if they can, but they may decline to play a role, participate in a particular moment, or share at the end if they feel that not doing so is best. The protagonist will wait until the following session to share what she or he has experienced.

The second key aspect concerns the primary role of the co-directors – that is, to lead psychodramas. Analysis, discussion, and commentary – by the co-directors or group members – are discouraged. Being present, attentive, and in the service of the protagonist is encouraged. The focus upon bringing to life in a dramatic enactment the critical matter that concerns the protagonist separates this form of group therapy from many others. Here, while the extraverted nature of group dramatic enactment is obvious, the being in the service and support of the protagonist brings in a significant element of introversion. The drama is not being put on for the group: rather, the group is there to help the protagonist to dramatize her or his critical concern. This is very different from what a theatrical group, or a process-oriented psychotherapy group, is attempting.

A third key aspect of Jungian psychodrama is its use of two facilitators: the director and the auxiliary ego.[4] The director is responsible first to the protagonist and second to the group. The director is striving for a psychodrama that is attentive to Psyche, allows encounter and movement, and is safe. The director comes physically close to the protagonist sometimes, but often stands at a distance – behind, in front of, or beside the protagonist. The director is the stage manager, the lighting director, the guide, and the anchor point. The director's attention can play back and forth between the group and the protagonist. Thus, for example, the director will signal when it is okay for members to step behind the protagonist to 'double' – that is, give voice to

44

feelings, thoughts, expressions that may be lying just below the surface of the protagonist's consciousness.

The auxiliary ego, by contrast, is present solely for the protagonist, literally walking in the protagonist's footsteps, often with one or both hands on the protagonist's back, supporting the protagonist and gaining the physical and emotional sense of the protagonist. The auxiliary ego is, in effect, the protagonist's auxiliary ego, voicing what may be lying just beneath the surface of consciousness that may need expression or support. Also, the auxiliary ego serves as a check on the director. If, for example, the director wants to try an idea that seems off to the auxiliary ego, who is always 'standing in the protagonist's shoes', the auxiliary ego might say, 'I am afraid to do that; maybe that's not such a good idea. Is that possible?' If the protagonist affirms this offering in any way, the director is alerted to withdraw or reframe the idea. Occasionally, the check works the other way. If, for example, the auxiliary ego becomes too identified with the conscious position of the protagonist, the director might ask a question that alerts the auxiliary ego to the over-identification. In such ways, the director and auxiliary protect the protagonist.

A final key aspect of this form of psychodrama is its Jungian quality. Archetypal figures and images arise from within the protagonist. I have witnessed, among others: King Arthur and King David, a great Mystical Bird, huge Snakes and Serpents, many Inner Children, many positive and negative mother and father complexes, the Pet in the form of cats, dogs, and rabbits, and many manifestations of Shadow, Anima, and Animus. The drama is directed so as to allow these figures to appear. Often they are not named. Insight and analysis are left to the protagonist, whether during the drama or upon later reflection.

Similarly, psychodramas may be used to enact a protagonist's dream, developmental issue, or next step in individuation. One sees traumas, scenes from key points in a protagonist's life, possible visions of the future, and striking dream figures and images. A protagonist may want to work on a dream by itself or enact both a dream scene and a scene from outer life. In the latter case, the protagonist is likely to experience and become more aware of connections between his or her inner and outer worlds.

With these few important general aspects in mind, we can turn to an actual Jungian psychodrama and let its particulars make other significant points.

One psychodrama: George's childhood asthma attacks

What follows is a full account of one psychodrama by a person I call 'George'.[5] I have changed everyone's identity to preserve confidentiality, as well as modified certain particulars to shorten the narrative, clarify certain moments, and, again, preserve confidentiality. I set the scene at the beginning, and I comment on the psychodrama at its conclusion, but most of the psychodrama session itself is narrated by the protagonist, 'George,' in the first person singular 'I' and in the present tense. It is drawn both from George's extensive contemporaneous notes (made by many who undertake psychodrama) and from details George has shared with me subsequently. As I originally read his account, I was struck by how much more George's narration brought me into his psychodrama than does the usual narration from the director's point of view.[6] When it is necessary for clarity, I have inserted comments or observations [*in italics, within brackets*] within George's narration.

George is in his early 40s. There are several issues he could work on in a psychodrama session. He is at mid-life, he is thinking of switching careers from architect to high school geography teacher, and he is unsure of his marriage. He is working both in this psychodrama group, which meets regularly, and in analysis. On this day, however, he is strongly moved to ask to be the protagonist and to re-enact his frightening experience of early childhood asthma attacks.

George's account starts with his walking to the new place where the group will meet.

Just before the psychodrama session[7]

Walking to our new meeting place, I find I want to go back to age two, when the bad asthma attacks began. I want to learn what happened, why the attacks occurred, and what they mean to me now? I want to do this, but I'm also afraid to try.

Initial phase of the psychodrama session

I enter the room – maybe 30 feet by 30 feet – larger than our usual room. Light floods in the windows along the far wall. No curtains, so no chance to darken the room. That's okay. Everyone is already seated in the central circle. I apologize for being a little late. Diane [*the director*] says something must be up, since I'm never late. Everybody laughs. There's a good feeling in the group. I very much trust Diane and Antoine [*the auxiliary ego*].

After check-ins, Diane asks Karen [*a group member*] if she has any feedback from her psychodrama last session. As Karen begins, I notice I'm not paying attention – too stirred up thinking about maybe doing a psychodrama today.

Who will work today?

I hear Diane asking, 'Would anyone else like to share with respect to Karen's psychodrama?' After no one responds, she asks, 'Okay, who would like to work today?'

My right hand shoots up. I look around – no other hands. Then, hesitantly, up comes David's hand. Oh no! I'll have to fight for this!

Diane asks: 'Anyone else? Just George and David? Okay, George, you go first since you raised your hand first, then David. The two of you decide for whom it is most important to work today.'

I explain my idea of revisiting my childhood asthma attacks, note that I have wondered about them for years, and say I am ready to do it today. I add that I can wait if David has an emergency, but I hope to go today. I feel nervous and eager. I am shaking. So is my voice.

David is my friend. He knows I am shy, and he's been encouraging me to do a drama for weeks. He says he just wants to speak about an issue briefly before yielding to me. He talks about a problem with his partner, says he wants to mull it over some more and then do a psychodrama next time. Then, he yields to me. Diane thanks him. So do I. I hope he gets to go next time.[8]

Warming up while seated: George telling his story to director Diane

Now Diane sits to my right. She asks me to describe in detail what happened when I was two years old. She is calm, accepting and encouraging. I notice the group less as she holds my gaze, and I tell my story.

> 'It happened several times between ages two and four. My mother cared for us in the country, while my father worked in town. Mom began having symptoms – headaches, depression, poor sleep. Her doctor ran tests and asked questions. He concluded that there was no medical problem, just a bad case of "cabin fever". She had changed from city-life and a great job with bright adults to country-life alone with two little boys (me and my brother Chad), and it was making her crazy. The doctor recommended that she find a part-time job and have us cared for by Mrs. P, a local caretaker of little children. Mom took his advice and soon began working mornings at the local college, leaving Chad and me at Mrs. P's.
>
> 'It was while Chad and I were at Mrs. P's that the first asthma attack came. I was two, and Chad was four. The attacks came several times over the next two years. I don't remember them well. But I recall like it was yesterday one final attack that I had many years later, at age 11. Also, Mom has told me what it was like when I was younger.'
>
> 'I'm sure Mrs. P was a good woman. Everyone says so. But I recall feeling she was a little too smothering. For example, she loved my dark, curly hair and put it up in ribbons. She wanted to have a daughter. At least by the time I was four, I didn't like the ribbons. Mrs. P liked me. But I didn't like the ribbons. I remember this, even though it is different from Mom's memory. She says I liked Mrs. P's attention. Maybe both memories are true, but I am sure of mine. I can even remember exactly where I was in her living room when I felt her smothering quality.

'Anyway, about two months after Mom began her job, Mrs. P telephoned her at the college and said I could hardly breathe and was turning blue. Mrs. P had called the doctor, who said, "Bring George to the hospital now." My mother sped to Mrs. P's, then rushed me to the hospital. I was put in an oxygen tent and given drugs to help me breathe. These attacks happened several times. One happened during a blizzard at night. Because Dad was away, Mom had to drive Chad and me to the hospital in the blizzard.

'Each time, I was put in an oxygen tent, given drugs, and stayed for several days. I'm sure I was afraid – just like when I was 11. That time, as we approached the hospital, I could only walk 15 feet before I had to rest, catch my breath, then walk another 15 feet. It was so hard to breathe. I was really scared. Again, there was an oxygen tent and medications.

'But today, I'd like to go back to the original attack and see what might be lying behind it. Mom thinks there was no psychological component. Dr. Y, my pediatrician at the time, also thought nothing psychological was involved. But I have a feeling there was. Why did this begin shortly after I went to Mrs. P's? What was it really like to be in her house?'

Diane shifts as she responds, 'Okay. Maybe it is time that we walk. How would that be for you?'

'Good! I feel like moving.'

George circling counterclockwise with Diane and Antoine

The group members stand up, move their chairs back, and sit along the walls. Diane, Antoine, and I begin circling. Diane walks next to me, Antoine behind me. His two hands are on my shoulders. I am glad he's here.

GEO [*George*]: It feels good to be moving. I'm a bit nervous. I hope I can do this, but I don't know.

AE: [*Antoine as George's auxiliary ego*]: But I really want to try, yes?

GEO: Yes, I want this a lot. I've been waiting for years to do this. (*Tears begin to form in my eyes. I am deeply moved.*)

AE: I have been afraid but today I am going to try.

GEO: Today, I try! (*I feel a surge of determination.*)

Notice how George's notes spontaneously take the form of dramatic dialogue here. This change marks a marked change that one is likely to experience at some point in a psychodrama. There is a shift from a more descriptive and objective story-telling mode to a more emotionally involved and entranced mode. The protagonist moves from story-teller to participant within the drama. You can often feel a shift in the room when this occurs. George experiences such a shift at this point. His notes reflect this shift, as

George modifies how he identifies himself and others. He becomes 'Geo' (for George). Diane becomes 'Di' (for director and Diane). Antoine becomes 'AE' (for auxiliary ego and Antoine). And George expresses in italicized parenthetical comments what is going on inside himself.

DI: Can you tell us a little about your father?

GEO: He is tall, with a strong personality. He worked hard and asked us to work hard. He moved here to sell real estate and renovate this old farm he and Mom bought. I loved to be with him, but he was away a lot. He was driven and restless. I think he and Mom were happy together then, but it was hard to make a living.

DI: Is he still alive?

GEO: Both of them are. But they got divorced later. Things got tense when I was a teenager. It was a mess. I loved him and respected him. So, it was a tremendous blow then.

DI: I am sure. (*Pause.*) George, let's go back to when you were little, if that is okay with you. Was it only your mother who took you to the hospital then?

GEO: (*I stop walking, try to remember. I can't believe Dad was absent. That doesn't seem right. I remember him in the hospital once.*)
I don't know. That time in the blizzard Mom had to drive because Dad was away. But I recall the last time I had to go to the hospital and see Dr. Y, Dad was there. Dr. Y was someone special, really wonderful. I had to go for some kind of injection. It was the last time I went. I remember my Dad saying I'd be okay. I hated shots. I was four years old. He and Mom took me that time.

AE: (*Antoine as auxiliary ego*): I really loved my Dad, didn't I?

GEO: Yes.

AE: But he let me down badly later, didn't he?

GEO: Yes . . . (*Here, I begin to walk again. I feel more tears.*) Yes, badly. But that's another story. It probably has nothing to do with my experience as a little boy.

DI: Maybe not. When you think of the asthma attacks, what place was important to you?

GEO: Mrs. P's house. I might have been fine going there at first, but after a while I am not sure I was so okay with it. (*Here, Di stops and turns to me. It's as if our minds meet.*)

DI: What if we set up two scenes in the room? The first will be Mrs. P's house, the second the hospital room. How would that be?

GEO: It seems just right.

DI: What if someone plays your mother, another person plays Mrs. P, a third plays Chad, and a fourth plays Dr. Y.

GEO: Yes, but what about my father?

DI: If he seems essential to you, we can add him, but I sense that it might be best to keep the drama as simple as possible.

GEO: (*Di is probably right. I am going way back in time. I want it to happen. I don't want it to be complex . . . even if part of me wants to include Dad.*) I can't see how he fits in, and I want to get back to that time.

Setting the scene

DI: Okay. Where do we place Mrs. P's house? And how do you want to set it up?

GEO: (*The windows are on my right, to the east; the far wall is ahead, to the north; the entry side is to my left, west; and the wall just behind me is to the south. I feel as if Mrs. P's should be in the middle of the room east and west, but somewhat to this southern end. The hospital should be at the northern end near the far wall. I set chairs for the four corners of Mrs. P's house. I tell Diane that the northern half is her upstairs, and the southern half her basement. I use chairs and blankets to indicate furniture.*)
Mrs. P's house had a ground floor and a basement. I hated the basement. I recall at least once being put in a caged area in the basement. I saw big, black bugs. They scared me. My brother Chad was there. He tried to reassure me. I wonder whether it was something like this that set off the first asthma attack. I clearly remember the cage and bugs. But I don't know what caused the asthma?

DI: What was Mrs. P's first floor like?

GEO: Wooden, one story, maybe four rooms, linoleum floors, the smell of coal. Mr. P was a carpenter. The house was okay. I was mostly happy there, I think. I remember being happy growing up. The Ps were good people. But some part of being there didn't work for me.

DI: And the basement?

GEO: Smooth, concrete floor and stone walls. The caged area was clean. I don't think we went down there often. I can't even believe it happened now, but my memory is so clear of one time there. What might make sense would be this. Maybe, Mrs. P put us down there once or twice when she had to go somewhere because Mr. P was away doing his carpentry. The cage was made of smooth, interwoven wire. It was big, like a little room.

DI: Is there anything else you feel you need to tell us about it?

GEO: No. That's enough. (*AE and I circle counterclockwise away from Mrs. P's. Di is standing at a distance. I can't remember when she stopped moving with us.*)

AE: How is it for me to be back in Mrs. P's?

GEO: It's not horrible. But I don't like the basement. I don't feel completely safe or comfortable there.

AE: I don't feel completely safe there.

GEO: No. (*I pause with this feeling. It is strange that the home of good people who were kind to me feels unsafe!*)

Introducing the key figures

DI: George, who should play Mrs. P?

GEO: Let me think. (*After a while, I ask Sylvia, because she is so motherly, though I don't tell her this. She accepts the role and takes the seat that I have set for Mrs. P. I stand behind Sylvia, but I 'see' Mrs. P more than 30 years ago, sitting in her living room armchair. I try to feel how Mrs. P must have felt and recall her body shape and her clothes. Finally, I place my hands on Sylvia's shoulders and begin to 'load' Mrs. P into her.*)

MRS. P: [*as introduced by George*]: I am Mrs. P. I am average-sized. My husband and I don't have much money, and we don't have children of our own. I love children. That is why I take care of kids like George and Chad and why we are foster parents. But I get frustrated because first we have a child, and then it is taken away for adoption.

AE: [*now as the auxiliary to Mrs. P, because George is introducing Mrs. P*]: How do I feel about George?

MRS. P: [*as introduced by George*]: Oh, he is so happy. He lights up our house. His dark curly hair is gorgeous, I sometimes put ribbons in his curls. He looks so cute. He doesn't seem to mind. I want a daughter so much. Now I have a new foster daughter. She's with George and Chad and the other kids. I hope we can adopt her. But I think we're too old.

DI: What is Mrs. P's sense of how George feels about her?

MRS. P: [*as introduced by George*]: Oh, I think George likes me. He's always smiling, except when he has those terrible asthma attacks.

AE: [*as the auxiliary to Mrs. P, as George introduces her*]: How is it for me at those times?

MRS. P: [*as introduced by George*]: Terrible! I thought he was going to die the first time. I was so scared. He was turning blue.

AE: [*as the auxiliary to Mrs. P as George introduces her*]: I was so scared. He was turning blue.

MRS. P: [*as introduced by George*]: Yes.

DI: Okay, I think that may be enough. How is it for you, George?

GEO: Yes, that's fine. (*Di then looks to Sylvia-Mrs. P, who asks, 'How old am I?' I answer for her, 'About 45.' Sylvia-Mrs. P gives a thumbs-up. I walk away just a little.*)

AE: [*returning to role as George's auxiliary ego*]: How is it for me to be near Mrs. P again?

GEO: I'm sure she was good to me, but I don't like that she put ribbons in my hair and pretended I was a girl. It feels a little sick somehow. It feels good to step away from her and the house. (*We circle a little more. I feel relieved to be moving away from the house*).

DI: Now the hospital room where you were in the oxygen tent. Where should it be?

GEO: Here! (*I stand near the northern end of the room, a little toward the windows to the east.*)

DI: Okay. Can you set up the bed and oxygen tent?

GEO: Let me see. How to do this? (*As I talk with AE, I begin to 'see' the hospital room in my mind. We take two chairs, turn their backs to face each other but about four feet apart. We stretch a big blanket over them and over the space between them. I get underneath to try it out. My head is under one chair, my feet under the other. The blanket comes almost to the floor on both sides.*)

Perfect! (*I slide out and stand.*)

DI: Now who will play Dr. Y?

GEO: Polly.

(*Polly is a friend. She's bright, competent and kind, just like Dr. Y. She is willing. I put a chair for her near the oxygen tent. She sits down. I recall and get a feeling for Dr. Y. Finally, I put my hands on Polly's shoulders and 'load' Dr. Y.*)

DR. Y: [*as introduced by George*]: I am Dr. Y, a pediatrician. I have practised here for thirty years. I like my work. Parents respect me and children like me. I am warm, but also a no-nonsense person. I had to be, to go to medical school and then start a practice thirty years ago. Not many women did that then.

DI: What does Dr. Y think of George?

DR. Y: [*as introduced by George*]: Oh, I like George! Such a sunny disposition! He is afraid of shots and pain, but he tries to be brave. He's bright like his Mom and Dad. It always hurts me when a child suffers this much. The first time George came in, I stayed with him through the night so that his Mom would not worry. I slept beside George to be sure he was okay. He was blue when he first came in. There were other episodes. But slowly he got better, and then his family moved.

AE: [*now as the auxiliary to Dr. Y, as George introduces her*]: I liked George very much, and I was worried. So I stayed with him all night.

DR. Y: [*as introduced by George*]: Yes. I was moved by his obvious suffering. I wanted to be there. It was important.

GEO: Just a moment. (*My eyes tear up again as I stand back and away from Dr. Y. She really did care. She spent the night with me.*)

DI: I think that's enough.

GEO: I agree. (*Di looks to Polly-Dr. Y. She nods okay. AE and I circle again.*)

AE: How is it just now for me, looking at Dr. Y sitting there?

GEO: It's moving. I really trusted her. She was so calm. I'm surprised that she was worried. I would never have known. She must have cared about me a great deal to stay all night. (*There is a long pause as I sit with these thoughts and feelings.*)

DI: Now, George, your brother Chad?

GEO: What about my Mom?

DI: What if we introduce her last?

GEO: Okay, let me put two chairs down here. (*I put two chairs near the doorway, in the southwest corner. This is my childhood home. I ask Perry to play Chad. Perry looks like Chad and keeps things to himself the way Chad does. Perry accepts the role and sits in Chad's chair. It is easy to introduce Chad.*)

CHAD: [*as introduced by George*]: I am Chad. I'm two years older than George, so I take care of him. But I also tease him some. George is friendly and kind. I am glad I have a brother. I show him things, and he likes to try the things I show him. He's happy most of the time. I mostly like him, but sometimes I don't like the extra attention he gets because he's younger.

DI: How was it for Chad to go to Mrs. P's house?

CHAD: [*as introduced by George*]: No big deal. It was fine. Mom had to work. There was no other way. The P's were nice folks.

DI: I think that's enough, unless you have more. Chad is just going to be with you at Mrs. P's, playing some and perhaps going down to the basement.

GEO: Okay. (*Perry-Chad and I both shake our heads in agreement. AE and I move away from Chad in his chair.*)

AE: How is it for me [*George*] just now?

GEO: You know, I remember how often Chad was there for me. We are very different. We often disagreed, and a few times even fought, but he has been very loyal to me at many points in my life. I am glad he is here. (*I look at Di, as if waiting for what's next.*)

DI: What if we introduce your mother now?

GEO: Yes, that seems right. (*I ask Elsa to play Mom. She's smart and thoughtful like Mom, has the same reserve and command. Elsa accepts and sits in the chair I placed next to Chad. I pause for a while behind her. This is my mother. I want to get her right. Okay, now.*)

MOM: [*as introduced by George*]: I am Nancy. I am 65 years old now. I was 28 when George's asthma attacks began. They were awful. I didn't have any difficulties like that when I grew up, only later in my marriage. As a student I did well academically. I also had early success in my career. Later, my sons became the center of my life. I became a teacher, first part-time, then full-time. But always, my boys meant the most to me. They helped me get through the hardest times.

DI: What happened when George got sick?

MOM: [*as introduced by George*]: It was very frightening. When I got to Mrs. P's the first time, George had turned blue and was gasping for air. I rushed him to the hospital. They got him oxygen immediately and gave him shots. Later, Dr. Y offered to stay with him overnight. We were lucky to have such an exceptional doctor. She was both medically competent and wonderful as a person.

DI: What did Mom feel about George in general?

MOM: [*as introduced by George*]: He was my sunshine baby. He was so happy. It was impossible not to like him. Everybody did. He was easy to be with. He added a lot of joy to all of our lives.

DI: How was George when these asthma attacks came?

MOM: [*as introduced by George*]: He was in pain and afraid. It was awful. The first time I thought he might die. The time in the blizzard, I just hoped we would all make it to the hospital and not slide off the road.

DI: Did you wonder if the attacks were a psychosomatic reaction to something?

MOM: [*as introduced by George*]: I worried about that. I asked Dr. Y. She didn't think so. I don't either. It may have been an allergic reaction to something. You know, I needed to start a part-time job. My doctor said that all of my symptoms – poor sleep, depression and all – were probably the result of cabin fever. He recommended I get a part-time job. And so I did.

DI: How was it after work began?

MOM: [*as introduced by George*]: It was much better. We needed money. I was going crazy stuck full-time in the middle of nowhere with two little boys. Before, I had spent lots of time with adult colleagues at my job in the city. All of that was gone. I feel badly that it might have been my leaving Chad and George at Mrs. P's, but I think it wasn't. I did what I could.

DI: That may be enough, George. Or is there more to add? (*Di looks at me {George} and at Elsa–Mom. We both nod we are ready. Then AE and I stand away and again circle before I pause.*)

GEO: I understand my Mom's situation even more. It was impossible. I know she cared. She was having psychosomatic reactions. She took the doctor's recommendation. I got asthma a little while later. She doesn't want to think it was what she did that set off the asthma. We'll never know. But what I can feel just now is how much she cared for me. I realize another mother might not have that need for adult contact and work, but Mom couldn't help that. She was bright and going stir-crazy.

AE: She was a good Mom.

GEO: Yup!

AE: But, she felt I might die.

GEO: Yes. It must have been awful. (*I am quiet with this for a while. Then, DI and I consider what is to come next. Together we decide: Chad and I will play upstairs at Mrs. P's before going down into the cage to the bugs and asthma attack. Then the emergency and rush to the hospital. Finally, the hospital, oxygen tent and Dr. Y helping me.*)

Enactment: playing in Mrs. P's living room

DI: Okay, George, you and Chad are at Mrs. P's, playing. You can begin. Mrs. P is in another room. Your Mom is at work.

GEO: (silence): (*I hesitate. I can't seem to play, even after Chad hands me a pillow and says it's a truck. I hesitate. Chad is playing. Callie {a group member} comes up and puts her hands on my shoulders after handing me a shoe, 'doubling' me.*)

CALLIE: [*doubling for George*]: Wow! Look at this neat train engine. I can go all around the room with it!

GEO: (*that does it: Chad and I love trains*): Look, Chad, it's a train!

CHAD: Choo, choo, choo, choo!!!

GEO: Cool! Trains! (*We play trains for quite a while, then we play shop. Then I get this idea there is a big ball in the room.*)

GEO: Whee! It's a big ball, Chad! Watch this. Watch me roll, Chad! (*I roll over to Chad. He rolls me along further. We cut loose. Amazing! I'm doing this in a room of adults. I hear laughter, but I'm so into the playing, I probably miss most of it. It's so much fun! But then, after a while, I hear Mrs. P coming.*)

Enactment: descent to Mrs. P's basement and asthma attack

MRS. P: There you are, boys! I'm glad you're having so much fun. Why don't you keep playing, but go on down to the basement. I have to go out for a few minutes. You can play there and take the toys with you. I'll just be gone for a few minutes.

GEO: Okay . . . (*Down we go – Mrs. P first, me next, Chad behind. I feel dread. She turns on the light. We're going into the cage.*)

AE: Suddenly, I am quiet. What's going on in me?

GEO: I . . . scared. Why this? We were having fun. Why we go down?

CHAD: It's okay, George. We can play here.

MRS. P: It will be okay, George. You boys can keep playing. I'll be right back.

GEO: Okay . . . (*Mrs. P closes the cage door and leaves. Chad plays with the toys. After a while I wander over to the wall. There, I see two huge, black bugs and begin to cry in terror.*)

GEO: Whaaaaaa!!! Chad!!! Whaaaaa!!!

CHAD: What is it?

GEO: I don't know. They're big.

CHAD: Let me see. Wow! They are big. But they are okay.

GEO: I scared. (*Just like Chad. Not afraid of critters. But I feel tightness in my chest. I am remembering the breathing problem. I feel it coming on. I am sucking hard to try to intake enough air. At first I play at this. Then it almost seems real. I fall to the floor, gasping for air and trying to cry out. Now, Chad is afraid. He's calling for Mrs. P – over and over. Finally, she's come down. Suddenly Mrs. P is next to me.*)

Enactment: emergency run and
first day in hospital

MRS. P: Oh my, God! George, what's the matter? What's wrong? Can you breathe? Let me get you upstairs and call the doctor. Come on, Chad!

GEO: Help me! (*Chad and Mrs. P help me 'up the stairs' and lay me down in the living room. Breathing is difficult. Mrs. P calls Mom. Soon Mom arrives. – This part is hard for me to remember. – Mom and Mrs. P put me in the back of the car – four chairs, two and two, serving as the car seats. – Mom gets in front. She 'drives' me to the hospital. There, I am 'carried' in – group members helping me walk in.*)

AE: What's going on for me?

GEO: Strange place. Where am I? White coats are asking questions. I can hardly breathe. Scared!

MOM: It's going to be okay, George.

GEO: (*I'm taken to a room and slid inside an oxygen tent. It's too cool. I ask for extra blankets. Mom is outside the tent, talking to me. At first, it's no better. But then Dr. Y comes. She is calm. I like her. I can barely talk to her and Mom. I gasp for air. It feels good to be in the bed, under the oxygen tent. But, they're out there. I am scared. Mom and Dr. Y calm me. Good that they are here. They tell me to breathe deeply. Sometimes I can. Sometimes I cough when I try. I am so deep into the drama here that, later, I can't recall many of Di's directions and forget much of what I say to Mom and to Dr. Y. I do recall feeling comforted when either of them comes to me. This part of the drama goes on a long time. At some point, I hear Di speaking.*)

DI: Now it is night time.

MOM: George, I have to go home now, to pick up Chad and take care of him. But Dr. Y is going to stay with you. Is that okay?

GEO: Okay, Mom. (*Mom gives me a kiss. I don't want her to go, but Dr. Y is staying. That's good. She lies down next to me, outside the clear plastic tent. I feel better. I fall asleep. A few minutes pass. Then, I awaken. I cry out afraid. My chest is still heavy. Dr. Y comforts me. I ask where Mommy is. Dr. Y says she'll come in the morning. She puts her hand on my belly and soothes me. I fall asleep again. More minutes pass. We are a long time in this overnight time. Slowly I feel better and sleep more.*)

Enactment: recovery, leaving hospital,
return to Mrs. P's home

DI: Now, George, what if we say this is the morning of the fourth day in the hospital. Mom is coming and you get to go home. Would that be okay?

GEO: Yes. It would be great!

MOM: George, you look so much better. You know, Dr. Y says you can come out of the oxygen tent today and come home.

GEO: Oh boy!

DR. Y: Good morning, George. How are you feeling?

GEO: Better.

DR. Y: Good! Will you help me, Nancy?

GEO: (*Dr. Y and Mom lift up the oxygen tent {the brown blanket}, light streams over me. It's like being reborn!*) Wow! So much light! Do I get to ride in the car?

MOM: Yes, of course.

GEO: Yeah! This is great!

DR. Y: Good-bye, George!

GEO: Good-bye, Dr. Y. Thank you. (*Dr. Y gives me a hug. Then, I get into the car with Chad and Mom. Mom drives us back toward home.*)

Enactment: extension of the original trauma, re-envisioning and healing

DI: Okay, George. We can stop here if you would like. Or we can go on. If we go on, it will be a few days later, when it is time for you to go back to Mrs. P's, because your Mom has to return to work.

GEO: Wow! I never pictured it like this. I did have to go back, didn't I? What a thud in the chest! Let me be with this for a moment. . . . (*Of course I had to go back to Mrs. P's, after each asthma attack. Of course, it happened this way! I better try it.*)

Okay, I want to go back to Mrs. P's.

DI: Okay, then, George. You, Mom, and Chad are already in the car. But now, Mom is driving you back to Mrs. P's. Take your time. You can do whatever you want with the scene. It's just for today. It may not have actually happened. But for today, you can do what you want.

GEO: Okay. (*But I don't say anything else. Mom is driving the car. She and Chad talk. They are fine.*)

MOM: George, how are you doing?

GEO: Fine! Fine! Are we going to Mrs. P's?

MOM: Yes, is that okay?

GEO: Okay! (*It must be okay. Mom has to go to work. Chad isn't upset. If it's okay for him, it should be okay for me.*)

AE: Am I sure it's okay? I seem awfully quiet and unsure. This is where the black bugs were. This is where I got sick.

GEO: Yeah, I'm okay.

MOM: Good! Here we are. And there's Mrs. P.

AE: Is this really okay? What's really going on in me right now? My back is so stiff. It's like a board.

MOM: Hi, Mrs. P. What a nice day! And George and Chad are coming back today.

MRS. P: Oh, it's great to see you both. George, you look so healthy. How do you feel?

GEO: I'm okay. (*Wow! I can't believe it. This is how it must have been. It's what my analysis is all about right now – not complaining, not making waves, not risking upsetting others, not claiming things for myself if doing so will bother others. Here I am taking care of Mom, Chad and Mrs. P, but I'm the one who almost died!*)

AE: Am I really okay? Is that true?

GEO: I think so.

DI: Take your time, George. Don't hurry. You can stop if you want, at any time. It's your psychodrama now. You can do what you want.

AE: What do I want? (*Exactly! What do I want? I'll bet I didn't make a fuss. But something is wrong here. Where am I in all this?*)

MOM: Come on, George. It's okay. You'll be okay here at Mrs. P's. Chad will be with you.

MRS. P: Oh yes! You'll be okay. You look so darling with your curls. If you like, I can put ribbons in them today.

GEO: No. . . . No. . . . NO! (*Later I realize Di must have whispered to the role players to say these lines, but in the moment, I don't notice. I just snap inside. I've had it!*)

MOM: What's the matter, George?

GEO: I don't like Mrs. P.

MOM: But she's so nice to you.

GEO: I don't want ribbons in my damn hair. I don't want black bugs on walls in a cage. I don't want to be smothered by her. I don't want you telling me what it's like here. Fine, she tries to be nice to me. She's a good person. But I don't want to go back.

DI: Switch. Slowly switch places. George, you are now playing your Mom and Elsa is going to play you. Elsa, please repeat George's last line. [*Here, Elsa and George slowly switch positions and roles, and Elsa repeats George's last-spoken words.*]

'GEO' [*as played by Elsa*]: Mrs. P is a good person. But I don't want to go back.

(*I {George} sink into Mom now, as I stand in her place. What would she be feeling and saying? It's important to get this right.*)

'MOM' [*now as played by Geo*]: George, I care about you, but I have to go to work. You'll be okay here. You said you'd be okay. I thought you were.

DI: Switch back. (*Again Elsa and I change places. This is critical. I can feel it. I need to take my stand now or never.*)

MOM: [*once again as played by Elsa, repeating the last lines*]: You'll be okay here. You have said you are okay. I thought you were

GEO: I know. But this is not what *I* want.

DI: What do you want, George? This is your time. If you want something, it's okay. It's just for today. (*Long silence as I go into a trance-like place. Then from the depths somewhere comes a line so improbable, it stuns me.*)

GEO: I want my Daddy. I want to go for a drive in the car with Daddy. I don't want to be with you, Mommy, or with Mrs. P. (*Where is this coming from? I'm weeping. I love Dad. I love to drive with him. Why isn't he here?*)

MOM: But he's not here now.

GEO: I know that. Okay, look. I know you have to go to work. And I know Mrs. P is a good person. And I will stay here, but only if she promises me one thing and you another.

MOM: What's that?

GEO: Tonight, Daddy takes me for a ride, just me and him, in the car. And no more ribbons in the hair!

MOM: Yes, of course. I'm sure Daddy will take you for a ride. I'm sure he'll agree.

MRS. P: And no more ribbons, George. I'm sorry. You didn't seem to mind. I didn't realize how much it bothered you.

GEO: All right, then! (*We all stop where we are. It's as if we all know the drama has come to its end. I feel good, and astounded it has led back to Dad! And back to today's issue — not standing up for myself, taking care of others too much. I almost died; yet, I'm so concerned about the others that I don't speak up. No wonder Mom's memories are different from mine. I didn't complain. How would she have known?*)

Ending the drama: Walking clockwise and closing the curtain

AE: Maybe I would like to walk for a moment.

GEO: Yes!

AE: How is it for me just now!

GEO: I am alive. I feel strong. (*We continue walking a little longer. Then I hear Diane.*)

DI: Good, George. I think we should end here.

GEO: Yes.

DI: Why don't you say good-bye to each person? You choose how.

GEO: Sounds good. (*Sometimes saying good-bye is complex for me, finding just the right gesture or words. But today it's easy. I take each of these people from my childhood and first say good-bye to them as a child; then I speak to them as the real persons they are as we walk back to their chairs on the perimeter, thanking them — in the order that seems right to me, with Mom–Elsa next-to-last and Dr. Y–Polly last.*)

Then, I break down the scene – folding blankets and setting them aside, returning 'toys' to their original state as shoes, pencils and pillows, and setting chairs in the beginning of a circle in the center of the room. Soon there is no hospital and no Mrs. P's home – only a few chairs in an arc near the room's center.)

DI: Can we all gather around in a circle then?

GEO: Yes.

Sharing: coming back into community

(We all re-make the original circle of chairs and sit down. Diane asks each role player to share what it was like to be in his or her role. I {George} listen carefully, but I remember only a little of their sharing, so deeply have I gone down, so little energy left to hear much. But I do hear some. They were afraid when I became sick. They felt helpless. 'Mom' speaks of how guilty she felt, but she did not know what else she could do. 'Dr. Y' speaks of how glad she was that I got well and how touched she was by my struggle to breathe. 'AE' says many things, but what strikes me most is his reflection of how frozen and silent I became upon returning to Mrs. P's and how I gained strength when I demanded time with my father. It was as if I were two different people. After each person shares from within role, Diane de-roles the person and helps the person come back into herself or himself.

Then, Diane asks each group member to share from his or her own life. The stories pour from them: illnesses as children, times of being left alone or with someone they were not comfortable with, other forms of trauma – deeply moving stories. We have so much more in common than I realized. What was so hard for me to contemplate – acting like a child in front of other adults – has moved them deeply. I am touched by their saying so and by their experiences. It's amazing how much darkness we all have experienced.

Diane thanks everyone and announces the session has ended. We slowly get up. I speak briefly with a few members, but feel the need to be alone. This experience has been extraordinary. I want to write it down and reflect on it.)

The following session: George's feedback from his experience

A week later, when we next meet, Diane begins by asking me for my feedback. I say words to this effect:

'I want to thank everyone for helping me with last week's drama. I was afraid to do it. But each of you who played roles helped so much, and everyone's sharing at the end helped me see how common is this feeling of being abandoned.

'There were three things that were extraordinary for me last week. The first was the fun that Chad and I had playing. I felt as if I were a child all over again. It was delightfully freeing.

60

'The second thing was how astonished I was to realize that, even when I had almost died and was returning to Mrs. P's, I ignored my own fear and tried to take care of everyone else. Mom had to go to work; so, why upset her? Chad wasn't upset; so, why should I be? And I didn't want to hurt Mrs. P's feelings. But my concern for everyone else was too much. This is the issue in my analysis today. And I see why my Mom has a rosier view of my childhood than I do – because I was not complaining then, just as I fail to do today when complaining is needed.

'After the psychodrama, I happened to speak to my Mom about it and the actual asthma attacks. Do you know what she said? She said that the strangest thing was that it looked as if I could not expel the air, as if my lungs could not express what was in them. What a perfect metaphor! I need to "express" myself in order to assert my standpoint in the world. I needed to express myself then. Apparently, I did not, and that may have been related to my trouble exhaling. I couldn't believe my mother when she told me this. I asked her to repeat it, just to be sure I'd heard her correctly.

'Finally, the most powerful moment of all came with the shock of crying out for my father, to get away from the women, away from the ribbons and the negating of my masculine identity. There is something that my father has that I very much want. What is it? This was completely unexpected. This is the cutting edge of my work today – some powerful complex that just leapt out at the end.'

The End

I later learned from George that the second and third insights that he gained from this psychodrama were to exert a profound and enduring effect on his analysis and his coming to terms with himself and with his parents. Recalling this psychodrama often helped him remember how important it was to stick up for himself and to attend more to his relationships with his father and other men.

Observations about George's psychodrama

Specific techniques

It is worth *naming and briefly explaining a few of the specific techniques* that we have seen in George's psychodrama.[9]

Warming up in psychodrama can take place in a number of ways. In George's case, it is done by Director Diane as she quietly and openly talks with George, lets him describe the outer situation at length, and asks questions to round out the picture. She does this first sitting with George in the group circle, and then later as George, auxiliary ego Antoine, and she walks counterclockwise in a circle. This stroll lets Diane and Antoine learn and feel much more as

George relaxes, his inhibitions lower, and the time of enacting the asthma attack approaches.

Setting the scene has the important effect of involving the protagonist in the re-creation and embodiment of the physical situation he was in and will now return to. Things become more real and embodied. In this psychodrama, George, Diane, and Antoine take great care setting up Mrs. P's house and the hospital room. This patience with the sensate details helps to make everything more real. You can hear this as George's account goes on. It's as if he is actually at Mrs. P's or in the hospital.

Choosing a group member to play a particular role brings us to one of the great mysteries in psychodrama. George picks Perry because he looks like Chad and because Perry 'keeps things to himself the way Chad does'. He picks Polly to play Dr. Y because both of them are 'bright, competent, and kind'. But often it is only after the drama has been enacted and the sharing is underway that the protagonist and group learn that a particular member has been asked to play a role that precisely re-enacts his or her own life experience. When this information comes out, it is like a lightning strike – a primal experience of synchronicity! The unconscious has played a powerful role in selecting the role player. This kind of numinous experience does not happen in George's drama, but you can see how carefully he chooses those who serve as role players.

Introducing the key figures can be very powerful in and of itself. Occasionally, a psychodrama will end with the introduction of a particularly important figure, perhaps a parent or lover, because so much emotion arises in the protagonist simply by being in this person's skin and 'loading' the person into a group member. While nothing this strong occurs for George, the people in his life come powerfully to life in the room as he introduces them.

Doubling is important in the enactment phase. The director invites a non-role member on the perimeter of the room to stand behind the protagonist (or one of the role players) and give voice to that which the protagonist (or role player) may be just shy of articulating. The 'Double' puts his/her hands on the person's shoulders and speaks as if playing that person for the moment and saying something the group member feels might serve the protagonist. The protagonist is encouraged to accept, reject, or simply ignore the input of the Double. In George's psychodrama, doubling occurs only once, when non-role player Callie steps behind George to help him let go and play like a child. The doubling helps George finally jump into playing.

Role reversal is another critical tool. When George and his mother confront each other in the final, critical scene, Diane asks George to reverse roles – to switch between himself and his mother. This example reveals the multiple purposes of role reversal. One purpose is to get the other figure right. Group member Elsa is playing George's mother. Elsa knows George's mother hardly at all; George knows his mother extremely well. It is a critical scene. He needs to get the conversation between himself and his mother right. Rather than unduly strain Elsa and risk turning the psychodrama false, Diane asks George to switch between himself and his mother. After each switch, Elsa repeats the last lines spoken by George in the role he has just left in order to help him orient to where he is and to decide how he wants to respond from the new role.

A second purpose of role reversal is to shift the protagonist 'into the other person's shoes'. This permits the protagonist feel what it's like to be the other person and see himself from the other person's perspective. Here George gets inside his mother and sees himself from her perspective.

A final purpose of role reversal is to slow down and deepen the encounter. The switches take time. This taking of time helps the protagonist deepen into both roles, to really dig inside to find what lies at the heart of the situation for self and other. Such a deepening clearly happens for George.

A final technique, *mirroring*, was not employed in George's drama. If there had been a moment when Diane thought George needed to see himself in a certain situation or posture, Diane could have asked George which non-role group member might play him for a few minutes. George could have chosen a member and observed that member imitating George's posture, voice, or movement. In such a moment George might have seen himself in a different light.

While there are other techniques, I hope that highlighting these few gives some appreciation for the various ways one can work with a protagonist.

General observations

I want to end by drawing several general points from George's psychodrama – those that go to the heart of psychodrama as a therapeutic method.

First is the *power of psychodrama*. Not unlike active imagination, psychodrama is an uncommonly powerful therapeutic tool. George is profoundly moved in this re-enactment of his childhood asthma attacks, and he learns much about himself, as his feedback a week later clearly shows.

Second is the corollary that comes with this power: the *need for caution*. The director and auxiliary ego must always exercise care and restraint. It would be easy to exhaust, strain, overwhelm, even abuse the protagonist. Helmut Barz spoke of his teacher, Dean Elefthery, cautioning him: 'As director, you cannot solve in one psychodrama a person's problems that have taken a lifetime to come into being.' And I remember Doreen Elefthery saying to us four times in one weekend, in effect, 'If you as director have a choice between trying an idea or not, and you don't know why you want to try it and how it will serve the protagonist, then don't do it. Almost always, less is better than more.'

George's drama shows this clearly. He has a simple goal: re-experience his childhood asthma attacks to see what is revealed. Diane and Antoine try to simplify the set, introduce only the figures who are essential, and intervene during the drama as little as they can. Yet, from this dramatization George experiences three breakthroughs: (a) re-living the delightful play of childhood; (b) seeing his tendency to put his concern for others ahead of his concern for himself (even to his own detriment) and realizing that now is the time to correct this one-sided way of relating; and (c) experiencing his great need to connect with his father. He also spontaneously discovers psychological connections between his asthma attacks as a toddler and his individuation needs almost forty years later.

Third is a point that many psychodramatists might mention first: *the capacity of psychodrama to enable the protagonist to enact and experience what has been, is, or will be of the greatest psychological significance.* The movement in space; the setting of the scene; the 'loading' of people key to the protagonist into group members; the energy, insights, and emotions that the role players bring to the drama; the interaction between them and the protagonist; the presence, energy, and gifts of the director as guide and the auxiliary ego as articulator of what lies just beneath the surface: all of these factors enable a coming into being that can be hard to engender in talk therapy.

In George's drama, for example, we are transported to a time and a place completely other than today. George and the group enter into his childhood: the crushing reality and fear of his asthma attack; the relief as he recovers; the anxiety and withdrawal as he returns to Mrs. P's; George's finding the will to stand up for himself; and his expressed need for a greater masculine presence. No one knew what to expect. Only by taking all of the steps of psychodrama is the original experience re-lived and a fuller picture realized.

Fourth is another source of healing in psychodrama, *how it shapes and reshapes one's sense of belonging in community.* There is the gathering in a circle and checking in by each group member, followed by the protagonist of the previous session giving feedback about her or his psychodrama. Finally, this session's psychodrama begins, and another group member brings something essential from her/his life. The others in the group are asked to stretch beyond their natural tendencies toward stereotyping and judgment, as the room is filled with a problem, situation, constellation, and complex of emotions that some might prefer to keep at bay. Because commentary is strongly discouraged and deep personal sharing encouraged, a vessel for depth and soul is created. The protagonist gives deeply from within; then, the group gives back. In this extraordinary exchange of gifts (the most difficult, wonderful, traumatic, joyful, awful, paradoxical stuff of their lives), the protagonist and group learn deeply about self and other. This builds community within the group and beyond.

In George's case, he sees how it is his natural disposition that has led to his feeling he is not being seen in his suffering. George overcomes his inhibition to play and to suffer as a child in front of others, which leads to their sharing of similar experiences. In this way, George re-joins the world. He is not so isolated as he has feared.

Fifth is the *need for analysis and reflection beyond psychodrama*. It is essential that everyone in George's group is in analysis or therapy. It is one thing to re-experience the asthma attacks, quite another to reflect upon that re-experiencing and become more conscious. George gains much more because he carefully writes out the account, reflects on it, and discusses his experience with his analyst and his mother. He thereby learns more about his past and more about what he needs to work on now.

Sixth, as Moreno points out (Fox 1987: 3–5), psychodrama engenders the *weaving of time past, with time present and time future*. In George's drama, it is difficult to know how the asthma attacks actually began when he was young, how much he did *not* complain, how present his father was or was not, and so on. Much of his 'memory' may really be imagination highly influenced by today's complexes. But in a real sense this does not matter if one recalls that any work going back into the past is done primarily to see how we are today. George's key insights – regarding his inability to stand up for himself and his need to connect with his father and the masculine – surely have as much to do with his present and future as they do with his childhood.

Seventh is a point that Helmut Barz discusses in his article *regarding psychodrama and the transcendent function*.[10] Just as every aspect of time is involved in psychodrama, so too is *every typological function*. Sensation is activated when describing and setting the scene, as well as when being in the scene and close to the key figures in one's life. Not only are the five obvious senses activated, but so, too, is the kinesthetic sense of body in motion and space. This strong sensation component and the embodiment of significant figures around an important issue or dream generate emotions and activate the feeling function. The pauses, the reflection of the auxiliary ego, the questions and any unexpected directions of the director, the doubling by group members, the switching of roles by the protagonist, and the sharing by role players and group members all enliven the thinking and intuition functions. And at moments in most dramas all four functions are in play. This leads to the rising of the transcendent function. At such moments profound insight and enduring healing can take place, as happens here for George.

Eighth is the critical *role of the director*. The director must do many of the things that an analyst does: create a safe vessel for the protagonist and group, maintain an open and empathic connection with the protagonist, serve as an anchor, and ask questions and listen to gain a sense of the protagonist (his or her story, ego strength, vulnerabilities, Persona, Shadow, Anima or Animus, activated complexes, what can safely be worked upon and what is best left alone, etc.). But some aspects of the director's role are unique: for example, helping to choose and set the scenes to be enacted; deciding when role reversal is appropriate; discerning when someone might stand in for the protagonist so that he/she can step out and see him/herself from a distance; and deciding when to end a scene, open the curtains or turn on a light, or encourage the non-role players to double.

Diane displays many of these skills as she directs George's psychodrama. I will highlight just one of them. Near the end of the drama, Diane makes one significant suggestion that George has never considered, and it leads to George's two most important experiences and insights. Diane suggests that George, after his hospitalization, return to Mrs. P's. It is not a difficult idea to think of, but the director cannot know whether the protagonist will accept it or where it will lead. Certainly, if George were tired or overwhelmed at this point, Diane's best option would be to suggest ending the drama. But what Diane sees is George's deep engagement in the drama, the tension lurking just under the surface, and the possibility of gaining insight. Diane makes it clear that George may stop or play the return to Mrs. P's in any way he wants. This *reality* hits George in his chest. 'I am stunned. Of course, it must have happened this way. . . . I never thought of this', he says. He realizes he needs to go with the idea, Diane and Antoine help him with it, and he comes to the most powerful experiences and insights of the session.

Ninth is the *role of auxiliary ego*. The auxiliary ego is the most important support figure in the room, serving as protector, encourager, articulator, and mirror. When a psychodrama becomes difficult, this is the person upon whom the protagonist relies for help, who signals to the director when there is a need for a change in course, who can sense when the protagonist is nearing a breakthrough, who can ask important questions, such as: 'What am I feeling right now?' or 'My muscles are tight, what's bothering me?' We see Antoine playing this role almost to perfection throughout the psychodrama. He does such a wonderful job that we hear George commenting on how supported he feels at several points.

Finally, there is the *spontaneity of psychodrama*. So many times the protagonist, director, auxiliary ego and group members are surprised by what happens in a psychodrama. To take but one example in George's enactment, it is obvious that no one foresaw that George would 'cut loose' with Chad and play with such delight, or that George would suddenly ask for his father or demand to ride in the car with him. These extraordinary moments arose because of, and in spite of, the careful work of everyone to re-enact George's childhood asthma attacks. Psychodrama invites the unlived into life, but how it comes into being, and from where, is often a mystery.

I hope this introduction to Jungian psychodrama, using George's experience as an example, gives some idea how this form of group psychotherapy can complement and add to individual analysis.

Notes

1 The Barzs trained in psychodrama with Americans Dean and Doreen Elefthery, who had trained with Jacob and Zerka Moreno. Jacob Moreno was, of course, the originator of psychodrama. He is to psychodrama what Freud is to free association and psychoanalysis and what Jung is to active imagination and analytical psychology.

2 Accessible introductions to Jacob Moreno and psychodrama include: *The Essential Moreno: Writings on Psychodrama, Group Method, and Spontaneity* by J. L. Moreno (Fox 1987); *Foundations of Psychodrama: History, Theory, and Practice* (Blatner 2000); and *Acting-In: Practical Applications of Psychodramatic Methods* (Blatner 1996).

3 If two or more members want to work in a session, then those members discuss for whom it is most important to work in that session. No one else may express an opinion: the director facilitates the discussion. On rare occasions, the interested members may resort to chance (e.g., the roll of a die) to determine the protagonist, but only if all competing to work agree to this process. It typically takes 5–15 minutes for those discussing the matter to discern who the protagonist will be for the session.

4 Rather more common in the world of psychodrama is to find one director working alone.

5 I am deeply indebted to the person who is 'George' for his willingness to share with others this psychodrama and the life experience that it portrays.

6 First-person narration is appropriate for another reason. One learns about psychodrama not so much by reading or studying but, rather, by participating in psychodrama groups over time. Thus, by hearing this psychodrama from the protagonist's voice, we come very close to what an initial encounter with psychodrama is like.

7 I have superimposed the headings onto George's narrative in order to identify and highlight the stages involved in a psychodrama, as well as to help readers orient themselves within this extended account of George's session.

8 Here we see one of the elements of uncertainty in psychodrama: one must struggle in the group, like a young bird in a nest of siblings, for the chance to partake of the nourishment. There is not that certainty of individual attention that one feels in analysis. There is *both* greater attention – from the group – if it is one's time to work *and* less attention and a duty that I attend to another – if it is that person's time to work.

9 For a more complete list of psychodramatic techniques, see 'A Compendium of Psychodramatic Terms and Techniques', in Blatner (2000) *Foundations of Psychodrama: History, Theory, and Practice*, New York: Springer Publishing Co.

10 Barz (1992). This article also contains a brief, clear description of Helmut and Ellynor Barz's approach to psychodrama.

References

Barz, H. (1992) 'The Transcendent Function and Psychodrama', in *The Transcendent Function: Proceedings of the Twelfth Annual IAAP*, Einsiedeln, Switzerland: Daimon Verlag, pp. 173–88.

Blatner, A. (1996) *Acting-In: Practical Applications of Psychodramatic Methods*, New York: Springer Publishing Co.

Blatner, A. (2000) *Foundations of Psychodrama: History, Theory, and Practice* (4th ed.), New York: Springer Publishing Co.

Fox, J. (ed.) (1987) *The Essential Moreno: Writings on Psychodrama, Group Method, and Spontaneity by J. L. Moreno,* New York: Springer Publishing Co.

5

THE DRUM TIME OF PSYCHODRAMA

Reflections on a Jungian psychodrama group

Siri Ness

Apparently it happened out of the blue. One day a fellow student at the C.G. Jung Institute Zürich announces that there is one opening in the English-language psychodrama group. The very next day I find myself in the group at the Barz Psychodrama Institute in Zumikon outside Zürich. Just so. Apparently.

The drama of psyche is everywhere, as if psyche in its essence is drama, to such an extent that strange questions may arise: whose 'drama' (or life) is this? Is it I who live my life, or my life that lives me? But, then, '. . . no one knows what "psyche" is, and one knows just as little how far into nature "psyche" extends' (Jung 1934, para. 806, p. 409). That is our drama.

As I reconnect now and open up to my experiences in that psychodrama group, what emerges in my mind, with an 'aha' in my body and *vice versa*, is the rhombus. I know it well – from dreams first, years back; then, later, it manifested as the centre of the shamanic drums of the Saami people when I wrote an introductory paper on those drums (Ness 1994). Oval drums they were, decorated with images of gods and goddesses, and of the shaman's experiences of other worlds and the everyday world with the dead nearby, all centred around a rhombus, called *beivve* [the sun]. During my work on that paper, this rhombus became strangely alive to me, opening up as it did to a kind of pulsating, centring and life-giving energy that was, at one and the same time, strengthening and calming; a matrix, as it were, a still point of being and becoming. And I also found that the placement of the decorations helped me to deepen and structure my understanding of the dynamic dimensions of (their) life. Traditional Saami life, religion and economy obviously were one living organism, rooted in nature and part of nature.[1]

The rhombus equals the smoke-hole of the nomad's tent: that is, the opening to the upper world, symbolizing the World Tree, the *axis mundi*, or – for the Saami – the World Pole,[2] as seen from above. According to this axis, the access to the lower world would then be through the fireplace, which may relate to the shaman's connection to fire. The drum was sacred and profane at the same time – a tool for the shaman's journey to the other worlds as well as for divination in all areas of everyday life.[3] Both in that respect and through the actual rhombus-axis, the drum contained horizontal and vertical levels in more than three dimensions.

For me, the rhombus became a symbol for these dimensions. Hence its emergence now, as I open up to my time with psychodrama and to the energy that brought the drama-journeys forth, is no surprise. A surprise it is, however, when I realize for the first time that the rhombus, in its various expressions, seems to have played an important part in those dramas that come back to me. Unawares, it seems, I lived in a drum time.[4]

Psyche has its own inscrutable ways. Better go with the journey of its drum, with as much awareness as possible.

I had read about classical Moreno psychodrama as early as 1978 (Røine 1978). I was much intrigued by the approach, but not ready to explore it further. Then, when I started my training at the C. G. Jung Institute, I was ready to sign up for Wilma Scategni's seminars.[5] And so it is that my fellow student announces an opening in an on-going psychodrama group.[6] Tired, if not exhausted, and in much need of peace and quiet (which is *not* what you get when you go with psyche and find yourself in a Jungian training programme), nevertheless I hurry up to him.

And so, all of a sudden, fifteen years after I first heard of Moreno, I am part of a psychodrama group. This, however, is Moreno psychodrama with a Jungian approach, according to Helmut and Ellynor Barz, Jungian analysts and lecturers at the C.G. Jung Institute and founders of their own psychodrama institute. They combine the two powerful approaches of Moreno and Jung: working on the personal level of consciousness and the personal unconscious, with a deep understanding of the mysterious ways of the collective unconscious, allowing for archetypal patterns and the degree to which these impersonal energies may work in our personal lives.

The participants of the group are fellow students, some whom I know a bit, others not at all. Some have been part of the group for a long time, others have joined recently. Part of the dynamic of the group is shaped by the fact that we all come from different continents, countries and cultures, some of us in the last part of training, others fairly new at it, all of us with our individual stories, backgrounds, professions and experiences, yet sharing that inner 'must' that has brought us to leave families, friends and work to reside in Zürich (with no commuting possible) for a training most of us cannot get otherwise: a very mixed group of people, indeed, converging here in a room at a very special time in our lives.

The basic rules and structure are explained to the newcomers, and then the drama starts.

I am in my second semester at the Institute, steeped in my version of 'the process'; already fed up with that term, it nevertheless seems the simplest one to label what each one of us goes through when life leads (or drags, depending on our willingness) a person onto her very own narrow road. Not unlike the process of the caterpillar that one day *has* to go into the cocoon, completely at the mercy of those forces of transformation and certainly 'not prepared for the agony of the transformation that goes on inside the chrysalis' (Woodman 1985, pp. 20–21). Some drum journey, that.

In this respect, our dramas have already started. There has been the drama of settling into a completely new way of life, of finding accommodation (quite a struggle for a lot of us) and money, of tentatively beginning to explore sand play, dream groups, authentic movement, taking part in special seminars on children's dreams and picture interpretation, writing papers and following lectures and more seminars, to say nothing of the training analysis itself, all of these persistently challenging old survival strategies, functional systems turning out to be only functional. We are all going through chaotic and frantic periods before some order emerges in the transitional chaos, before we settle into the chrysalis of the immersion training.

But this is a different kind of drama, even if it is very much part of it all. This is a drama delimited in space and time, in Zumikon once a week, with a director and an auxiliary ego, a drama of life and psyche certainly, but with a supportive grid and structure that holds you, and that persists if you try to make it (too) easy for yourself, as it dawns upon me during the drama this very first morning in the group. It also gives me a lively introduction to the elements of psychodrama: the stepping forward of a protagonist, the choosing of actors, the presentation of the characters they are to play, and how the director and auxiliary ego actually work. I like what I see. What is more, the feeling of the group is good, particularly during the sharing after the drama. I take part, yet stay somewhat on the distant side.

The second psychodrama, the following week, hits me with an astounding and unexpected power. Suddenly being so close to another person's real pain and struggles touches off my own. And what hits just as much, if not more, is the underlying impersonal archetypal aspects of that personal drama – or, rather, the combination of the two. What you go through within and how you cope with this is one thing; another is what others see, and what you see or don't see in them and their challenges. Suddenly you recognize something in the drama of others in ways your 'head' may not understand. Suddenly something opens up and will not let go. Luckily that is the case!

So, given the way psyche works, in the wake of these inner eruptions triggered by the second psychodrama, further eruptions come in a seminar the very same day, these followed by powerful images in dreams, memories and drawings. I accept that I 'think' in images: only when I have an inner image am I able to remember, to understand, and to see. In this particular instance, a hole opens up, and with it a jungle and much uneasiness. And the eruption continues, and the hole grows, and the hole widens underneath me in a seminar on the liminal phases of life and brings to mind a dream, an example of a childhood dream, from another seminar, of trying not to fall and the hole comes closer. Strangely, Jung's descent into the chasm does not occur to me (Jung 1961, p. 205) – but, then, this hole is clearly no chasm, and I do not understand its persistent presence. Slowly, from within – from within the hole? – a strange urge stirs: *Work on the hole in psychodrama*. A *hole*? Work on a hole in psychodrama?!?

I work on the hole in psychodrama, the very next day. That morning, the hole has increased in size, and so has the unease. I make up my mind. If no one else wants to do a drama, I will. No one does. As my hand starts to move – I never get around to putting it up – Helmut notices, and there I am, doing my very first drama after only two sessions. Time and experience are not the issue: the urge and the need are – and the chance. So, I have my drama.

And I discover more about psychodrama. Such as choosing persons for your drama, how intriguing that is: the conscious reason for your choice is only one part of it, the unconscious having its own reasons. Surprisingly often it seems that the two meet in the persons chosen. Intriguing, too, and powerful, is what happens when you present your characters – even a hole. Particularly the hole, I find – as if the hole presents itself through me. I know that the person I want to play this part has a knowledge of holes, that it may be too difficult for her to embody the role, but I ask, and she accepts. Is this the hole working through both of us? And this, too, is part of a whole: not only the protagonist is facing her inner and outer challenges, but the persons she picks have their own issues, which may be triggered by the roles they are asked to play, so that unwittingly I may put them in roles that mean more for them in their own lives and dramas than for me in mine – and that, of course, gives even more depth to my own.

As the protagonist, I choose and present the characters, they 'belong' to me – but I am not the director. And there's the auxiliary ego, too. Between them, they open up and extend and bring new energies and voices into the enigma of the drama. I find myself between my characters, I hear and partly receive what the auxiliary ego says, what my characters say, even what I, the protagonist, say and do.

> . . . on the floor . . . my hand creeps towards the hole – gets in touch. Gets in touch . . . brown feathers . . . and blue . . . brushes a cheek . . . the cheek of the hole . . . lovely . . . the lovely hole . . . there's gold to be found . . . light . . . and a jungle . . . lush, green jungle . . .

The *lovely* hole . . . ?!? I was expecting the hole to be full of painful, no-longer available memories and experiences. To my huge surprise, that is not what the

71

journey of the psychodrama brings. *This* hole is a black pillar with cracks of golden light. With reflection, I see that a hole can just as well be seen as a pillar, an axis, depending on the point of view. Like a tube that is a pillar and a hole both, bringing light . . .?

What becomes obvious in the days following the psychodrama is that the hole actually contains an astonishing amount of light and joy, a joy in living that reverberates within a background of pain, a dark pain that gives joy depth, if I'm able to stay at the balancing point between the two.

In retrospect now, I think of that rhombus called *beivve* – the sun – that axis of light as coming from the depths above and below. At that time, I have not started my research on the drum. I have not started reading the book on Saami shamans that I will eventually pick up at around this time (Pollan 1993). The rhombic images from my dreams stay at home and out of mind, in old drawings. The hole has nevertheless worked its way into my awareness, with a strange uneasiness and, stranger still, the jungle – this epitome of wild, green nature – which, thanks to the psychodrama, turns out to be a positive presence in my life for the time being.

The words spoken during the psychodrama, during the sharing, somehow disappear afterwards, even if they touch and stay in the unconscious, in the body, working from within. Work from within. Work from without. There is a pat on the shoulder, a big hug, two cards expressing fundamental trust, strong verbal responses, and she who played the hole has also won some important insights.

A few days after my psychodrama, I look at a photo of my drawing of a face, which I always have at hand. It is a strikingly beautiful face from a dream some years ago, a face I first feared, until I dared to stop and to face that face, and was struck by its serene, penetrating beauty. It radiates out of the darkness, yet contains it. Light is not to be had just like that, darkness is not at all to be kicked out: without darkness, light has no meaning. A sudden urge makes me open Jung's *Mysterium Coniunctionis* at random, and my eyes fall on the following passage:

> The eye that hitherto saw only the darkness and danger of evil turns towards the circle of the moon, where the eternal realm of the immortals begins, and the gloomy deep can be left to its own devices, for the spirit now moves it from within, convulses and transforms it. . . .The 'light' that shines at the end is . . . the new widening of consciousness. . . .
>
> (Jung 1955, para 211, p. 172)

The psychodrama told me that the hole is an opening, a solid, flexible aperture, part pillar, part container of light, all in one. In my body there now is a sense of 'fullness' and of warmth under the sternum, as if the unease is somewhat less and the jungle more in place. It is reminiscent of an experience during a shamanic drum weekend a year or two earlier, when I found, to my huge surprise, what an important tool my 'stomach' is, that I have to be in touch with it and 'consult' it, as it were, to listen inwards. 'Gut feeling', some would say; this, however, is more. Instead of suppressing the uneasy 'flickering' evoked by the drumming that grew to a next-to excruciating pain, I stayed with it and listened. Listened and trusted, and on the other side of the pain I saw what the person alongside me suffered. It was an instant of penetrating presence of the other and myself. Without trust, this is impossible, I realize.

As if on cue, up comes *trust* in the very next psychodrama. I see that the uneasiness I have picked up from the protagonist is no figment of my imagination; it is also something I recognize in myself and can share. The dramas are so concrete, and so are the archetypal images and energies that come through them and through us, not least during the sharing. This makes the dimensions of psyche and its symbols alive, many-faceted and rich and turns the drama into a weaving we are all part of, adding our threads to the plait of the protagonist.

The connection between us grows. Suddenly we know who'll have a drama today, before anyone has said a word. And we know who will be asked to act a part. To be asked to act a part – or not – is a dynamic too. Does this influence us? Are some asked more often than others? Does that matter? And if yes, is it a question of trust? Just by being present, each one of us takes part in the drama. All join in the sharing. But what if I lack impressions or images to share? Does anyone else experience a 'sharing block'? I know that I do only when I start *thinking* about what to share, but when I simply trust the images that come, and for me there are always *some* images, then there is no block. The 'closed' book falls open and reveals connections, movements, images, some to be shared. Mostly I don't remember afterwards what I share. If it stays, it stays in the psychodrama room, in some of the members of the group, in the protagonist, for a while.

We continue to meet for a psychodrama session once a week. The impressions last, are as much a part of the 'process' as the outer practicalities of our lives, slowly settling into workable patterns of the quotidian that become a necessary grid for the powerful energies we live within and are lived by, thanks to this chance to explore soul and psyche the best way we can. All of it is interwoven, and the hole now seems to be ever-present, so that during a seminar on adoption, when we are asked to do an exercise – to fall into a bottomless hole – I suddenly 'fall' into a deep-seated lack of trust. The exercise is meant to illustrate how an adopted child will carry a 'break' or 'hole' in the body, having experienced a rupture from the mother-body and its well-known sounds of heartbeat and voice, all of which is suddenly gone – a loss of grounding in the child-body self. Denial of emotions, feelings and senses in relation to life experiences, be they adoption, divorce, death, alcoholism, abuse, or simply being in the world, can create this loss of ground, loss of trust, hidden in (and revealed by) body-tensions long before they can be experienced and translated into words.

Where is 'body' at the Institute at this time? Not obvious. The lectures and seminars are intriguing, challenging, and demanding; lots of intellectualizing and reflecting, insightful descriptions of experience. We sit and we listen and we discuss. Body as ground, as grounding, embodiment that includes the head, is mostly found on the fringes, as 'extras': sand play, a drawing weekend, an authentic movement workshop, and psychodrama.

Psychodrama provides a chance to re-connect to body-ground, through trusting the urge to step into a drama, to present characters, to touch and move around in the room. It is experienced first in breath, in lack of breath, with heartbeats, sweat, uneasiness, eagerness, postures, emotions. Participating in the psychodrama group, you take part, and through the energy you bring to the group and to the protagonist, forgotten images, dreams and experiences now re-emerge in a broader context and with a deeper understanding.

Then, one day I realize that I've lost touch with the hole – such a loss! And through that I fall. In this state, some days later, I am asked to be the Eye in a drama. The Eye? The *Eye*?!?

It is too much. It is not possible to play an Eye. It feels like an archetypal dream, hard to grasp, hard to remember, hard to make sense of, and its energy is awesome. And yet I accept. Its energy feels more than human. It needs to be taken on and acted by a human.

The archetypes work through us. Only through our openness to their images and patterns can we understand *something* of their energies. This, however, demands that we manage to build an inner vessel – or for some, an inner axis – strong and flexible enough to hold and transform these energies, which in turn transform us. We bring something to the archetype when we relate to it: the archetype needs us (to paraphrase Jung[7]), but for that we need an awareness that comes with a strong and flexible-enough vessel (or pillar-hole-axis), a necessity if we are not to be taken over by the archetype, as in an inflation, identification, or possession.

What comes with the Eye through me in the actual psychodrama never stays. The more-than-human energy is too much and not 'mine' to keep, as if I truly am only a tool to 'embody' it in the here and now, and then that is it: 'mine' to hold is the before and after, it seems – that is, what the Eye touches in my life.[8]

That very morning I read Jung on the hero and the dragon (Jung 1935, para 192, p. 92), having more than their fight in common, according to Jung, stating that in Scandinavian mythology, the hero is recognized through his eyes that are the eyes of the serpent – that is, the hero and the serpent are one. Whether the Eye I am asked to embody had any connection with a dragon or serpent's eye, I cannot say. Strangely enough, what I read is not on my mind at all, before, during and even after the drama. I can hardly believe my eyes when I return home and find the book open on just this passage.

At the time, however, I did not connect to the strange passage in *Mysterium Coniunctionis* that was there for me after my own psychodrama, '. . . (t)he eye that hitherto saw only the darkness . . .' In retrospect, it seems that the 'eye' was stirring also in my life. And I see that we touch aspects of the archetype and we are touched by it and we need time, a lifetime even, to open up to what it stirs and moves in our lives.

Through a dream that arrives in the wake of the Eye-drama, I find my topic for a research on symbolic understanding: the bird of 'eyes' – that is to say, the peacock – who is a transformer of poison as I discover later, connected with the wisdom of seeing things as they are.[9] This whole accumulation of events is astounding and strangely archetypal, hence I assume there remains so much that I don't see. To see things as they are – without judgement – how easy is that? And what is it like, to be seen in that way? Do we feel seen, truly, as we are, un-judged, or do we meet such an eye with our own judgemental projections?

What did the protagonist see that made him choose me, I wonder, as the psychodrama continues to work on in me and, in my dream, an eye-specialist shows me-the-dream-ego a picture of my pupils that are not like ordinary pupils, but 'cut' in a way that makes me-the-dream-ego particularly open to religion, he says. I-the-dream-ego am astonished . . . Well, outside the dream, I too am astonished. I know the 'cut' or 'dent', though, from some of my drawings, gleaned from a Tibetan way of rendering the eyes of holy persons. This, too, is too much.

What is an eye? A hole, an opening . . . taking in, giving out . . . a two-way mirror of soul.

We do not see with our eyes only.

The energy of the psychodrama work once a week has been profound, densely interwoven with all that goes on through the overall intensity of the immersion analytical training. This is taken further when two weekends of psychodrama are scheduled, five dramas each weekend. These will be our last psychodramas, as the Barzs have decided to work in Swiss-German only. We never did a psychodrama on our reaction to that decision when it was first announced: now we are happy for this possibility of ten more dramas. Some have left the group in the meantime, others join in – a new group is constellated yet is somehow the same.

The first drama of the first weekend, on a Friday evening, is on a dream. I have the impression that the protagonist thinks that it will be an easy and short drama, but psyche has its own agenda, and the work turns out to be deep, powerful and long. A person brings a topic but has to go with its energies as the topic takes its own course within the given time. In this tension, whatever it is that needs to be worked on and worked out, will reveal itself: the transcendent function (Jung 1958) is very much present in the soul work of psychodrama.

The following day brings us three dramas of enormous strength and fun! Part of the impact is, for me, the experience of playing roles in all three: from pillar, to gatekeeper, to mother; the previous day I was wife. The most astounding experience, however, is the introduction of a white dog that I am not and yet instantly am when the protagonist describes the dog that is to be part of his drama. I so feel that dog jumping and prancing and skipping with joy that I am flabbergasted when the protagonist does not pick me to embody it. Instead I am asked to play the gatekeeper – a good thing, I feel afterwards.[10] And yet I have never experienced such an 'explosive' identification with a particular energy in any of the parts I have had in various psychodramas as I did with the white dog. It takes time before I see that its joy hit me with such force! Its joy in life and mine.

That evening I am exhausted and yet also dancing. I realize that the work is not 'simply' to 'struggle' and 'hold the tension'. At times what is needed is to surrender, to 'let go', to release the joy and playfulness, when the right moment – that *kairos*[11] moment – opens up.

Next day I notice an urge to bringing forward a week-old dream I cannot make head nor tail of. However, sensing that one of the other participants is brewing something, I decide against this, and we have a drama on four dreams in one. A completely new and very puzzling experience comes with this: I feel estranged. I have problems relating to the dreams of the drama, as if I am not able to see past the protagonist and relate to what is presented, at least on the conscious level. Later, back home, I restlessly pick up Erich Neumann's *The Great Mother* (1955). There I find the archetypal pattern woven into those dreams, and suddenly the life of the psychodrama is there, touching on something partly within me, partly in the research I am presently working on, about poison. Strangest of all, though, in spite of the intensity of the weekend, I am surprisingly relaxed.

Five more dramas to go. The fact that this is the last psychodrama weekend with the Barzs adds to the energy. Saturday morning, the urge from that dream stirring some weekends ago, is stronger. I feel ready to work – so ready, I find, that when it turns out that I have to fight to do it, even fight with the person I appreciate most in the group, I do. I fight for my drama.

I have to argue for my drama, come up with the good reason and necessity to do the work *now* and not at another time, if at all. When we are first told this, it feels impossible to trust, to not employ the 'Oh no, I don't matter, please go ahead' trick, spoken through more or less clenched teeth. I have to claim a space.

That same morning, before the fight, as we listen to the reflections of the protagonist from the previous evening, a voice within me suddenly tells her, 'You have to let people be stupid; otherwise they'll never get out of the stupidity!' The corollary follows: 'You have to let people be bitches, you know, otherwise they'll simply stay stuck in it!' It is a statement about meeting people as they are, without judgement, without thinking, 'You're not good enough, you need to change, I'll show you how to, as I know better than you!' The jolt of energy that accompanies this inner voice carries over into the fight

I now find myself in thanks to the group and my friend who needs to do his drama. It feels strange to fight for my psychodrama, to find that urge in spite of my ambivalence and to let it, the urge, speak. And I 'win'. Or rather, the dream wins.

Strange too, it is, to work on a dream, so different from working on the hole, however much of psyche was there too. A dream in itself is movement and strange dimensions, only partly conscious, full of symbols, rich, furtive, and alive.[12] Just by starting work on a dream in psychodrama, you step into a halfway world:

> . . . an older sister lives in poverty in the countryside. . . . The younger sister left for town where she sold something that belongs to the older sister which made the youngest one rich . . . the hate and bitterness are strong and all contact broken . . . but somehow I-the-dream-ego see the story and what the youngest sister stole – a flat oblong piece of wood or stone with a line of strange signs on each side – through something I-the-dream-ego says or does, a contact is created to the youngest sister's youngest son, who brings what the youngest sister really stole – the square, white base of a baking oven of rough wood, which he reconstructs . . . the square main part is the important part . . . so far there is no open contact yet . . .

For all the vital 'props' of the dream, I find myself picking unexpected things that bear no resemblance to the dream images, but they are full of the 'right' energy and somehow perform their own amplification: for the stolen 'secret', a small Buddha signals to me from his seat under a calligraphy; for the base of the baking oven, four books by four mystics (no doubt, with 'dented eyes' as well; after the drama, I note the choices: Teresa of Avila, Hildegard von Bingen, Meister Eckhart, and Bernhard of Clairvaux).

The actors for the three characters – the oldest sister, the youngest sister, and the youngest sister's youngest son – also seem to choose themselves. As for endowing the actors with these completely unknown figures from a dream-story that the dream-ego merely watched, I find that the characters simply step forward and present themselves through me: the oldest sister is a shock with her tremendous energy, *she* who is stuck in the countryside, in poverty, in apathy in spite of her hate; as for the youngest sister, the apparently energetic one, she who left for town where she lives in prosperity, thanks to selling what she had stolen from the oldest sister, *her* energy is flat in comparison.

The way the three characters act in the drama, particularly the son (enacted by he who 'lost' the morning's fight), amplifies and elaborates the dream. There is also the group member who doubles out of his own intuition and not from the director's intervention, adding just the right element, and so subtly that I first asked myself: where did he come from? was he a part of the drama? part of the dream he was not, but what a significant contribution!

In the drama a broken axis emerges, the axis between the oldest sister of the countryside and the youngest sister of the city. The break or split caused by the theft has rendered both the old and the young females deprived and negative, a split only to be healed by the youngest son of the youngest sister, who goes against his mother, introducing a positive masculine energy that brings the base needed for a transformation of the broken feminine constellation to take place. The story lives its own life 'outside' the-dream-ego, but it is through the witnessing energy of the-dream-ego that contact to this positive and urgently needed masculine energy is constellated. Only in this respect is I-the-dream-ego truly the protagonist.

The first time the stolen secret is presented to the oldest sister, riveted as she is to the ground by her overwhelming hate and pain, the protagonist is struck and awed by its numinosity, which breaks the freezing spell of negativity. The tremendous shock, when in the doubling the presenter of the stolen object presents it once more, as if on the spur of the moment, moved by the *kairos* and bringing forward as he does the *peripeteia*, enables the protagonist to touch the secret this time; in this instant she experiences a sacredness, the still point of something being and becoming, just before or just when the youngest son arrives, a moment of pure joy.

The base that he brings was, after all, never lost. This mysterious base is for the oven that can 'bake' whatever is to be baked. In the drama the four parts of the broken base are concretized with the four books by the four mystics. The impact of all this coming together – this oven, this container, in this drama – renders the protagonist speechless and totally open and totally empty and in that instant touched by the mystery of healing, the self-healing aspect of the psyche, part of the mystery of life.

And just then it turns out that reconstructing the oven is not the end of the drama. The director puts a frame around the work: pointing out to me a row of seats for a concert, he tells me as protagonist to be seated, and to wait, and I find myself, of my own volition and to my great surprise, turning down various people who want the free seats, so they are still free when the oldest sister, the youngest sister, and the youngest sister's youngest son suddenly arrive. They are freed, for the healing to happen. With so much joy, and love.

This is what can result from going with what comes, from going through the opening, honouring that hole.

The directing, acting and enigma of the dream have given the drama a profound intensity. The auxiliary ego, embodied by the co-director Ellynor Barz, repeatedly sensed and expressed what the protagonist could not say or gave her the possibility of words when she needed them (Ellynor's exceptional gift!) and so supported her through the drama. During the sharing, Ellynor reminds us of the myth of the Greek goddess Demeter, who struck the earth barren in her grief-rage over the abduction and loss of her daughter Kore/ Persephone, a barrenness that lasted until Hermes (Mercurius) managed to bring forth a reconciling change. This helps me to understand why my work on the dream had come to nothing; only by realizing its archetypal roots, as Ellynor made clear, could a more personal understanding be gleaned from it. The strangeness of this dream, which had kept it so insistently present in my mind, became meaningful in this archetypal context, and the urgency I had felt calmed down. Something felt released.

After a powerful psychodrama it takes some effort, particularly for the protagonist, to come back into the group and take part in another person's drama. This is yet another part of the psychodrama challenge, and it is astonishing how possible it is to manoeuvre.

We work so deeply in all the dramas, going with archetypal images and patterns more often than not, and at the same time we are held and supported through the work in the group. I know some of what the work brings me, and how it furthers the process I find myself in at that stage in my life. I find the psychodrama work powerful, invigorating and deeply meaningful, not only through my own psychodramas, but very much too through taking part in the dramas of others, also in being part of that group and its dynamic.

Working on this dream feels so special – not so much as an 'interpretation' but as a powerfully emotional experience stirring some deep-seated unconscious knowledge that was next to impossible to relate to at the time. Its archetypal roots are made clear to me, the amplifications coming through the props and through the characters and their interaction, the enactment fathoming the deeper dimensions of the dream. There is a release, yet the dream goes on, I realize one morning some days after the drama, as I come out of a dream knowing what I have forgotten to do during the psychodrama: namely, to put the stolen and returned secret into the 'baking oven', the secret being the spark needed to set the fire going and to make the transformation happen. So, when it feels right, I do this on my own. Events in dreams and psychodramas can be re-constellated in body-soul when the time is right, even as Helmut had creatively given a conciliatory shape to my drama of the sisters, and in that way they can be taken even further as 'inner' psychodramas. When the dream first came to me, it demanded to be related to and did not leave me in peace, even after the dramatization, until I had performed the last gesture in an adequate way. Then, after the drama and my private work placing the secret in the oven, the dream somehow let me be for years.

The dream slipped away, but its archetypal energies re-emerged later through another myth that became central to my research (Ness 1998). That is the way of psyche. These energies are collective and unconscious and come to us in various ways, through dreams, symbols, stories, life patterns, illnesses. In themselves they are too much for humans. They have to be related to, humanized. In the dream, the split was stuck. The presence of the dream-ego who saw the story and gave it energy was needed for the release to happen. The psychodrama turned the possibility of release in the dream into an enacted psychic reality. The psychodramatic work emphasized being present, and open enough to see and relate to what comes, in preparation for changes to happen; in that delimited time and space, more aspects and connections reveal themselves. And then, also, some aspect of the dream slips away.

What we witnessed and embodied that day, on the collective level, was a splitting of the archetypal feminine, through the denial of the dark feminine of an older order rooted in nature (the oldest sister in the countryside) by the bright feminine of a newer order supported by technology (the youngest sister's city life). The stolen secret that I came to see, after the drama, as a symbol of the mysterious 'spark' of the feminine archetype, had through the theft been separated from its mysterious container. The psychodrama not only exemplified the split and what was needed for its healing, it placed the mystery of life and psyche and nature at its very centre. And for that a positive masculine energy, or a positive, flexible consciousness able to hold the tension of the opposites, is a must.

The splitting of the archetypal feminine did happen, ages ago. It is a reality in which we still live, with which we still struggle today – women and men, to various degrees, more or less unawares, depending on our cultures. I meet this struggle every day in my work as an analyst. It expresses itself in various ways in the lives of individuals, who are called upon to meet the challenge according to who they are and the stories they live. As Marion Woodman emphasizes: 'A life that is being truly lived is constantly burning away the veils of illusion, gradually revealing the essence of the individual' (Woodman 1985, p. 20). It takes time and generations to work on archetypal issues.

Part of that mystery in my life was the sequence of events during that psychodrama time, 'as if' the psychodramas of the hole and of the eye, together with those halfway forgotten rhombic images from older dreams, brought me to that strange openness for the pulsating energy of the rhombus of the Saamic drums. That I had the dream and the psychodrama of the broken sister-axis during the actual research on and writing about the drum was no coincidence. At the time, however, I did not make all these connections. It is in retrospect that I now realize how that mysterious energy of the centre, rooted in psyche's nature, manifested itself in the context of psychodrama and my writing about the shamanic drum.

> Or perhaps we could put it the other way round and say that the centre – itself virtually unknowable – acts like a magnet on the disparate materials and processes of the unconscious and gradually captures them as in a crystal lattice –
>
> (Jung 1944, para 325, p. 217)

– or in a rhombus of many dimensions. Truly a drum journey.

Only in retrospect has it been possible to 'burn away' the multifarious veils, not so much of illusions, but of all the other meaningful demanding painful joyful experiences with which life was jam-packed during that time: a veritable 'feast', in which all the dishes – bitter or sweet, sour or salty, harsh or fresh, like them or not – had to be eaten, one way or another, perhaps a lot of them simply gulped down. It takes time, to digest.

That last weekend of psychodrama was the last time our group worked together. I did other psychodramas with other directors, often without the co-director as auxiliary ego. I very much missed, however, working with the Barzs. There was something very special in their work: together, they created so safe a vessel and such a wise approach that it seemed natural to open up and to trust, even in a group of people who did not know each other well. Psychodramatic techniques may be fine, but it is the people who make of them healing experiences – or not.

So, I did not take psychodrama further. It has remained with me, though, and I am deeply grateful for that time, and for the work we did together. And I would not mind another psychodrama, the Moreno and Jung way, I think – as I suddenly realize that this is just what I have had now somehow, working on this essay. It reminds me somehow of what Jung says: 'I do not imagine for a moment that the psychological interpretation of a mystery must necessarily be the last word. If it is a mystery it must have still other aspects' (Jung 1955, para 213, p. 173). Drum time goes on, indeed.

Notes

1 The disruption of this organism was the main complaint of the Saami against Christianity. The time after 1740 is called 'the time when one had to hide the drums': this was the end of drum-time (Rydving 1993). A religious-symbolic life formerly collective and all-embracing had turned private and concealed.

2 The Polar Star in Saami is called *weralden tjuold*, literally meaning the World Pole.

3 It was said that there was a drum in every tent ('like a Bible in every Christian home') and that the male head of family would ask the drum about all kinds of undertakings, such as if he was to go fishing or not. The shaman was only called in cases of serious illnesses and death.

4 'Drum time' signifies the time when the drums were alive – i.e. the era of the indigenous religion. Losing their drums was like losing their way in the wilderness. In the context of this chapter, it signifies those inner journeys and that openness towards the unconscious that was so much part of the psychodrama work and the immersion analytical training, and that is so much part of soul work.

5 'An Approach to Psychosis'; 'The Dramatic Structure of Dreams' – Summer Semester, 1993.

6 This group was not part of the training at the C.G. Jung Institute; psychodrama was one of more group activities students could attend outside of, yet related to, the Institute.

7 For instance his discussion in 'Answer to Job' (Jung 1952) on God's relationship to man and His need to become conscious.

8 I thank the protagonist of this psychodrama of the Eye for permission to refer to this material.

9 '. . . discriminating awareness wisdom . . . does not mean discriminating in terms of acceptance and rejection, but simply seeing things as they are' (Chögyam Trungpa, Rinpoche, in the 'Commentary', *The Tibetan Book of the Dead*, 1985, p. 21).

10 I thank the protagonist of this psychodrama of the white dog for permission to use this material.

11 *Kairos* is what the Greeks called *the right moment* '. . . for a "metamorphosis of the gods", of the fundamental principles and symbols' (Jung 1957, para 585, p. 304).

12 A dream, too, is a symbol – i.e. the best possible expression for something unknown or only partly conscious. 'Every psychological expression is a symbol if we assume that it states or signifies something more and other than itself which eludes our present knowledge' (Jung 1921, para 817, p. 475).

References

Jung, C. G. (1921) *Psychological Types, Collected Works 6,* London: Routledge, 1989.

Jung, C. G. (1934) 'The Soul and Death', in *The Structure and Dynamics of the Psyche, Collected Works 8*, London: Routledge, 1991, pp. 404–15.

Jung, C. G. (1935) 'The Tavistock Lectures', in *The Symbolic Life, Collected Works 18,* London: Routledge, 1993, pp. 5–182.

Jung, C. G. (1944) *Psychology and Alchemy, Collected Works 12,* London: Routledge, 1992.

Jung, C. G. (1952) 'Answer to Job', in *Psychology and Religion: West and East, Collected Works 11,* London: Routledge, 1991, pp. 355–470.

Jung, C. G. (1955) *Mysterium Coniunctionis, Collected Works 14,* London: Routledge, 1992.

Jung, C. G. (1957) 'The Undiscovered Self', in *Civilization in Transition, Collected Works 10,* London: Routledge, 1991, pp. 245–305.

Jung, C. G. (1958) 'The Transcendent Function', *The Structure and Dynamics of the Psyche, Collected Works 8,* London: Routledge,1991, pp. 67–91.

Jung, C. G. (1961) *Memories, Dreams, Reflections,* ed. A. Jaffé, London: Fontana Paperbacks, 1983.

Ness, S. (1994) 'Saami Shamanism and the Use of Decorated Drums', unpublished paper, C.G. Jung Institute, Zürich.

Ness, S. (1998) *The Torn Cloth and Other Spider Stories,* unpublished Diploma Thesis, C.G. Jung Institute, Zürich.

Neumann, E. (1955) *The Great Mother: An Analysis of the Archetype,* Princeton, NJ: Princeton University Press, 1991.

Pollan, B. (1993) *Samiske sjamaner,* Oslo: Gyldendal.

Rydving, H. (1993) *The End of Drum Time,* Uppsala: Acta Universitatis Upsaliensis.

Røine, E. (1978) *Psykodrama: psykoterapi som eksperimentelt teater,* Oslo: Aschehoug.

The Tibetan Book of the Dead (1985) transl. and commentaries F. Freemantle and C. Trungpa, Boston and London: Shambhala.

Woodman, M. (1985) *The Pregnant Virgin,* Toronto: Inner City Books.

6

JUNG, MORENO AND DREAM ENACTMENT

Wilma Scategni

Introduction

Jungian psychodrama is a psychodramatic technique and theory. It is action as well as observation, articulated into a complex model along the lines of Jung's analytical theory. It flows from two wellsprings: the brilliant work of Jacob Moreno and the depth psychology of Carl Gustav Jung. Moreno introduced his techniques: enacting, mirroring, doubling, soliloquizing, role reversing, and group sharing. Jung introduced his concepts: dreams, the collective unconscious, archetypal images and the individuation process.

It may seem ironic that an activity such as Jungian psychodrama could exist, in as much as Jung had strong reservations about psychotherapeutic work in groups. Groups could make their members vulnerable to suggestion from one or more of the others. Their members could lose their critical acumen or develop regressive tendencies. They could lose themselves, their personal tension and their growth. When Jung maintained this, he was thinking mainly in terms of large groups and their potential to make their members lose their ability to reason for themselves. Finally, in 1955, Jung came to the point where he began to stress that polar opposites could actually co-exist as complementary. In this sense, an individual and a group are opposites that could coexist and become complementary. Individual analysis was to work on the individual in his or her archetypal polarity, while group therapy was to explore the collective, to explore individuals – but individuals as they were in relation with others.

Jungian psychodrama is versatile in method and has always kept its distance from dogmatism. Consequently, it has increased in importance as a worthwhile therapeutic tool in public and private health practices for the prevention of psychiatric and psychological disease. It has spread in socio-pedagogical contexts and is an essential tool in the supervision of therapists, medical doctors, teachers and social workers.

Furthermore, Jungian psychodrama can be used to explore the potential for dreams to express the unconscious of an institution such as a school. An example of this is the research project conducted jointly by the University of Bologna, the University of Brescia, and COIRAG.[1] In this research project, 49 dreams of conference participants were collected in two ways. Participants dropped them into a so-called Dream Box, and an hour-long Social Dreaming Matrix was held every morning for each of the three three-day conferences, in which participants shared their dreams. (A Social Dreaming Matrix is a group held throughout a conference, where group members reflect on the nightly echoes of the day's sessions.) The researchers drew the connections among dreams that seemed similar as they searched for links among the oneiric themes that emerged. This research stimulated an intense curiosity towards what could be called the night processes of the institution, and a more intense and warm social life emerged among members of the institutional group. In addition, there was a turning towards Jungian analytical psychology and its connections with other kinds of dream research. (To examine this project in detail, see Pani, Ronchi and Scategni 2006.)

The dream as inner theatre: narration and enactment

I will now re-examine the psychodramatic enactment of one particular dream from a Jungian point of view in order to explore issues raised by Jung and Moreno in a specific context. I will first very briefly examine the hypotheses that underlie my work. There are several themes that emerge in the analytical processes of the dreamer–protagonist in question. These emerge at different times and in different ways: in the enactment or the sharing, in later sessions in the form of fragments or connections, and in individual analytical sessions. As I put these parts together, I will illustrate how I work. It is more useful to say I have an outlook on working rather than a method of working, in that a method is something that may often become a stiff and determined a priori. My outlook responds differently to different contexts, questions, intuitions, and images shaping my mind, but it is something that is always present in the connections that I draw from the dream, the group, the protagonist, the auxiliary ego, and, naturally, myself too as director.

As we know well, Jung considered the dream a sort of private theatre where the characters are made up from the range of the dreamer's feelings and emotions. These are what he termed the dreamer's autonomous complexes, the psychic entities that we can define as unknown guests of our conscious ego, which may or may not be welcomed. They are entities that conduct a powerful affective charge that can catalyse our attention intensely. In dreams, the conscious ego is called on explicitly to measure itself against these expressions of the unconscious.

The dream in question here belongs to A, then a 34-year-old woman. She was a teacher of artistic education – and also an artist – who had been attending a group for about a year and a half and was, at the same time, also working in individual analysis. It is with the dreamer's authorization that I write about the personal contents of her dream and her reflections on its enactment.

> After walking down a long and tiring way, I meet B and C [*two group members*] at a crossroads. I exchange a few words with them, but I don't know about what. They point out a way to go that takes me in front of the house where I grew up as a little kid. There is something very strong that attracts me inside, and maybe this was what I was looking for. I find myself in front of three rooms. The first is the playroom of my childhood. There's my sister inside, absorbed in her play with some stuffed puppets that we used to fight over when we were little. A little bit down from that there is my parents' room, which I see from the window as they go away in the distance. The room has remained empty, but there is a table in the middle of it with two clay busts on it. I recognize the images of my parents, which I sculpted, and I feel that I have to finish them. The third is the room of a newborn baby. There is an empty cradle, but I feel that there is a presence behind the curtains. It is something ethereal and fleeting. I have the feeling that it has something to do with my maternity.

In every psychodrama session, the first step is to choose the protagonist. In this particular session, after an introductive sharing, the issues raised by A seemed the more 'active' in claiming the energy of the group, especially because two participants of the group played roles in her dream. The presence of any member of a group in a dream is always a relevant, even a seductive, element for the group itself. When it was clear for me and for the group that the protagonist and the group itself were ready to enact the dream, I, as the director, moved us toward the scene in order to express the themes of the dream more deeply. The protagonist narrated the dream. The next step was to build the scene concretely, as if on a stage.

This step in the enactment of A's dream entailed warming up the protagonist and the group to the dream's contents. The dream was enacted in a group that meets for two sessions each week for ten months in the year. In this case, as usual, the warming-up consisted in the protagonist and me walking together in a circle inside the group's circle of chairs. Then the protagonist closed her eyes and kept the memory of her dream images in focus. This helped some of her potential feelings come to the fore, which she experienced as open questions. She opened her eyes, and we built the scene. I asked where she would like to put the bed in which she was dreaming and where the space for the representation of the dream should be. We then explored her feelings in relation to the different locations of the playing space. She then identified the person who could be her 'auxiliary ego' and play specific roles in the dream. As always happens when we have to stage-manage a long dream, we had to focus on that part of the dream that held the strongest energy, the part that could seemingly best express the central theme of the protagonist and of the group. Then we could go on with our enactment.

In this particular case, the dream was staged focusing essentially on the final scene, the encounter with the clay busts and the empty cradle. This was the point where the story seemed to reach its highest emotional pitch, the point that could perhaps best reveal the particularly acute issues in conflict. The other aspects of the dream – the road, the meetings, and the playroom – were staged and run through quickly in very short skits, so that their eventual links to the climactic moments could emerge.

The house was a setting that the protagonist had mentioned in previous psychodrama sessions. She presented it as a place that she could escape to in order to grow in every way and rediscover her own autonomy. In this dream, the house took on an unusual warmth and evoked a sort of fascination. It was welcoming and, at the same time, turned out to be enigmatic and disquieting. In fact, a rather corpulent woman was chosen to play the role of the house. In the group, she represented affective features, even though these features were sometimes absorbing and sometimes fleeting. This had to do, above all, with the way this group member related to the others.

The dreamer chose B and C to play the roles of the people who had shown her the way, and this was the same choice that A's unconscious had suggested – that is to say, the participants in the group played themselves as they had appeared in the dream. Both of them, a man and a woman, were representatives of a kind of historical memory of the group because they had been participating in it for a very long time. They had also demonstrated, even though they had taken different paths, that they were rather determined in the choices they had made and that they were able to offer themselves affectionately without giving up their own autonomy and without being absorbed in or manipulated by their own personal and family relationships. At least, this was the sense that the dreamer communicated in the sharing after the dramatization.

A young man who had entered the group recently and an adult woman who had not by then demonstrated any 'maternal attitude' were chosen to play the dreamer's parents as well as the clay busts in the parents' room. It became clear to the dreamer only later, during the dramatization of the dream, that she had been looking for a connection between her parents in the dream and the clay busts that she had to re-sculpt. It became equally clear to her that it was through this kind of 'ritual' that she would become able to meet with her real parents again and accept their limits. (The dreamer experienced her mother as someone who was not very affectionate, even though she was absorbing. She experienced her father as someone who had shown many immature and unpredictable features in relation to the responsibility that his fatherly role required. He demonstrated this despite the fact that he was already very old even at the time when A was born.)

A female group member who had frequently demonstrated that she had problems with 'becoming an adult' was chosen to play the role of the sister.

There was a brief flashback to the 'play room' and an encounter with the sister in which the dreamer exchanged roles with her. This made her realize that a part of herself was lingering in the playroom and could remain imprisoned there. At the same time, she realized that perhaps this fear was at the root of her later problems with not being able to abandon herself in play.

This was a dream that could be delved into on three levels – the level of everyday life, the metaphorical level of the dreamer, and the metaphorical level of the group. On the level of everyday life, the dream again brought up the issues that the dreamer was confronting at that time: her maternity and her presumed sterility, which was disproved several years later when she gave birth to a son. On a metaphorical level, she was furthermore seeking some renewed creative potential in both her personal and her professional lives. Likewise, the group as a whole was seeking the same thing. My delicate task as group director was to choose which feature of the dream to focus on.

The protagonist of the dream, A, played an emotionally demanding role that was very personal. Doing so, she set up a deeper relationship with her own inner world while becoming more 'available' to the other group members, especially to those involved in the scene. She reached out to E, another member, with whom she shared the problem of waiting for a pregnancy.

The dreamer, who became the protagonist of the psychodramatic play, raised a question – that of getting pregnant and giving birth to a baby – which had a deep resonance among all the group members, both literally and metaphorically. Even I, as director, was led to ask myself whether I could find a newborn creativity in working with psychodrama and whether this group was something that could promote it. This deeply felt theme, as well as the presence of two group members in the dream, seemingly catalysed the group's interest. In the play, all this potential was changed into psychodramatic images and thereby amplified. As the scene was being constructed and dramatized, the memories of the group members, even in detail, came to the fore. Aspects of their experiences were seen again through their memories with nuances and details that had been long put aside or forgotten. The dreamer, in the role of protagonist, had evoked a kind of 'return to the origins' that was echoed in the recollections of other group members both during the dramatization and in the subsequent sessions.

This dream, like any dream, could be looked on as having some sort of message. In psychodrama, this is something that becomes explicit at the end when the director recounts his or her observations to the protagonist and the group as a sort of plot summary, which often serves to bring out some of the many potential meanings in the dream. At the end of the dream the dreamer found herself in front of an empty cradle. In the dramatization the dreamer, playing the role of protagonist, realized that the cradle was waiting for a newborn child, which was felt perhaps as the fleeting presence behind the curtains. She realized that the child would take shape and come to life only once she had finished sculpting the busts of her parents, again with the help of the group. In real life, she felt this sculpting would help her to approach her parents again in a deeper way. Taking a step towards her parents was exactly what would enable her to take a step towards becoming a parent herself. Only by touching the roots could the branches bloom.

Jungian psychodrama: the outlook or method

When dealing with a dream like that of A, I approach it from a particular outlook that is expressed in what could be described as a method. Here, I will reflect on the kinds of atmosphere and the language in psychodrama. Then I will list some key words in Morenian psychodrama, which, in fact, are consonant with a Jungian approach.

The general atmosphere and the transcendent function

The director must first build a scene and create the atmosphere appropriate for expressing the dream. He or she must do this in light of the experience and the involvement of the whole group. This can only happen when the unconscious is moving, when what Jung called the transcendent function is activated by the individual or group unconscious, when the conscious can meet the unconscious. In this way the psychodramatic space, the space where the play is performed, is transformed into a kind of shelter, a rough equivalent of what the ancient Greeks called a *temenos*, a temple for rituals. Here Jungian psychodrama rests on an analogy with ritual. The director and group members act as sorts of celebrants in a kind of heirophany, a sacred ritual where the 'gods' manifest themselves. In this case, the 'gods' are the heretofore hidden impulses and emotions of the group members. This is a kind of intensity that does not always take place in psychodramatic play. However, when it happens, the whole atmosphere helps to get the group members involved, kindling their attention and focus and helping to open their minds to thousands of memories, associations and feelings. We can call these revelatory moments 'insight'. Moreno called them moments of the 'magic of psychodrama'. Jung called them 'mana'. Jaime Rojas-Bermudez (1997) calls them instances of the 'sacredness' in group 'celebration.' Yet, these moments can be fleeting. Cinderella's carriage can easily turn back into a pumpkin.

Language in dreams and in the temenos of psychodrama

The language of dreams has often been described as a kind of twilight language, something crepuscular and symbolic that may seem to delve into the deepest meanings of things. The language of the psychodramatic stage is something unique in that it tries to blend this twilight language with the language of the here and now that reflects the meanings of everyday life. The director has to blend these two languages into one language. This is a language of the 'as if'. The director has to feel which way the wind of psychic energy is blowing, where it is headed. He or she has to read the messages emerging from the group's unconscious in the array of images, dreams, and interactions emerging from the group and from these intuit the individuation of the group. When a director chooses a protagonist and suggests scenes for enactment, he or she has to make choices that will also move the group towards its individuation. All this happens, to a great extent, through the use of language. However, the language of a psychodrama enactment gathers together that of the dreams that emerge in response to other dreams during the nights between sessions, during the enactment, or during the sharing, when group members provide their feedback to their experiences. Other dreams may emerge from the deepest forgotten corners of the members' memories. These sorts of experiences are often expressed in the language of autonomous complexes and archetypal images, which pits itself against the logical and rational language that the conscious ego uses to engage in a conversation with so-called reality. There is a danger that rational language can become babble, that the ego is swept away. Jungian psychodrama strives to find a symbolic language of unconscious images that does not give up all links with the real world.

A group member, or even a director, may feel a little bit like Alice on the Queen's croquet ground, as recounted in Chapter VIII of Lewis Carroll's *Alice's Adventures in Wonderland*. Alice finds herself playing croquet with the Queen of Hearts. Live soldiers, who are cards, stand on their hands and feet to make croquet arches, but they move around all the time. The mallets are live flamingos, and the balls are curled-up live hedgehogs that can get back upon their legs and walk away. Likewise, psychodramatic play raises questions that are not answered, or potential questions that are not even formulated. Questions are ceaselessly reformulated about the perennial problems of the group members. New answers are often given. Sometimes they are clear and sometimes enigmatic and contradictory.

The language of psychodrama echoes the sounds of the members' everyday battles, hopes, illusions, frustrations and wounds. The coin of this realm has neither heads nor tails, as banal images give way to solemn revelations, and vice versa. The most essential point in psychodramatic work is the inclusion of opposites – symbolical and archetypal images as well as concrete reality. This is a hard act to follow, but it can work as long as the group can forge a sheltering *temenos*, and in that shelter get in touch with the mana, or magic, of this symbolic space, a place where they can become more aware of the influence of archetypal forces in their everyday lives.

The warming up

A warming up is an element that contributes to the correct atmosphere of psychodrama, usually done at the beginning of the group session. The warming up consists in a cluster of techniques that aim to facilitate communication among group participants. Warming up is rarely turned to in continuous psychodrama groups, but it can be used when situations seem to be stalled. As in individual analysis, it is more often preferable to face silences, even long ones, in which contents take shape in the participants' minds. These may be more difficult and sometimes more painful to take on, but also more significant. Facing moments of emptiness and expectation in the group can therefore cause deeper themes to emerge. However, a warming-up technique can be used frequently, although not obligatorily, in workshops where the participants hardly know each other, in situations where the group is not homogenous and its participants need to be better integrated, or in situations where the group participants are not at all used to working with psychodramatic techniques and so need a more gentle start. Warming up allows the participants to relate to each other, coming closer to each other progressively.

The psychodramatic stage

I work in a psychodramatic space in the shape of a circle. I use a circle as a mandala, an image of wholeness as well as a symbol of completeness and equidistance from a centre. This shape demarcates an enclosed space where psychodramatic images take on real-life shapes. The characters in the enactment, the group members, are the living forms of the psychic forces and energies moving in the inner world of the dreamer–protagonist. The dreamer–protagonist thus concretely expresses his or her own unconscious, which becomes, in turn, the unconscious of the group as a whole.

Jungian psychodrama refers to this space as a stage. The stage where the dramatic action takes place is the physical space marked off by the participants sitting in a circle. In this position they all are equidistant from the centre where the scenes take place. At the same time they all can see the others' faces and likewise be seen. The circle has a kind of magic capacity to involve people. Each participant knows that he or she is part of the group and so is particularly important to it. Thus the space assumes the aspects of a *temenos*. On stage there are some elements that remain fixed: the timed recurrence of the sessions, their constant duration, and the physical space that borders them. All these contribute to create a kind of frame. In this way, the scenic space is transformed into a *temenos* in which the element of change is represented by the scenes that are enacted. These are in a continuous development that narrates and reflects the group's history through the participants' experiences and dreams. Images from the participants' lives and fantasies find room for themselves on stage, where they are joined by images coming out of the unconscious as dream images and then incarnated in the concrete reality of the psychodramatic play. Thus the stage functions as the meeting place of the concrete reality represented, on the one hand, by the group as a whole that marks its borders and its individual participants and, on the other hand, by the reality of the inner world of the protagonists. Their unconscious images in their subjective reality are expressed through scenic representation. Inasmuch as the stage is a symbolic space representing the heart or centre of the group's space where its energies gather, it sometimes appears in the participants' dreams transfigured by the emotions that have been projected onto it.

This is something different from the stage in classical Morenian psychodrama (Ancelin Schützenberger 1970; Boria 1997). Its stage is not circular, but more like that of a little proscenium theatre. There is space for the group members not directly involved in the enactment, and there is an area where the protagonist can see the role of him- or herself played by another member of the group, an auxiliary ego.

The psychodramatic space marks out the borders of the frame. Inside, a stage temporarily protects the reality of the world of 'as if' and of psychic forces. Outside, there is the world where all the members live and which they will all go back to after a session. Actually, the psychodramatic space is set up to explore, aside from dreams, that same outer world from which it is demarcated. The borders around the space thus are not meant to block out the outer world but, rather, to provide a sheltered space from which to explore it, a space protected by the ritual-like enactment of psychodrama. Therefore the oneiric images that may seem to belong just to the private dimension of a dreamer enter the space of psychodrama when the dreamer shares them with his or her fellow group members. They become part of the conscious here and now, but the here and now within the *temenos*. In Jungian psychodrama, these images become a means of communication among group members, a real relationship in the real world. Obviously, a group member can choose to keep some images or reflections to him or herself and eventually explore them in the future through personal analysis. The psychodramatic space is a catalyst where the potential energy of memories and reflections can be sparked and sometimes seen in a new light and where, as Moreno put it, the group members may find 'new solutions to old unsolved problems'. This goes not only for the members who share their images or reflections but also for those who do not work directly, whose memories, fantasies and emotions may be moved as they observe. In a way, they all share in three dimensions of time: the here and now of the psychodrama session, the time evoked in memory, and the archetypal time of the dreams. In groups that are held continuously, there is also the memory of past sessions that form a kind of mythical history of the group itself, which is buffered by the group's geography, its return to the same physical space.

Individuation and groups

In Jungian terms, individuation means the realization of the potential innate in each individual. Thus the term is connected with the development of the individual's personality through distinguishing one's own uniqueness from collective thought and values. In social relationships the process of individuation assumes that an individual relates to others in his or her own unique way and experiences the values of the group he belongs to in a more inner-directed and personal way. Group values are not accepted passively but re-claimed and worked out again in a spontaneous way, keeping a certain dose of innovative energy alive. In the broadest sense of the term, individuation guides a person towards the realization of the Self as the complete expression of himself as a whole and also stands in relation to a person's fulfilling his own human destiny. The function that pushes an individual towards this goal is identified as the transcendent function. During the course of an individual's entire existence, the transcendent function relates the consciousness of the ego to the contents of the unconscious, which manifest themselves through a continual transformation.

Likewise, every group can be thought of as a single individual entity with its own collective attitudes and potential development, which are expressed in the social life of the group itself. The members may or may not be skilled in building relationships in a social life or may or may not be open to the world outside. In any case, a group can only progress towards individuation within the sheltered time and space of its *temenos*. In a way, the individuation of a group consists in the history and possible destiny of a group at a particular moment, where they are and where they may be headed, no matter what kind of group it is.

The protagonist and the enactment

The protagonist is the narrator and actor of one or more scenes that are enacted in psychodrama. Usually the director selects the protagonist or protagonists to work in the individual sessions. The choice is instinctive but based on the sociometry of the group itself. (Sociometry, a term coined by Moreno, is the study of the relationships among individuals within the realm of their interactions.) The protagonist chosen is the one whose themes seem to best catalyse the group's energy and attention and create the most resonance. The sociometric choice can be made more or less explicitly through questions or play. However, the director's choice is based on what he or she seems to be picking up from the group – the attitudes, mimicked expressions, postures, associations or other less explicit messages that seemingly indicate the themes that have more widespread emotional impact at that time. Substantially, the attention focused on the protagonist is always constantly balanced by an attention towards the group as a whole. Likewise, the themes played on stage by individual participants are the themes of the protagonist that simultaneously reflect those of the group as a whole. The images that emerge and the scenes that are enacted represent in themselves a kind of response that is always an opening towards other questions and towards the problems or conflict that the first protagonist introduced. This theme will be returned to him or her enhanced by the new resonance and the faceting revealed by the group and opened towards new creative potential and chances to formulate new hypotheses.

For the most part, the scenes that are played are proposed by the protagonist, who has introduced the theme or the dream that he or she is interested in working on. At times, however, the director may invite the protagonist to focus on something that may have merely seemed tangential and so cause the protagonist to play a scene different from the one he had been set on – sometimes involving a detail or something that was mentioned as an association. For example, participants can pass from a dream to the playing of a scene from real life, or vice versa. This occurs mainly when the director feels the need to overcome rationalizing defences. The content of the scene that is played can involve differing time frames: a recent recollection, an impression or fantasy that has to do with the here and now, a memory that dates back to several months or many years ago, or a sequence from a dream that belongs to the timeless space of the world of dreams. It often happens that a scene from a dream may be followed by a scene from a protagonist's real-life experiences that the dream seems to evoke. Sometimes the scenes – both those involving dreams and those from real life – may seem to be evoked by the very reality of the group as a whole and its history, which continually intertwines with the history and reality of the individual participants. Analytical work can be directed along parallel lines towards the protagonist, the group as a whole, and the individual participants and can focus on the inner- or outer-world aspects in the individual group members. The actors are the protagonists – the narrator of what the scene is about – and the auxiliary egos chosen by the protagonist him or herself from among the participants in order to play the various parts, defined as roles. During the dramatic playing of the scenes the director focuses on the emotional states and subsequent transformations that seem most significant in order to gather in the most profound and complex aspects of what has been narrated. Over the course of the play the protagonist is invited to make successive 'role exchanges' with one or more characters that are participating in the scene itself, thus giving him or her the chance to experience personally the emotional states and perspectives of even his or her antagonists and to gather new nuances from them. After the play, the actor-participants recount their feedback – the moods, feelings, and emotions that they experienced in the roles that they played.

Choosing the focus of the enactment

It is up to the director to choose which feature or scene to focus on when a protagonist-dreamer recounts a rather long and involved dream. Despite this focus, the rest of the dream should help provide the context for the enactment. One approach that I have taken is to present the contents expressed in the other sequences of the dream as a short vignette or series of vignettes. Then one of the group members is chosen as an auxiliary ego to stay in the scene physically as a living reminder for the other events, a kind of frame for the central focus. As the scene to be focused on is being enacted, the director and the group as a whole should be flexible enough to shift this focus to another part of the dream, if this other part begins to be felt in a more intense way.

Auxiliary egos and their roles: casting the characters

The role is the part that the protagonist of the scene to be played assigns to some of the other group participants. A scene is chosen and then constructed. Here the characters, the feelings in the air, the objects, and the atmosphere take shape bit by bit on the psychodramatic stage as the setting is described and structured. The participants thus function as auxiliary egos, interpreting the various roles, the parts that the protagonist assigns. Aside from human characters, some participants may often be called upon to play the roles of inanimate objects in order to explore the symbolic and emotional significance that these can have for the protagonist. Emotions, feelings, or somatic symptoms can be represented for the same reason.

An example of how this works concretely can be seen in the enactment of A's dream. A played the role of herself, and then switched into the role of the unfinished clay bust of her mother. In this role, A conceived of herself (the mother) as 'not perfect, but good enough'. A, as the mother, realized that she was subject to her daughter's manipulations. When she realized that her mother was not perfect, A herself realized that she herself did not need to be perfect as a potential mother. Therefore getting pregnant ceased being an impossible dream: it became something good-enough. She was ready to accept her own limits. It was only through switching roles that A managed to realize this.

The term 'auxiliary ego' indicates the participants in the group whom the protagonist chooses to play the various roles in an upcoming scene. It is worth noting that the protagonist can opt to have another participant in the group – who acts as an auxiliary ego – play the role of him or herself. The protagonist expects to hear some significant response from the participant who was chosen. In this way the protagonist has the chance to see him or herself from the outside – at least in a part of the scene. The group takes on a two-fold function. First, they are a chorus who participate and comment on the protagonist's actions and so function as an emotional and affective container. Second, they are a gathering of auxiliary egos who have been called into the scene to make the protagonist's inner world material and concrete, the world that is represented through their physical and emotional presence.

Usually the protagonist him or herself chooses the auxiliary egos to play the various roles. However, the director may sometimes sense that another group member may be more valuable in a specific role; in this case, the director may suggest this to the protagonist as another choice. However, the protagonist always has the last word. There are various approaches to psychodrama, and these may have various approaches to the auxiliary ego. In the approach of Helmut and Ellynor Barz, for example, the co-director or co-therapist may play the role of auxiliary ego as long as a session lasts (E. Barz 1988, H. Barz 1990).

The function of the director

The director (or leader) performs a variety of tasks. In fact, he or she is the one who guides the group in its incessant explorations inside the labyrinth of relationships, fantasies, encounters, feelings, emotions, images and memories that come out in psychodrama. At the same time, this is the person who looks for some sort of sense in all these phenomena and aims to give them back their form and set them off in some direction. On this pathway he or she reflects a world that is simultaneously that of the relationships among the protagonists/participants and that of the relationships among the figures from their inner worlds who continuously enrich and transform themselves. Formulating hypotheses about how themes may develop, a director handles the direction of the scenes together with the protagonist and the group while maintaining the analytic and therapeutic function that will allow her or him to have the awareness and responsibility for what is happening and what she or he is doing at that moment. All this is carried out in the group by going in two directions: towards every one of the individual participants and towards the group as a whole. Analytical psychology recognizes four fundamental functions in the individual: intuition, thought, feeling, and sensation. Conducting a group requires that all these functions be involved at the same time. In fact, it is important that a director participate letting herself or himself be guided by the sentiment and the emotions that are flowing through the protagonist and the participants without letting herself be overwhelmed, maintaining her analytic and therapeutic function intact through thought. In the same way it is important that a director is able to pick the possible roads to go down intuitively, and she or he can at the same time recognize the language of the feelings that emerge. Besides constructing the scenes along with the protagonist, the director also takes on the function of the auxiliary ego by prompting the protagonist during the dramatization of the scenes.

Every director may have a slightly different approach, so it may be illustrative to sketch out my own. I approach the space in this way. I sit in a circle with the group members, if possible – always in the same place in continuing groups. In shorter workshops, I like briefly to get the lay of the land, as it were, in advance, in the space reserved for the group session. This helps me become aware of a particular context as a kind of preliminary mediation. In effect, the lighting, windows, doors, furniture, pictures or decoration and carpets often work together to create a kind of spirit of the place, a *genius loci*, which can be evoked during a session. But I often am not able to scout out a space before a workshop session, in which case I hope to depend on some degree of flexibility. These features of the ambiance can sometimes be used to set up a foothold that helps the group members enter the psychodramatic space. In continuous groups these features become part of the group history.

Peter Kellerman (1992) describes four roles that the director plays: analyst, therapist, producer and group leader. As an analyst, the director empathizes with the protagonist, helping emotions to emerge and memories to be looked at again, more deeply, re-reading events in search of new links. As therapist, the director aims to heal by considering which content of the dream is most healthful for the protagonist and the group to enact. Often a group is not yet ready or strong enough to confront deep issues. Analytical work is therapeutic, but analysis requires more time than therapy; a director can turn over the soil, as it were, to prepare the group to confront some issues later on. Sometimes the protagonist is ready, but the group is not, in which case the director may choose to broach the issue softly or indirectly and go back to it in a subsequent session, or simply wait until the right time comes, if it comes at all. As a producer, the director must combine the efforts of director, stage manager, and set designer, as if in an aesthetic performance. He or she must, in effect, put the play on concretely, focusing on the core problem of the protagonist, building a stage, and suggesting group members for specific roles in collaboration with the protagonist (who is nevertheless the ultimate casting director). And as group leader, a director faces three main dangers. First, she must never neglect the group by concentrating too much on the protagonist: she must remain receptive to the emotional reactions of the individual group members as well as the group as a whole, both during the enactment and during the sharing – a difficult thing to do when the protagonist gets deeply into emotions. Second, the director must beware of any charismatic members who, acting consciously out of a narcissistic or histrionic personality or completely unawares, may steal the centring control of the group away from the director, leaving members feeling unsheltered and disoriented. There is the same danger when a group member carries into the work a pathology that a director may not be able to control. Third, the director must not be swept away by unconscious contents or deep emotions that come up in the sessions. One can understand why Jaime Rojas-Bermudez (1997) prefers that the director occupy a position in the centre of the circle at the very beginning of sessions; this goes along with his emphasis on the anchoring mandala as emblematic of the sacred in psychodrama.

Sharing and observations

Sharing usually follows the dramatization of every scene. However, a director may sometimes choose to pass quickly on to another scene when she or he thinks that another scene would be more likely to exploit the emotional energy that has just been mobilized while it is still hot. In this case, the director would take up the sharing later. Essentially, sharing goes in two directions. The first has to do with the emotions, sentiments and feelings experienced in the scenes in relation to the roles that were assigned in the play and in the eventual role exchanges. At this stage it is important, as much as possible, that the protagonists work as auxiliary egos and thus are able to give back what they imagine is faithful to the script assigned them while avoiding personal interference and projections. This is done in order to give the protagonists the feedback that would allow them more deeply to grasp the meaning of the relationship that was played in the scene. The other direction of the sharing enters the real situation of the individual group members as such: that is to say, it is more related to their own personalities. It therefore can pertain to feelings and emotions experienced that seem to each of the participants to be more related to him or herself than to the protagonist. It can also pertain to personal associations that may or may not be the topics of successive scenes. Usually sharing does not involve all the potential feedback in reaction to the scenes played in a session. Here too the director has to choose to make more room for those instances of feedback that seem to be most meaningful, most emotionally charged and most pertinent to the theme of the session and to the problems that the protagonist brought. It is usually the protagonists themselves who choose either to speak first or to hear the group's feedback at the end of the dramatization of a scene. At the end of every session it is customary to leave some space for feelings that some participants might feel are still up in the air – those that are strictly personal and those that come as the feedback of an auxiliary ego. Other feelings that may be less immediate return, instead, in successive sessions in the form of thoughts, reflections or dreams.

The observations conclude the sessions after the sharing. When there are two group directors who alternate in leading the sessions, the one conducts while the second stays apart in a corner of the group taking some notes to be fed back at the end of the session. The observations represent a kind of thread that binds the scenes together and, to a certain extent, represents the development of the group's theme. The observations claim to be neither a detailed description of the session nor an interpretation of what has been happening according to logical and rational interpretative tools. These would risk yielding a reductive reading that would follow the patterns of predetermined analytical models. The observations are simply limited to giving back images and connections that are open to more than one reading and reflect the individual participants' different ways of seeing and feeling. In this way, the end-of-session observations end up opening new questioning and again fostering a steady dialogue between the conscious and the unconscious of the individual participants, of the group as a whole, and of the collective. This is a dialogue that stays at the centre of the analytical journey. When a director works alone, she or he gives possibly briefer impressions to the group as a sort of device that ties in the collected work done and gives it back to the participants.

Jung, Moreno and dream work: conjuring up a common thread

Dreams have always been the object of interpretation, but sometimes they can be said to interpret us. In sorting out Jung and Moreno's approaches to dreams, we need to put them into the context of several other approaches that are most relevant to Jungian psychodrama. Jung's thought comes closest to Moreno's when he talks about dreams. Jung holds that dreams can be interpreted in a way he calls objective – that is to say, pertinent to what the dream gets across in metaphorical language in relation to the objective reality of the dreamer's life. Jung also allows for a subjective interpretation (Jung 1916). At the same time, James Hillman holds that we, as dreamers, are 'interpreted' or, better, 'lived by our dreams', which are based on 'personal myths'. In this, Hillman treats dreams in a way that is opposite to Jung's. Helmut Barz criticizes the concept of 'interpretation' in that it implies the discovery of one unequivocal secret meaning and closes the doors to the multitude of possibilities that the dream offers our mind. Rather, he emphasizes the dream as a glimpse into the mystery of the *unus mundu*s, the dream as a mystery that he prefers to 'circumambulate', alluding to the meditative walking around the mystery of life that is performed at Buddhist temples. In this way, Jung's four psychological functions are engaged. I think that the objective and subjective approaches do not clash, nor they do not exclude each other: rather, they are complementary, adding strength to each other as they add new nuances of meaning. If we take a good look not only at Moreno's writings but at his practice, we can realize that while Moreno writes only about what Jung would have considered the objective level of dreams, in his practical method Moreno explores the subjective level. In his writings, he treats the outer roles only and even rejects the word 'unconscious' completely, but, in practice, he works with the inner world constantly. Jung was no Jungian, it has been said, and Moreno may not be very Morenian either. Flying in the face of Jung's and Moreno's own words, Jungian psychodramatic practice makes its way by balancing Jung and Moreno in relation to dreams. Doubling, mirroring and role reversing are just so many ways of exploring the subjective level and giving group members a chance to live all kinds of realities in the 'as if' of the psychodramatic stage.

Jungian psychodrama technique: its effect in view of analytical psychology

We can assess how effective this technique is by looking at some of its typical results, when positive. Group members become more aware of themselves as they discover that there is some continuity among the different roles they have played in psychodrama. In the dream used as example here, A recognized herself in all the different roles she played and thereby discovered a new sense of unity in herself. Group members share concrete experiences with the group and develop their ability to work as a team. They can typically do this through role reversals, which give them a chance to see and feel how they are seen by the other group members as well as what facets of their own personalities are more evident to the others, often in different ways to different people. They can also observe the dynamics of their own relationships by observing themselves as they work in psychodrama. They develop their ability to empathize with each other through prompting and role reversal. In prompting, they stand behind the protagonist and talk the talk of their potential inner voices, giving voice to the thoughts that the protagonist's conscious ego does not express. This can happen in preparing the enactment of the scene. Usually, the director acts as the prompter and suggests an auxiliary ego. In role reversal, the protagonist plays the role of an antagonist or antagonists, so that she or he can experience the scene from another point of view (Scategni 1994, Scategni and Gasseau 2007).

Group members work to let the creative skills of their psyche come to the fore, giving them a chance to find new answers to old questions. They put two kinds of thinking face to face, thinking through images and thinking through reason and logic. In other words, they enact the images in scenes, and then they reflect on their enactment logically. In the sample dream, A experienced images in their deeper meanings through enacting them and then had the chance to reflect rationally on the emotions she went through. She could do this because her emotions had been transformed into the concrete reality of the psychodrama enactment.

Group members find out how images are linked to emotions by experiencing their links on the psychodrama stage. As members act, they reacquire their memories and the intense emotions linked with them. They live through them again in an as-if world and are given the chance to distinguish between what happened to them in the past and what happened to them as they re-experienced the past, which is something completely different, as well as what happened to them as they shared all this with the group. Finally, they become aware that their own individual paths are also open to the reality of others.

Note

1 COIRAG is the Italian Confederation of Associations of Group Therapists. It has a post-graduate school of psychotherapy affiliated with IGAP, the International Association for Group Psychotherapy and Group Processes.

References

Ancelin Schützenberger, A. (1970) *Précis de Psychodrame*, Paris: Editions Universitaires, 1992; *Lo Psicodramma* [Italian trans.], Firenze: Martinelli, 1972.

Barz, E. (1988) *Selbstbegegnung im Spiel*, Zurich: Kreuz.

Barz, H. (1990) 'Dream and Psychodrama', in N. Schwarz-Salant and M. Stein (eds.), *Dreams in Analysis*, Wilmette, IL: Chiron.

Boria, G. (1997) *Lo psicodrama classico*, Milan: Franco Angeli.

Jung, C. G. (1916) 'General Aspects of Dream Psychology' in *The Structure and Dynamics of the Psyche, Collected Works 8*, Princeton, NJ: Princeton University Press, 1969.

Jung, C. G. (1945) 'On the Nature of Dreams', in *The Structure and Dynamics of the Psyche, Collected Works 8*, Princeton, NJ: Princeton University Press, 1969.

Kellerman, P. F. (1992) *Focus on Psychodrama*, London: J. Kingsley.

Pani, R., Ronchi, E. and Scategni, W. (2006) *Sogni e processi conoscitivi delle istituzioni* [Dreams and the reasoning processes of institutions], Bologna: Clueb.

Rojas-Bermudez, J. (1997) *Teoría y Tecnica Psicodramaticas,* Barcelona: Paidos Iberica.

Scategni, W. (1994) *Das Psychodrama zwischen alltäglicher und archetypischer Erfahrungswelt*, Solothurn & Dusseldorf: Walter, 1994; *Psicodramma e terapia di gruppo: Spazio e tempo dell'anima*, 1996, Como: RED; *Psychodrama, Group Processes and Dreams: Archetypal Images of Individuation,* Hove, East Sussex: Brunner-Routledge, 2002.

Scategni, W. and Gasseau, M. (2007) 'Jungian Psychodrama: From Theoretical to Creative Roots', in C. Baim, J. Burmeister and M. Manuela (eds.), *Psychodrama: Advances in Theory and Practice*, London: Routledge.

7

FAIRY TALE DRAMA
Enacting rituals of play, laughter and tears

John Hill

When an archetype becomes conscious it is a process of incarnation.
(von Franz 1979, p. 1)

Reawakening the playful mind

I was six years old, just recovering from a long illness, when my parents decided to send me to a private boarding school, consisting of six male pupils. We lived in a house of bygone centuries, surrounded by rivers, lakes, woods and some open fields. The sole owner, director and teacher of the school was a German baron. The baroness organized the kitchen and the sporting events of the afternoon. Every night the old baron would read us fairy tales, often in candlelight. It was not difficult for us to see, hear and feel fairies, dwarfs or beautiful nymphs in the wild flowers, gnarled trees, or sparkling waters of our surroundings. One focus of attention was the house of the next-door neighbour about one mile away. Here lived seven brothers. We were told to be careful and could only talk with one of them, because he was the only one who could be seen. Apparently the six other brothers were missing something: each was either deaf, blind, dumb, lacking an arm, having a crooked leg, or not having a mind at all. We encountered those mysterious brothers in many of our childhood games. They terrified us, imprisoned us or changed one of us into one of them. Sometimes we would be rescued; other times we would be left to rot in their evil-smelling house. At that time we lived in the world of fairy tales, and it lived in us.

There was a period when my interest waned in examining candidates of the C.G. Jung Institute on their ability to interpret fairy tales from a Jungian point of view. My body was telling me that something was missing. All too often a concept, such as self, anima, or shadow, would be applied in a rather abstract way. My mind was outside the tale, examining it, objectifying it, but not really living it. I missed the dream world of my youth. Luckily the institute was generous enough in allowing me to offer courses on fairy tale drama that would not be part of the required curriculum. The following quotation from Jung was one of many that supported my endeavour to link fairy tales with psychodrama:

> We are apt to forget that in psychic matters we are dealing with processes of experience, that is, with transformations, which should never be given hard and fast names if their living movement is not to petrify into something static.
>
> (Jung 1942: para 199)

One day a Japanese client brought to analysis a most remarkable dream that re-awakened old memories of playing with those strange figures of the storyteller's imagination:

> I dreamt that I saw a big fish moving around in black waters. It looked fierce and aggressive. I peck at him with my umbrella to keep him at a distance. He tries again and again to bite at the umbrella. It is a very interesting game for me, so I play with him, forgetting all about time. Then I feel someone look down at us. I look up and see an old man smiling at the fish and me. He is standing at the edge of a road and murmurs with a smile: 'Nowadays nobody in Europe has such a mind that you still have.' I ask: 'What kind of mind?' He answers: 'The playful mind that makes you play with the "water tiger" for so long that you forget all about time.' Then he leaves us to go somewhere. Both fish and me see him leave, and we are so surprised that we forget to fight.

The dreamer knew that the fish symbolized a world not identical with his conscious self. As we gathered the relevant associations, he recognized the umbrella to be a defensive attitude that kept dreams at a distance. He also understood the old man to be a symbol of wisdom, linking him to the sages and ancestors of his cultural heritage.

Up to now, the Japanese man had maintained a scientific attitude to dreams. He would apply learned, intellectual interpretations without emotional involvement, 'without getting wet.' He could not let go and play with the images. He was enamoured by the scientific progress of the Western world and as a 'scientist' believed he had to be serious, detached and apply psychological interpretations in an objective way. I remain grateful to him and his dream. It seemed to reveal the very nature and purpose of the playful mind. In emphasizing the tension between the mythopoetic and discursive, we were both awakened to older ways to approach the unconscious, still to be found in many cultures. The dreaming mind here appears as playful and trickster-like, lifting us out of bondage to ordinary time and conventional routine and placing us in the 'once-upon-a-time' of storytelling.

In fairy tales we find vestiges of the oldest religion of humankind. Unlike myth, they do not explain life, but they do make the world come alive. They provide a narrative structure, in which the universe takes on significance that is different from the universe that is perceived through a discursive mind. In fairy tales every object – a rock, plant, animal, man – is invested with a vitality transcending its usual functional pattern. This phenomenon corresponds to the earliest religious experiences of humankind. Animism is a religion through which humans perceived the spiritual world of gods and demons in all that surrounded them. Humans could invest kinship energy in the people, animals, and objects of their environment. According to James Hillman, such a personified world is not just a 'what' but a 'who' (Hillman 1983: p. 129).

Using the objects of our surroundings, our imagination creates a parallel mythic world, one that reflects the deeper purpose of human life. The sun is not simply an object that gives warmth and light: it also can represent the need to create a centre of existence. A tree does not only give food and shelter, but can symbolize the recurrent cycles of life and death. Water does not simply wash the body, but becomes part of a purification ritual. Gods, goddesses, dwarfs, nymphs and other creatures of the imagination have always personified basic human needs. In the realm of the imagination, there is no strict separation between man, animal and nature; between mind, heart and body; between the individual and the cosmos. Having been trained in psychodrama, I soon realized that its microcosmic arena could contain a personified cosmos, or what Moreno called a 'surplus reality'. He applied this principle to all stages of life, psychodrama being an instrument to bring out 'the invisible dimensions in the reality of living' and embody them in the potentials of a space, time and destiny in a cosmos that is alive (Moreno 1961: pp. 7–12).

Fairy tale drama represents an attempt to render visible what has been invisible and to re-create the lost world of childhood in both its light and dark aspects. Such a world is not made up of isolated, clearly defined objects. Through the enactment of a tale we try to connect with the inner child who still lives in the world of fantasy. For that child the universe is a malleable reality. All is interchangeable. A well becomes an entrance to another world, a tree speaks, a frog is restored to human form. The world of fauna and flora takes on supernatural significance. In fairy tale drama, however, we may also encounter those dark moments of violence, bewitchment or betrayal when some fairy tale figure represents a caretaker who has abused an innocent child, banishing its heart and mind to the soul's underworld.

The purpose of fairy tales is to make the world come alive again, or, inversely, to overcome those antagonistic forces that restrain its full blossoming. Perhaps its most recent offspring, our modern novel, is still attempting to achieve this goal. D. H. Lawrence, in his essay called 'Why the Novel Matters', claims that a well-written novel is like a cardiograph of a life that is lived or, inversely, it sensitizes us to the deadness of inauthentic existence (Lawrence 1936: pp. 533–8).

Choice of the tale

Humans need the archetypal landscape of a living universe in order to tolerate or even cope with the injustice, violence or abuse that many encounter in those formative years of childhood. Fairy tales portray family patterns of relationships that are embedded in the background presence of the supernatural. The interaction between family members and the supernatural forces that they are likely to encounter facilitates a transformation that is embodied in the hero and heroine who represent a model of change and development. Hence the person who chooses a particular tale to be enacted often identifies with the hero or heroine and may take on the main role in the improvisation of a tale.

In choosing a tale, one needs to consider the presence or absence of one or both parents, which obviously has biographical significance. The potential protagonist might choose a tale with a powerful mother and weak father (*The Juniper Tree, Hansel and Gretel*[1]) or a cruel father and absent mother (*The Goose Girl at the Well, Thousandfurs*). While deliberating on a tale, the potential protagonist might already sense a possible resolution in the presence of a mysterious otherworldly figure that brings healing and transformation to the young hero and heroine who find themselves threatened by an omnipotent mother or father (the white dove in *Ashputtle*, the old woman in *The Shoes that were Danced Through*, the dwarf in *The Water of Life*, the well in *Mother Holle*).

Relevant to the choice of tale are the multiple forms of anxiety that are rooted in childhood, which tend to curtail one's life's potentials, often undermining healthy relationships in later life. Fear appears in narratives of abandonment (*Ashputtle, Hans my Hedgehog*), betrayal (*The Girl without Hands*), incest (*Thousandfurs*), scapegoating (*One-eye, Two-eyes, Three-eyes*), loneliness and depression (*Maid Maleen*), or guilt (*The Juniper Tree*). These are but a few examples of the complex faces of anxiety that are graphically illustrated in the initial scenes of most tales. Other narratives may have a direct bearing on the later stages of life: sexuality without the heart (*The Frog Prince*), symbiosis with a princess whose husband has to be buried with her (*The Three Snake Leaves*), aggression and rage when deception is unveiled (the quills in *Hans my Hedgehog*), innocence (*Little Red Cap*) and defence systems as illustrated in the many layers of skin of an enchanted prince (*The Linden Worm*[2]). Many motifs touch on partnership and professional identity: romantic idealizing love (*Jorinda and Joringle*), woman as an object to be possessed (*Thousandfurs, Maid Maleen*), woman who judges by appearances (*King Thrushbeard*), man who has to learn to be a man (*Iron Hans*) and the young man who has to follow his own path, despite disappointing his father (*The Spirit in the Bottle*).

In preparing a seminar on fairy tale drama, I usually arrange a preliminary meeting some weeks before the actual event in order to help participants to organize themselves into smaller groups. Each group then decides on a tale they would like to enact. As director of a seminar, I have found it useful to have prior knowledge of the tale. I read it several times to fathom its content and gain awareness of its symbolic significance, bearing in mind that I might activate one of its figures, which could be a source of inspiration for the protagonist. In psychodrama the protagonist is the person who eventually takes on the main role. As the psychodrama progresses, the protagonist chooses a member of the group to be the antagonist. There may be several antagonists, performing various functions, destructive or creative, personal or archetypal. I shall elaborate more on technique in the next section. May it suffice to enable the reader to understand why the director of a fairy tale drama should be cued into the archetypal motif of a chosen tale in order to make a quick decision. The director must act spontaneously and intuitively. This is possible if one is connected to both the embryonic aspirations of the protagonist's psyche and the symbolic intentions of the chosen tale, as illustrated in the following vignette.

In a recent improvised enactment of *The Spirit in the Bottle* the protagonist, a young man in his thirties, takes on the role of the woodcutter's son. He finds himself immersed in an endless conflict with his father. The father is irritated that his son is not practical and cannot cut wood properly. The son tries to persuade the father of the importance of philosophy in order to set limits to the rabid materialism that is destroying the world. The father is convinced that he had foolishly wasted his savings on his son's education. There seemed to be no way out of this conflict, despite several attempts at role-reversal and doubling from other participants. It suddenly occurred to me that the spirit in the bottle, identified as the god Mercurius in the original tale, might be a source of inspiration. As director of the psychodrama, I instructed the protagonist to step out of his role as son and choose a member of the group to be that spirit. He warms her up as a wise Mercurial figure who can see beyond the moment and bring healing to the damaged father/son relationship. The antagonist, now embodied as the spirit, tunes right into the archetypal dimension of Mercurius. In the dialogue with the son, she speaks directly to his soul, momentarily distracting him away from the struggle with his father and awakening him to his deeper intentions and destiny to become a philosopher. In re-connecting with the tale's Mercurial energy, the son can calmly and convincingly speak to his father about the importance of his future profession, without being caught in the snares of fruitless argument. The subtle wisdom of this archetypal figure inspired the protagonist to gain a firm standpoint that prevented him from identifying with the splitting forces of a puer/senex feud.

105

The technique

There are, of course, many ways of enacting fairy tale drama. I usually choose a setting that takes place over a weekend with persons who have experienced or are currently in some form of therapy. The structure is relatively simple. During a weekend there may be enough time for at least three specific fairy tale dramas. Each of these three slots is divided into four sections: enactment of the actual text, improvisation out of a role, sharing as in classical psychodrama, and finally reflection on the meaning of the tale.

Initial preparation

For the enactment of the original text, three or four members form a smaller group within the larger psychodrama gathering (usually twelve participants). They choose one fairy tale, possibly a favourite story, divide the main roles among themselves and organize at least one rehearsal before the seminar begins. If one member has to play two or three roles, one should select those figures where there is a continuity or transformation of the role. (If there is a negligent mother in the beginning, she may be a witch or a fairy godmother later in the tale. If a father is cruel in the initial scene, the same person can choose the role of the prince who redeems the heroine.) Symbolic animals and objects (trees, animals, wells) may also be enacted. If there are too many roles or the text is too long, the group may invite a narrator to link the enacted scenes. Participants are encouraged not to read the text on stage. It inhibits action and spontaneity. Spoken dialogue is minimal in fairy tales, so there is not much to learn. One can always improvise. Fairy tale enactment is not just about entertainment. The energy in the role inevitably embodies not only some element of the participant's personal life, but also an archetypal figure of our common cultural heritage. Masks, music or some costume, suggesting the fairy tale figure, are permitted to help maintain the role. The presentation of the original tale is a moving experience, inviting all present to participate in a world of laughter and tears.

Improvised enactment

After the presentation of the original tale, one member of the smaller group decides to become a protagonist. This role cannot be rehearsed. Sometimes the protagonist wants to enact a scene in the classical manner of psychodrama. I will focus only on those improvised enactments that are created within the framework of a fairy tale. We start with silence and an empty space. Gradually this space becomes a scene, sometimes resembling the protagonist's personal life, more often one from the enacted fairy tale. The director of fairy tale drama stands behind the protagonist and warms that person up to become whoever he or she chooses to be. The protagonist now finds himself or herself becoming some figure or object in the tale. After choosing a participant from the group, the protagonist warms up that person as the antagonist to become a figure that the protagonist needs to confront. These roles are both personal and impersonal. They may resemble a scene from one's personal life, but now enacted in the context of a fairy tale.

Role-reversal is the technique that is most commonly used in both psychodrama and fairy tale drama. It provides an opportunity to allow the protagonist to feel, think and behave like the antagonist. In fairy tale drama we explore Moreno's quandary concerning relationships with a wide cultural distance where role reversal cannot be presumed as in intimate personal relationships but must come 'from a still deeper reality in which the unconscious states of two or several individuals are interlocked within a system of co-conscious states' (Moreno 1961, p. 64). Differing from psychodrama that focuses on personal relationships, fairy tale drama elaborates Moreno's description of role not only as a representation of past personal experiences but also as an exploration of 'cultural patterns of the society in which the individual lives' (Moreno 1961, p. 62). For Jung the cultural patterns of a society rest on earlier foundations. Reflecting on the phenomenon of spirit in fairy tales, he elaborates the archetypal nature of the 'primordial image, which is universally present in the preconscious makeup of the human psyche' (Jung 1948, para 396). The role of a sorcerer, an angel, a heartless king, a haughty princess or a crafty fox in fairy tale drama provides a framework for the protagonist to communicate with figures that have populated the folklore imagination of a wide variety of cultures. Through role-reversal the protagonist internalizes those figures, a process that is not without danger.

Whenever an archetypal figure is introduced in fairy tale drama, the director risks activating powerful, transpersonal affects in the protagonist. The teamwork between the director and the group member representing the protagonist's auxiliary ego is crucial in assessing the protagonist's capacity to work with such material. The auxiliary ego's role is to maintain an empathic and therapeutic connection with the well-being of the protagonist's deeper self. They read the protagonist's alarm signals. Working between the director and protagonist, they communicate to the director the dangers of inflation, identification, malignant regression or traumatic re-activation. In one fairy tale drama, the protagonist encountered a figure of violence, flew into a rage and might have beaten up the antagonist, had not the teamwork between the director and auxiliary ego initiated a more appropriate ritual to contain the protagonist's need to act out. In another fairy tale drama, the protagonist was about to enter into dialogue with a ruthless king. The auxiliary ego picked up a pressure coming from the director and the group to continue, but also felt that the protagonist was not ready to confront such a figure. The focus then switched to the protagonist's fear of violence, who then expressed relief and gratitude that her inhibition and fear of violence were respected.

According to Moreno, 'Every role is a fusion of private and collective elements' (Moreno 1961, p. 62). When the protagonist encounters an antagonist who unexpectedly is endowed with supernatural power, it may be helpful to embody that energy in a second antagonist. Separating the personal from the archetypal helps the protagonist to establish clear boundaries, see through the archetypal projection and thus gain awareness that he/she is confronting a numinous figure, be it divine or demonic. Self-disclosure becomes appropriately contained within a narrative context common to humankind. The protagonist not only confronts the personal mother or father, but also faces the embodiment of an archetypal figure that has structured those personal relationships. It may appear as a figure of love, wisdom, violence, hate or greed, representing any of the virtues or vices that one is likely to encounter in a lifetime. The virtues and vices are common to humanity; their embodiment in fairy tale drama can facilitate a process of internalization. Provided the ego boundaries are maintained, the protagonist can withdraw the projection, identify the virtues and vices as inner archetypal forces and relate to them in a more conscious and differentiated way.

We have already seen how the fairy tale's archetypal narrative structure provides an unexpected cue that helps the protagonist to find resolution to what seems like an impossible conflict. As in classical psychodrama, techniques will be used to facilitate a resolution: not only do we resort to role-reversal and the creation of an auxiliary ego (sometimes termed, in fairy tale drama, 'the empathic self'), but also to the techniques of warming up the antagonist, mirroring, doubling and careful de-roling at the end of each enactment. Provided there is enough time, other members of the group may become protagonists, creating new scenes and possibly new resolutions.

Sharing

The third section of each fairy tale drama invites the participants to share what has been activated in their own lives on witnessing the drama, following the classical method of psychodrama. Self-disclosure must be articulated in the first person, the 'I' form. This episode of fairy tale drama creates solidarity with the protagonist and the other group members. It also has a grounding effect, encouraging each person to tell his or her own story, as the narratives become more personal and less veiled in mythic imagery.

Reflection

In the final section, we examine the meaning of the fairy tale by drawing on the participants' levels of experience. Here we try to elucidate the significance of what has been enacted. It is important to consider the archetypal structure that has implicitly determined the dramatic scenes and events, often providing a resolution to the improvised enactment. We now have the opportunity to see the universal in the particular, the narrative in an embodied context and the archetypal in a constellated complex.

The technique of fairy tale drama provides a framework through which we can weave together strands of our personality that would otherwise go unnoticed or be acted out in an unconscious manner. On letting go of our persona to behave somewhat differently from our usual self, we gain courage and freedom to express those exiled parts of the self that would otherwise remain silent. The playful process that links bodily sensations, emotions, memory and mind corresponds with the four basic techniques described above. Enacting the original tale stimulates the vitality of body, expressed in mime, gesture and voice intonation, and locates us in the 'as if' world of imagination that is less inhibited by the constraints of everyday life. In the improvised enactment we encounter in face-to-face bodily form those affect-toned complexes that have determined our emotional behaviour in unconscious ways. In sharing, we connect with the past; memories are awakened that might be associated with shame, guilt or remorse, but now become humanized, explicit and relational as we affirm our identity in a group setting. Finally, reflection on the enactment of the tale allows the participants to place their bodily experiences, emotions and memories in a universe of meaning, enabling each person to affirm a narrative identity of coherence and continuity and to connect with other group members in deeper ways. Fairy tale drama allows for an organic process that grows out of a well-defined containing structure. Feeling safe and confident, each person welcomes new experiences that allow for the possibility of a transformation that is authentic, has archetypal significance and is rooted in a unique personal biography.

Fairy tales in action

Thresholds

In conducting fairy tale drama I have found that the protagonists usually move quickly into the role they have selected. This is probably because the archetypal energy of the figure they have chosen has already been constellated through the enactment of the original tale. *Mother Holle* is a tale about Gold Marie[3] who loses her spindle in a deep well. Her cruel mother insists that she goes after it. She jumps into the well, loses consciousness and awakes in a beautiful landscape ruled over by an old woman who possesses the powers of an ancient mother goddess. In the improvised enactment, the protagonist, a woman in midlife, chooses the role of Gold Marie. Fear and resistance soon become visible as she begins to explore the deeper levels of the scene and figures that she has created. She can hardly go beyond the encounter with the well, symbolizing an entrance to another world, which is personified by a member of the group. A long conversation – including several role reversals – takes place between the heroine and the mysterious well. Gold Marie is

109

terrified to enter that black hole. The wise well does not pressure her, allows her time to move backwards and forwards, and check out if this is the right time to descend into the darkness. While the protagonist is deliberating, memories of her brother's tragic death surface to consciousness. The well consoles her and assures her that she is in no way responsible for his untimely death. Gradually the last vestiges of an innocent child's guilt are lifted, and Gold Marie can enter the realm of Mother Holle. Here both the living and the dead are welcomed, and the protagonist once more embraces her beloved brother.

The resolution might not have been possible without the combined teamwork of the antagonist, auxiliary ego and director. Without knowing why the protagonist hesitated, they respected her resistance and thus facilitated her slow descent into the underworld.

Facing the dark

In the tale *The White Snake* the hero risks his life to perform three difficult tasks in order to win the heart of a haughty princess. The enactment of this tale constellated dark memories in a female participant. In an improvised enactment she takes on the role of a prince. 'He' is with a baby. The antagonist personifies a figure in black who is at first the haughty princess, but then the protagonist lets her become a much darker being – the goddess Kali. Behind Kali is another personage in white whom the protagonist designates as 'Wisdom'. A ritualized battle of words starts when Kali attacks the prince. In one scene Kali takes on the shape of the prince's mother. He pleads with his mother to help him, otherwise he will die, but she does not care if her son will die. Next Kali, as mother, wants to kill the baby. The prince feels terror but, through role reversal with Kali, the protagonist knows what gives the antagonist her power. The more Kali tries to kill the baby, the more the prince connects with his own aggression. After several role reversals, the prince begins to integrate Kali's rage. Finally he puts his arms around the baby and walks away. Kali no longer controls his life. The prince now finds support in the arms of 'wisdom' who becomes a figure of love.

In the sharing time, the female participant who had assumed the role of the prince said she needed to express the rage she still felt towards her mother. The mother had dominated her life. The protagonist was made to feel guilty whenever she criticized her mother. The baby represented her new life but also expressed a vulnerability that was in need of protection. The moment she felt vulnerable, the mother gained power over her. In order to protect the baby, she had to feel her aggression, here personified as a strong animus who could challenge the mother.

The enactment supported the protagonist's struggle with her mother, a process that she had been working on during previous years in analysis. A good conclusion might not have been achieved, had we not resorted to the technique of role-reversal and a ritualized form of aggression. The ritualized battle of words was activated only when the protagonist stood within a yard of the antagonist. This allowed the protagonist to maintain boundaries and ego responsibility in letting her decide to what extent she could tolerate this kind of confrontation. It proved highly effective in internalizing the power of Kali without loss of ego boundaries.

The missing one

In interpreting fairy tales, we usually pay attention to the presence or absence of a parent. All too often this becomes a major issue in improvised enactments. Following a group presentation of *Snow White*, the protagonist decides to confront her domineering mother. Personifying 'Snow White', the protagonist seems to get nowhere in a long struggle with her mother, the evil queen, who cares for no one but herself and her position in society. The director recalls the helpful dwarfs of the original tale and suggests that the protagonist makes contact with one of them. Only after a conversation with a helpful dwarf does Snow White realize that the strange little figure embodies the few memories of her absent father, who had abandoned the family when she was a little girl. Now she begins to understand the rage of her disowned mother. After several heated scenes solidarity develops between Snow White and the mother, and together they confront the father who had so cruelly left the family in the lurch. The dialogue activates an old trauma that had opened a void in the protagonist's soul. She had split off powerful Oedipal emotions and thus became a victim of her mother's resentfulness. In the enactment the presence of the chthonic dwarf helps her connect with her gut feelings that had been infested with the mother's rage. In the final scene she is alone, except for her father. She confronts him, expresses her anger, but also her love for him. The family tragedy begins to heal.

Thanks to the archetypal structure of the original tale, the director and auxiliary ego could see a connection between the missing father and the helpful dwarf, the latter representing a diminutive animus that could not develop after the father had left the family. This insight proved decisive in helping the protagonist come to terms with the family trauma.

The friendly animal

Marie Louise von Franz once said that there is one golden rule in fairy tales to which there is no exception. When a friendly animal appears in a tale, the outcome of the heroic quest will be successful. *The Cast-iron Stove* is a fairy tale that tells about a prince who was bewitched, locked up in an iron stove and deceived by a reluctant princess who eventually redeemed him with the help of a friendly animal. The initial scene inspires the protagonist, a woman in midlife, to set up two chairs. In one chair she sits as a princess who personifies that part of her who is always busy, writing papers, feeling important but essentially afraid of expressing her deeper self. That other self, a chosen antagonist, sits in the second chair and becomes a representation of the protagonist's totem animal. A conversation ensues without eye contact. The totem animal wants to participate more in the protagonist's social activities and not just as the companion of her wild, secret life. Alarmed by this proposal, the princess becomes afraid that she will be misunderstood and even be ridiculed by her friends. In the end they turn and face each other. The princess, looking into the eyes of her totem animal, suddenly makes a deep connection. At that moment she gains courage to speak out the name of her totem animal. In the section on sharing with the group, it turned out that this is the protagonist's First Nations[4'] name. It had been given to her at birth, but being afraid of it, she kept it hidden. Now, through fairy tale drama, she remembers what an elder once told her: The name connects her to her land, her people and her ancestors; she has to create the meaning of that name in her real life; she has to live it out in her own way.

That night the protagonist writes a poem in honour of her totem animal and does not hesitate to share it with the group the next day. Inspired by the friendly animal of *The Cast-iron Stove,* the protagonist's psychodrama opened up a new perspective on group participation. She could share something of her life's secrets in a way that she had not done before.

The animal within

Verifying von Franz's golden rule might prove daunting, especially at the outset of an enactment when the protagonist starts roaring like a lion, hissing like a snake or braying like a wild ass. Voicing the beast within, however, can be a way of connecting with a deeper self that has been silenced by outer authority. In the Grimms' tale *Old Sultan,* a domestic dog is about to be shot, even though it had served his master all its life. A wolf prevents this, but the dog remains faithful to his master and betrays his next-of-kin, the helpful wolf. Consequently the dog's owner whips the wolf mercilessly. In the improvised enactment, the protagonist, a young academic, takes on the role of a professor who has lost contact with his animal soul. He chooses a member of the group to be his younger brother, a wolf who leads a wild, outrageous life. After a fierce argument the professor shoots the wolf. In the next scene the dead wolf is lying on the floor, surrounded by several howling wolves who mourn their dead brother. Very soon everybody in the room is howling. The emotional outpouring emerges quite spontaneously and unexpectedly, and we are left dumbfounded.

In a later group discussion it dawned upon us all that we were mourning the dead animal within. In the sharing, each person had something to say about how they too had become over-domesticated and, like so many academics of our times, have participated in the betrayal of the animal soul.

Conclusion

In fairy tales we find expression of an ancient dialogue between humans and the mysteries of their environment. The purpose of this short outline of fairy tale drama is not only to awaken the imagination and bring back to life the 'once-upon-a-time' of fairy tales. My intention is to convey to the reader the transformative magic of an improvised drama that is inspired by the containing structure of a fairy tale. Fairy tales harbour collective and cultural treasures that have nourished the human soul over generations. They offer modern man and woman patterns of individuation that have withstood the test of time and may prove helpful in finding answers to life's enigmas. Expressing a common archetypal heritage, they encourage us to explore the subtle depth of human relationship. In the examples selected above we have encountered the crafty advice of the god Mercurius, the consoling power of Dame Holle's well, the violent energy of Kali, the gut wisdom of a chthonic dwarf, and the transformative power of the friendly animal, all reflecting new perspectives on the protagonist's present pattern of relationships. Through internalizing the symbolic intentions of these archetypal figures and amplifying them through mind, memory, emotion and body, we become aware of the deeper levels of the personal psyche that are embedded in an impersonal, universal landscape, essential for survival, health and fulfilment. Within this matrix, the human becomes truly human.

As outlined in the section on technique, one should never forget that enactments in fairy tale drama are powerful, spontaneous and unpredictable. The roles of the director and auxiliary ego need to be carefully adjusted in order to protect the integrity of the protagonist's ego, as it encounters the soul's numinous and sometimes all-consuming archetypal dimensions.

Fairy tale drama attempts to connect the personal with the archetypal in ways that address the plight of contemporary humanity who cannot find home in a purely functional world of artefacts. Enactments express not only the soul's hidden pathologies but also innovative narratives addressing universal themes that have occupied humankind since the beginning of time. Through role-play the participant has the opportunity to sort out and differentiate what belongs to parents, what belongs to society and what belongs to the gods. Letting go is a way of opening up to the symbol-creating mind that is continually active, playfully casting and recasting its encounters with self and the world into meaningful representations. Fairy tale drama initiates a shared group experience among individuals who come alive to themselves and others, in learning to play, laugh and cry together.

Notes

1 All the fairy tales and their titles in this chapter have been selected from Ralph Manheim's translation of *Grimms' Tales for Young and Old* (Manheim, 1979). The exception is Prince Lindenworm.

2 'Prince Lindenworm' in *Scandinavian Legends and Folk-Tales* (Jones, 1992, p. 3).
3 Gold Marie is the heroine's original name in the German editions of Grimms' tales.
4 First Nations: Aboriginal peoples in Canada.

References

Manheim, R. (trans.) (1979) *Grimms' Tales for Young and Old*. London: Victor Golanz.

Hillman, J., with Pozzo, L. (1983) *Inter Views*. Dallas: Spring Publications.

Jones, G. (1992) *Scandinavian Legends and Folk-Tales*. Oxford: Oxford University Press.

Jung, C. G. (1942) 'Paracelsus as a Spiritual Phenomenon', in *Alchemical Studies, Collected Works 13*, Princeton, NJ: Princeton University Press.

Jung, C. G. (1948) 'The Phenomenology of the Spirit in Fairytales', in *The Archetypes and the Collective Unconscious, Collected Works 9i,* Princeton, NJ: Princeton University Press.

Lawrence, D. H. (1936) 'Why the Novel Matters', in E. D. McDonald (ed.), *Phoenix: The Posthumous Papers of D. H. Lawrence*, New York: Viking Press, 1968, pp. 533–8.

Moreno, J. L. (1961) 'The Role Concept, a Bridge between Psychiatry and Sociology', in J. Fox (ed.), *The Essential Moreno,* New York: Springer Publishing, 1987.

von Franz, M. L. (1979) *Apuleius' Golden Ass.* New York: Spring Publications.

8

USING PSYCHODRAMA
IN ANALYSIS

Christopher Beach

Introduction

I first brought together the ideas of Jacob Moreno and C. G. Jung by participating in a psychodrama group as I was undertaking a Jungian analysis. The experience of working in both of these modes led to my later using some of Moreno's psychodrama techniques in my work as a Jungian analyst.[1] This chapter describes an extended example of such work with one of my analysands, referred to hereafter as 'Sofia'.

Before turning to that work, it will help if I explain in general terms how I have used psychodrama in analysis. It has been done infrequently, and only with analysands who have had the ego strength and interest to try it. In those instances, I have worked for as many as thirty hours without resort to psychodrama techniques, and normally at least three or four hours of regular analysis have passed between sessions in which these techniques have been used.

When using psychodrama techniques in analysis, my guiding principle has been *less is more*, the guiding principle for psychodrama itself. Both psychodrama and active imagination powerfully affect the subject – the protagonist in psychodrama or the analysand in analysis. Careful analysts encourage analysands initially to stay within an active imagination for only twenty to thirty minutes and, thereafter, to reflect upon what they have experienced. Similarly, careful psychodrama directors guard against asking too much of the protagonist during the psychodrama and encourage reflection upon it in the days that follow.

Psychodrama in its classic form is a group process wherein most of each two-and-one-half-hour session is devoted primarily to one protagonist. The other group members work in the service of the protagonist, under the guidance of two trained co-directors. This contrasts with analysis in its classic form, wherein an analysand works for one hour with one trained psychoanalyst. Thus, while psychodrama is primarily an extraverted form of psychotherapy, analysis is primarily an introverted form.

As for using psychodrama techniques in analysis, it works like this: An 'enactment' occurs when an analysand chooses to enact a small psycho-dramatic scene involving material from his/her life. These enactments are very basic. For example, Bob (the analysand) might choose one chair in the room to represent his mother and another chair to represent himself. If it is a diffi-cult scene for Bob, I might ask him if he would like to introduce a third person to serve as his ally in the enactment. Bob might, in that case, choose a blanket to represent his best friend. He places the chairs and blanket – his mother, himself, and his friend – in the room where he wants to. I then ask Bob if he would be willing to 'introduce' his mother. When Bob feels he is ready, he stands behind the designated chair and speaks as if he is his mother, saying, for example, 'I am Bob's Mom. My name is Clara. I don't like Bob's father, William', etc. In this way Bob 'loads' his mother into the chair, and she becomes a presence in the room.

If Bob becomes very emotional introducing his mother, we might end the enactment at this point. *Less is more.* There is already plenty of emotional material to work with in regular analysis. If, however, the introduction has not been too unsettling and Bob is willing, we might go to the next step. Bob takes turns standing behind each chair or near the blanket, playing the role symbolized by the object and conducting a 'conversation' between his mother, himself, and his friend. At some point, the enactment will be brought to a close – at either Bob's or my suggestion. Time remaining in the session and subsequent sessions will then be used to reflect upon what Bob has experienced during the enactment.

In this part of the session, I serve the dual role of analyst and psychodrama director, helping Bob with questions of who might be introduced, how the scene might be set, deciding which figure/person might speak first, and so on. Almost without exception, I remain in my analytic chair and play no part in the enactment. My role as analyst is primary: so, I provide a grounding point and a container for Bob's enactment and subsequent reflection.

More about the use of psychodrama in analysis will become clear as we now turn to Sofia's work at three points in her analysis. I will tell her story in the present tense, even though the analysis concluded, after about eighteen months, many years ago.

The analysand, Sofia[2]

When Sofia first comes to analysis, she is a 40-year-old single mother living in an apartment in Zurich with her 15 year-old son, Sam. She works full-time as a translator and is very good at her work. Nine years ago she divorced Sam's father, Ivan, but he still lives nearby. He is generous with Sam and Sofia. An émigré from an Eastern European country, Ivan often travels on business outside Switzerland, sometimes taking Sam with him. He is very intelligent and can be very charming, but he is also unpredictable, intimidating and choleric. His payments of child-support vary with his business fortunes, ranging from much more than the divorce decree requires to nothing.

Four years ago, Ivan suggested that Sofia attend an alcohol rehabilitation program, and then paid for most of her seven months there. This resulted in Sofia's recovery from the lowest, most dysfunctional point in her life. She has been abstinent ever since, regularly attending AA meetings. Although still suffering from an eating disorder and excessive smoking, Sofia functions effectively in the outer world.

Growing up, Sofia was an only child. Her parents had met in Santiago, Chile. Both parents were Jewish, her mother having fled from the Nazis in Vienna, her father from the Nazis in Leipzig. Neither parent attended synagogue, and Sofia reports having gone herself perhaps only twice. While her father was more sympathetic to Jewish traditions, her mother would have nothing to do with them.

By the time her family finally settled in Italy when she was seven, they had already lived in two South American countries and Switzerland. Sofia had become, in her words, 'the child without a motherland, the child without a mother tongue'. She still wonders whether it is the German of her parents or the Italian of the country where she spent most of her school years. Although brilliant with language, speaking five languages fluently, Sofia cannot identify one that feels like home.

Sofia's parents provided for her materially, but much else was lacking. Her father traveled world-wide, coming home infrequently. Her mother, obsessed with cleanliness and order, was given to angry outbursts. Both parents had extramarital affairs, leaving them with even less time for Sofia. They employed nannies to help. One Swiss nanny 'caring' for five-year-old Sofia in South America once made her eat what she threw up when she got sick at the table and, on another occasion, made Sofia walk so far her feet became numb. The nanny ordered Sofia to keep walking even after she complained. Sofia's parents were unaware of the nanny's abuse because Sofia felt that she (as the bad girl) could not tell them. This nanny was left behind when the family moved to Europe. Thereafter, Sofia continued to endure years of an emotionally and physically absent father and an obsessive and over-controlling mother. Sofia tells me, for example, of how much she hated it when her mother regularly made her comb out the fringes of the living room carpets with a hair-comb.

Sofia did not feel as if she could confide in her mother. Once, while playing with a friend, Sofia fell and cut herself. She asked to go to the friend's home to wash and have the cut treated because she feared her mother's anger if she came home dirty. When Sofia later did return home, her mother asked her why she had not come home first. When, she told her mother of her fear, her mother denied that she would have been angry, even as her coldness spoke otherwise. It is her mother's anger and her father's failure to stand up to it that Sofia repeatedly cites as having upset and angered her.

Once Sofia started school, she excelled. She recalls her school days as the best time of her life. But it was also the time when her bulimia, back pain, cigarette use, and drug and alcohol abuse all first manifested.

As Sofia begins analysis with me, she has been alcohol- and drug-free for three years, and she will remain so. It bothers her, though, that she still smokes cigarettes and suffers from bulimia. Her weight is normal for her height, but she binges in the evenings and believes her weight is excessive. It is as if there is a sharp battle between her Dionysian self, which wants to eat, drink and be merry (like her father), and her Apollonian self, which wants to maintain order and control (like her mother).

Over the initial months of analysis, Sofia goes through major employment shifts: from part-time work, through four months of unemployment and job-searching, to full employment. Although often tired and depressed, she manages these shifts well, even winning a desirable new job against stiff competition. Her response to these difficult challenges shows Sofia's marked instinct for self-preservation, which counter-balances her self-destructive side.

Her dreams reflect this same tension – even the initial dream of her analysis:

> There was a star over me. It caught my attention. It was technical. Then it was falling, and I was running. I tried to avoid it. It kept coming. I was very scared. It was very bright, like a falling star. Then I realized it was mechanical, metallic, with a definite shape, following me like a heat-seeking missile.

When we discuss this dream, Sofia draws an elongated, diamond-shaped object to represent the star and adds that it crashed onto her, waking her up. She doesn't recall whether it hurt her. Her associations include the fact that her father was a diamond and jewelry broker-merchant. Also, she reports that this dream is much less frightening than a recurring nightmare experienced from age 16 until her mid-thirties – in which an airplane violently crashed into her house.

When I first hear this dream, I see it in different ways. First, it may be reflecting her unconscious attitude toward the analysis she is starting: a star that initially attracts her becomes a diamond attacking from the sky. I make a mental note to restrain my tendencies to make penetrating observations and be overly enthusiastic. (Sofia will, indeed, express her ambivalence toward analysis over time.) Second, the dream may be reflecting her ambivalence between two attitudes as she faces an ambiguous cosmic object, something from above and away, possibly of a spiritual nature. This ambivalence is also seen in the two different ways she presents: sometimes as a curious and open child, at other times as an adult who has been overly 'parentified' – having had to protect herself against verbal and emotional assaults. Third, I am reminded of her attitude toward her father, in whom she often initially took delight but who would then disappoint her. A vain playboy-athlete, he regularly commented about his trim weight and her less-than-perfect weight. Thus, he could be like the cutting diamond from the sky, at first beautiful and orienting like a star, but then attacking with criticism. Sofia agrees with this and adds that her mother could also attack like this diamond.

During her analysis, Sofia has two brief but important intimate relationships. Each man is younger than she and has serious substance abuse issues. In the first relationship, with 'Hal', Sofia has for only the second time in her life deeply satisfying sexual relations without herself being under the influence of either drugs or alcohol. This relationship ends relatively early in her analysis, while the relationship with 'Amos' does not begin until over a year later, near the end of the analysis.

Psychodramatic enactments within Sofia's analysis

An early, aborted enactment

About a month after her relationship with Hal ends, Sofia tries a short psychodrama enactment, the third in her analysis. Although she has just learned that her job will soon terminate, it is the loss of Hal that she mourns. She clearly sees the drawbacks of his young age, addiction, unstable personality, and lack of employment; yet her grief is great. She can express her feelings of sadness, hurt, abandonment, and her fear of being lonely again, but she has not cried, which concerns her. She knows that, in the past, her addictions have been a way to cut herself off from painful emotions.

In our 25th session, after she closes her eyes to contact the sadness and see if tears will come, she reports that her thoughts scatter. Then comes an image of herself as a hurt child at age three, which was captured in a prized family photograph. She speaks of the present divide in her. She says that with her head she thinks of the positive things in her life – that she loves and is loved by her son, Sam, that he needs her, that she has caring friends and that most people like her, and that Hal is *not* the right person for her because of all his problems. But then there are her guts: they say, 'Fuck it! I *want* Hal.'

I ask her if she feels it might be useful to introduce those two parts of herself – head and guts – into the room, using a different chair to represent each, and perhaps have a dialogue with them. Sofia decides she would like to try this.

As she gets ready, I begin to make notes – a transcript, in effect. I do this each time an analysand does an enactment, primarily as the drama unfolds. At key points, it is verbatim. At others, I paraphrase. At still others, I reconstruct later parts that I could not note down during the session. The transcript enhances reflection and analysis after the enactment.

Sofia places two chairs facing each other, in front of me but turned sideways to me, about six feet from each other and from me. I suggest that she start with what she calls the 'rational' part of herself, that which sees the blessings in Hal's departure. I think to myself that this aspect may be less emotionally

119

loaded and so easier to begin with. Sofia moves behind the chair to my left, puts her hands on its back, and begins to speak:

SOFIA: I am the *rational part* of Sofia, trying to talk to her.
CHRIS: Where is this part located?
SOFIA: I don't know!
(*There is a pause. Then Sofia begins to weep – the first time she has ever cried in analysis!*)
CHRIS: You can sit down if you want to.
SOFIA: It's okay.
(*Suddenly Sofia is very angry. She takes first one chair and then the other, shoving them with fury back to where they were when the analytic hour began.*)
CHRIS: You seem as if you are angry. Are you?
SOFIA: I am angry – that I cry. I feel anger when I cry. There is anger at the crying, anger in the chest. It's not at anybody in particular.
(*Long pause.*)
    It reminds me of when I was a child. When I got depressed and would cry, my mother would say I had *Weltschmerz* – the pain of the world. Now I have anger at the world. My substance-abuse rehabilitation counselor used to say that having the pain of the world allows me not to have the pain of myself.

Sofia and I discuss what has happened here. Being young as an analyst, I talk more about psychological theory than I will later in my years of practice. But what I see and what I express at this moment will usefully inform the rest of Sofia's analysis.

In classical Freudian terms, it is as if the two chairs represent Sofia's ego (the rational part of her) and id (the libidinous part). Although I have asked her to introduce the ego first because I think it will be less emotionally loaded, within moments Sofia is quietly crying for the first time. Her sadness is palpable. Then something even more remarkable happens: a prohibitive and punitive giant enters the room, entirely taking over Sofia and the psychodrama. Again in Freudian terms, I see this as her superego – a combination of her mother's prohibition of any mess and her father's critical commentary. This harsh superego dominates the ego and id. It will have none of 'this self-pity' (Sofia's words). It bans feelings of loss and grief. Thus, in Freudian terms, the superego is dominating and squashing the ego and id.

From a more Jungian view, I see the situation somewhat differently. The 'rational part' of Sofia is her conscious ego attitude. The second part of her, her 'guts', which we barely begin to glimpse, I think of as her child-within. And the domineering intruder I see as her inner Critic. It attacks the child, overrides the ego, belittles feelings of loss and sadness, stuffs Sofia's crying, and kills the small psychodrama itself – the coming into being of playful imagination. This lethal force has been running Sofia's life for a long time.

(Only later will I connect it to the diamond descending from the night sky in Sofia's initial dream.)

From the perspectives of both psychodramatist and analyst, I am alerted to the enormous power that the inner Critic has over Sofia's ego. It is keeping her from a more natural and spontaneous living of her life. It is a force so powerful that it both stops the dramatic enactment and warns me that now is not a time for Sofia to work in this way. It is too loaded for her. We have been getting too close to her vulnerability, and this force has dropped down the curtain on the drama. 'Too close to home, too soon' is what I conclude. *Less is more.*

In the session, Sofia and I discuss the different ways of viewing the two parts represented by the chairs, as well as the third force that has taken over the room. I refer to it mostly as 'the Critic' as I talk with her. I do not say to her that it has killed the drama.

With these images and thoughts in the back of my mind, I continue to work with Sofia for another 33 sessions before we again use psychodrama. During this period of several months, she engages in another form of imaginal work: closing her eyes and bringing back scenes from her past. One of these moments proves critical. She remembers and tells the fuller story of her mother's referring to her *Weltschmerz* (pain of the world). Sofia was 11, staying with her mother at a hotel in a foreign city. Her mother wanted to take in a late-night movie, leaving Sofia alone. When Sofia began to cry, her mother decided to skip the movie and tried to comfort Sofia, saying that what had come over Sofia was just her *Weltschmerz*. Sofia ended up feeling guilty for keeping her mother from her favored activity.

Something about this childhood scene catches both Sofia and me. After she closes her eyes to go back into it twice and we discuss it for a while, I ask Sofia to close her eyes again and imagine what a positive mother would have done in this situation. Sofia answers, 'Not go to the movies in the first place.' Then she changes her mind, because she thinks that would be asking too much. She becomes stuck and says, 'It's a pretty lousy place – can't have feelings one way or the other.' I reframe the question, 'If you had an eleven-year-old daughter and you were the positive mother, what would you do?' Sofia answers instantly: 'Ask her what her feelings are, "What's coming up for you?".'

This is a key moment. Although not using psychodramatic *per se*, we are bringing back a distant memory in detail and imagining how else it might have gone. What Sofia and I suddenly see is threefold: (1) by calling Sofia's suffering '*Weltschmerz*', her mother misnamed Sofia's pain, stole her power to name her own pain, and distorted her self-image (Sofia's rehabilitation counselor was right: by feeling the pain of the world, Sofia unconsciously avoids feeling her own pain); (2) her mother also avoided taking responsibility for causing Sofia's pain and missed the opportunity to have a serious mother–daughter dialogue; and (3) in this analytic hour, Sofia expresses her own positive mothering from within. She plays the positive mother to her crying

11-year-old-child-self. Sofia inhabits both mother and child, first remembering herself at 11, then imagining how she would mother that child. Sofia-as-mother honors Sofia-as-child's right to have her feelings and to express them.

With this session, Sofia takes a significant step. We see its impact soon thereafter, when Sofia's mother comes for a two-week visit. She appears to Sofia to be older, more frail, more human, no longer like a tyrant. For the first time that Sofia can remember, her mother does not criticize or bother her. Sofia wonders whether there has been a change within herself that has somehow affected how they experience one another. Sofia is encouraged by this development.

Sofia confronts Ivan

The next psychodramatic enactment that Sofia tries occurs soon thereafter, in the 58th session, a little more than a year into the analysis. Sofia arrives at the session angry at her ex-husband, Ivan. Within earshot of their son, Sam, Ivan has asked a friend, 'How can anyone go to a movie about "homos"?' The friend, Gina, was about to join Sofia and go to a highly acclaimed film portraying homosexual men. Later that day, as Sofia and Gina were leaving for the film, Sam repeated what his father had said earlier. The more Sofia thought about this, the angrier she became. Ivan knew that she and Gina both had good friends who were homosexuals. And to say this in front of Sam!

Now, Sofia is in my office – angry at Ivan, and angry at herself for not having expressed her feelings to him directly. Earlier in the analysis, she has explained that she is unable to say 'No' to strong, authoritarian figures like Ivan, and that this problem first appeared in her childhood in relation to her mother. Both her mother and Ivan like to control those around them and are given to unpredictable outbursts of anger. One of Sofia's goals is to find the courage to confront, rather than appease, them. Hence, Sofia wants to change, to confront Ivan the next time something like this happens. She is upset that the father of her son is modeling intolerance of homosexuality.

Sofia says, 'I was enraged. I don't know what to do with this rage . . . I think it is quite healthy that I can feel rage toward Ivan. For years, I was only afraid of him. Now, I can see a change.' I sense that Sofia wants to find a way to channel her rage, and that psychodrama might be helpful. I ask her whether she wants to go into the rage and imagine how she might confront Ivan. She says she would like to try. Together we decide to have her introduce Ivan and engage him in an imaginary conversation.

Sofia rises from her usual armchair, takes a simple, straight-backed chair and places it in the room where she wishes. She stands behind that chair, places her hands on its back, and, in effect, 'loads' Ivan into the chair. Thus, she begins: 'I am Ivan Hyatt. I am the greatest. . . .' With this introduction, Ivan enters the analytic space:

IVAN: (*as played by Sofia*): I am the greatest. I am the most handsome. I am a high-stakes businessman.

(*Here Ivan turns 'his' head toward me to address me as Sofia's analyst. In a sense a rupture occurs, a crossing between the drama and analysis and between the relationships within each of those worlds.*)

IVAN: And you are Chris. You're milking my ex-wife for all you can get from her. All she's doing is telling you her problems. So what!

SOFIA: (*as herself, though still standing behind Ivan-chair*): You [Ivan] should look at yourself. You're disgusting. Why are you so prejudiced?

IVAN: What are you trying to say?

SOFIA: I am trying to talk to you.

IVAN: Well, talk then. I'm listening.

SOFIA: I can't. I don't know why I can't . . . .[3]

CHRIS: Maybe we should pause for a moment, Sofia. I have made a mistake here by not helping you set this up clearly. Let me explain first, and then we can try again, if you still want to. You are standing behind the chair and introducing Ivan. As long as your hands are on the chair, you should speak in the first person 'I', as if you are Ivan and speaking as he speaks. If you, as yourself, need to say something to me, please lift your hands off the chair and step back one step. This will help both you and me keep clear which role you are in at a given moment. And if you want to address Ivan, speaking as yourself, you can lift your hands off the chair, come around in front of it, and address it as if it's Ivan and he's right in front of you. How would this be for you?

SOFIA: It may help. I know I was having trouble getting into Ivan because it makes me uncomfortable.

CHRIS: Are you sure it's okay to go ahead? You don't have to if you don't want to.

SOFIA: No, it's okay. I want to figure out how to deal with him.

CHRIS: If it would help, you can take one of the pillows there on the couch and pretend it is the one person who most gives you courage and strength to stand up for yourself. Who would that be?

SOFIA: Rachel, for sure. Can I do that? That would be good.

(*Sofia takes a pillow to serve as her closest friend Rachel and puts the pillow nearby as she prepares to start over.*)[4]

CHRIS: Is it okay for you to try again?

(*Sofia nods, and we continue. Sofia takes her time introducing Ivan, with long pauses interspersed between her sentences.*)

IVAN: I am Ivan Hyatt. I am fat and bald. I can't help being bald. It runs in my family. I am losing weight. I am a businessman. I travel a lot. I am a wheeler-dealer. I live in luxury. I've made a lot of money in my time, and I've lost a lot, too. I have an absolutely lovely son. He's called Sam. He's 15. His Mom, my ex-wife, is a very smart, lovely lady. I have a lot of respect for her. My son lives with her. Before, he lived with me for a while, because her alcohol problems got so bad. I helped her sober up. I have married again. Women like me because I am very charming.

CHRIS: What do you think about homosexuality, Ivan?

IVAN: I think homosexuality is totally disgusting. Bloody queers! Effeminate monkeys! You've got to be a man. Those fucking homos!

(*Sofia stops. She takes her hands from the back of the Ivan chair and steps back. She looks troubled.*)

CHRIS: Sofia, how does it feel now, introducing Ivan?

SOFIA: It is absolutely horrible to be Ivan. He's just acting all the time. Once, many years ago, he cried and said how unhappy he was. But only once did this happen. He's so out of touch with his feelings, his desires, everything. Whenever he says anything, it's as if the opposite is true or also true. I feel totally anxious and uneasy. Blech! (*Sofia shakes her whole body.*) I want to shake him off, to get out of his skin. I often feel like shaking him, to help him out. It's like I've got fleas. It's a hard place to be, in his skin. He's totally false.

CHRIS: (*after letting her last lines sink in for a moment*): Sofia, what if you try now to confront Ivan about what is bothering you?

SOFIA: (*coming around in front of the Ivan chair to confront him*): You're a fake. Don't you see? Don't you see that people see through you? You're just showing off and pompous.

(*Sofia pauses as if waiting for his response.*)

CHRIS: Slowly switch roles.

(*Sofia slowly goes behind the Ivan chair, puts her hands on it, then speaks as if Ivan.*)

IVAN: What's the matter, Baby? What are you talking about?

(*At this point in the mini-drama, Sofia begins to switch roles on her own, shifting between herself and Ivan, each time changing her position physically in the room so that she literally steps into the appropriate role.*)

SOFIA: Why are you so judgmental? Why are you so critical of others?

IVAN: Oh, but Baby, you know I'm only joking. Don't take me seriously.

SOFIA: Why did you say in front of Sam, 'How can anyone go to see movies with homosexuals?'

IVAN: You know these issues are very complex, Baby, and you have to think about them carefully. They have a lot of consequences for society. . . .

Here Sofia's and Ivan's conversation turns into what she calls 'his socio-political babble', which, she says, makes her sick. When she gets caught in such discussions, her feelings and emotions get left behind. I feel a little ill myself. I stop writing as I listen to their conversation, a mix of sickly sweet syrup and ungrounded socio-political theories. Ivan is acting like an unreformed macho-man, not like an ex-husband of nine years. He accords Sofia little respect as an equal. They are not addressing the real issues that are upsetting Sofia. Because of this, I suggest that we pause.

I want to share my impression that Sofia and Ivan are avoiding a real conversation about real emotions and feelings, but do so in a way that does not sound as if I am criticizing Sofia. So, I begin by asking questions. As Sofia answers, I learn that she feels she typically falls into the trap of trying to keep up with Ivan's clever theoretical points and then gets lost. She feels she has to be as 'smart' as he, even though she knows he is false.

With this explanation, I realize that Sofia simply does not know how to express her emotions (gut responses) or her feelings (what she values and will not easily compromise) and how to stay with them. I decide to tell her a story, much as one might share a fairy tale, except this is a modern tale. In this short, dramatic story, another woman who looks as if she cannot stand up for herself does so by simply stating and staying with her feelings in front of a class of thirty adults, despite being told by other women in the class that her feelings are not politically correct. It is a story of an event that I have recently witnessed, a story that is powerfully moving.

And Sofia is moved by it. She sees the parallel to her own situation. She holds certain values that are valid, but in her 'conversation' with Ivan, she is pulled away from them. They are where she is, but she is losing them and herself in Ivan's whirlwind of ideas.

Sofia and I discuss how she might speak with the real Ivan *and* stay close to her feelings. We reach the conclusion that she need only tell him something like, 'Look, Ivan! I am very upset by the fact that you said, in front of Sam, "How can anyone go to a movie about homos?" You know very well that some of my best friends are homosexuals, and you even like them. I am very angry that you did this. It is not a good message to teach Sam.' Sofia and I also agree that if Ivan does go into his 'socio-political babble', she can say, 'Look, Ivan, I don't want to get into a verbal battle with you. What you did upset me, and I want you to know that.' As the session ends, Sofia is perceptibly stronger and calmer.

What I do not expect is that Sofia will confront Ivan almost immediately. A few days later, however, when Ivan himself brings up what he has said about homosexuals, Sofia tries what we have rehearsed. When Ivan begins his usual rationalizations, Sofia repeats what her feeling response has been and says she does not want to argue the point. She just wants him to know that his intolerant comment is very upsetting. He acknowledges her point, then changes the subject. Sofia reports all of this in her next analytic session. She adds that, although she wishes more could have happened, she feels good about the small change. For once, she has directly expressed her feelings to him and stuck to them. She is smiling as she reports this.

There are, of course, many ways of looking at this 58th session. For example, one might ask who in Sofia is telling me that I am just pretending to be of help to her while really only taking her money. Reflection upon this in subsequent months will enable me to see that a part of Sofia does not want to pay for analysis and feels that it is a waste of time. This part says, 'You just come and talk about your problems. So what?' This part seems to be a mixture of her internalized father as dismissive critic and internalized mother's as scornful 'realist'.

At the time of the 58th session, I do not direct Sofia's attention to this inner aspect of herself or to other aspects within. Nor do I wonder aloud what her transference might be. What is of immediate concern is her relationship with Ivan. Because she focuses on it in an enactment with me as witness, several things occur. First, the symbiotic relationship of Sofia and Ivan comes alive in the room; each person's voice, words, mannerisms and attitudes are embodied. Second, how Sofia and Ivan fail to talk about what matters most to Sofia is realized. Third, I experience how Sofia becomes distracted and de-potentiated in Ivan's presence. She knows her feelings at the start, but she loses track of them. Fourth, I realize that Sofia does not know how to take a stand. Neither parents, nor friends, nor anyone else has modeled for her a way of speaking up for herself without fear of chaos, retribution, diminishment or abandonment. Sofia does not have a clue how to proceed in this type of situation. Fifth, I recognize that my skills as a teacher and coach might prove useful: telling her a story that models a response different from hers might help her see a better way. Thus, by reviewing both her enactment and the story of the other woman, we find a new way she can respond to Ivan at his worst. Sofia then shows her readiness to act on her learning. She stands up to Ivan, expresses her feelings, sticks by them, and feels better afterwards. It is a small but important step in her attempt to assert herself in the face of authoritarian figures.

In significant part, we are working at a basic and behavioral level in this session. It seems to be what is needed. It reminds me of Jung's tenet that the forms that analyses take are as varied as the individuals who come into analysis:

> I always find it cheering when businesslike physicians and fashionable consultants aver that they treat patients along the lines of 'Adler', . . . or of 'Freud', or even of 'Jung.' There simply is not and cannot be any such treatment, and even if there could be, one would be on the surest road to failure. When I treat Mr. X, I have of necessity to use method X, just as with Mrs. Z I have to use method Z. This means that the method of treatment is determined primarily by the nature of the case.
>
> (Jung 1964, para 203)

A little later in the analysis, the mini-psychodramas that Sofia undertakes work more on the inner level, and are more like active imaginations. As Sofia slowly is learning to confront people who undermine her with their charm, intelligence, or authoritarian tone, she begins to engage similar inner figures. Psychodrama methods in analysis become a key tool in these inner encounters, as well.

Sofia confronts her inner critic

Here, I report only the first enactment of Sofia's several encounters with her inner figures in the last phase of her analysis. It is a double-hour session, the 63rd and 64th hours of her analysis. She begins the session by saying, 'My life is shit.' She feels exhausted from working her full-time job, doing part-time work on the side, and taking care of Sam. Her brief but intense relationship with Hal ended a year ago; there is no man on the horizon. She observes that so much of what she does seems like a 'duty – a big climb uphill'.

She says that she's gained two kilograms and needs to lose weight. She adds that I am the only person who has a positive attitude towards her eating, having asked her, 'What good things might lie in this bingeing at night?' Then she reports seeing a severely anorexic woman in a sauna, feeling concern for her, and remembering my long-ago comment that she has a strong survival instinct. She thinks she does have that instinct.

The negativity in the room, except for this last observation, is palpable. She talks of the 'Critic' inside herself. I ask her whether there is a situation that she might enact today in order to engage the Critic. She pictures her favorite time of the day – evening, lying in bed, reading a good detective novel, munching whenever she wants on whatever food she has. She sets the scene. She designates her usual analytic chair as the Critic's seat.[5] She designates the couch as her bed.[6] Then Sofia begins in the role of the Critic.

(*Sofia plays all of the roles in what follows, switching positions as she switches roles.*)

SOFIA'S INNER CRITIC: (*sitting in Sofia's usual analytic chair and looking critically at the 'bed', where Sofia has said she is lying, reading and eating*): Well! Well! You're back on the same track. When things don't go right, you go to your food. And then you look in the mirror and you look fat. You're getting old. Big tummy and bent back.

SOFIA: (*lying down on the couch-bed, holding up her imaginary book, back of her head to the Critic, voice fairly low and weak, almost whining*): Ah, leave me alone! (Big sigh.) It doesn't matter if I'm not that good-looking. I never was. I like to eat. I only eat because you put me down. So if you would shut up, I'd break this vicious cycle. And anyway, do you want me to look like the anorexic woman I saw in the sauna?

CRITIC: (*sitting in Sofia's analytic chair*): Don't be silly. That was a monster. You know the way you want to look.

SOFIA: (*lying on the couch-bed*): Sometimes I think you're wrong. Sometimes I know how I want to look. Sometimes I don't. You're always telling me to look thin. There was a girl with a Rubens figure. But she looked good even though she did not have the body of a model. And so what! I have a little tummy and I have a bent back, I'm not firm. So what! I'm forty. And if any man likes me, he should like me inside and out, as I am.

CRITIC: (*sitting in Sofia's analytic chair*): Oh come on! You're talking a lot of shit. You know how it is. You have to look good outside. Besides, you never believe people when they say you're too thin. You are too fat, you better believe *me*.

(*Here, Sofia suddenly comes out of the enactment and says, while sitting as herself in her analytic chair, 'This is worthless tonight.' Sofia and I then discuss what is going on for her. I tell her we can stop here if she would like, but I also note how she is speaking to the Critic in much the same weak and unassertive tone of voice that we first saw in her exchanges with Ivan. I wonder aloud what would happen if she spoke from her guts simply and directly to the Critic. I note that in the dialogue so far, her back is to the Critic and she is lying down, while the Critic is sitting up, above her. Sofia hears this and all but leaps back to the couch.*)

SOFIA: (*sitting on the edge of the couch, turned half-way toward the Critic's chair, speaking in a soft, child-like voice and beginning to cry ever so slightly after speaking only one or two sentences*): You really hurt me. Why are you doing this to me? I feel lost enough without your contribution. You oppress me. You don't leave me any room to be myself or to be what I think I am or want to become. I really wish you'd leave me alone sometimes, give me a break. (*Pause.*) You're always complaining, always criticizing. You're not that great. You're really not that great. Everybody can criticize. But help is different.

Here, for the first time with any analysand, I decide to take the risk that is inherent in 'mirroring' the analysand in a psychodramatic way during an enactment. One of my rules has been always to stay in my chair and maintain the stance of analyst–director during an analysand's enactment, in order to anchor the process and give the analysand a fixed point of reference and sense of security. In this moment, though, I realize that Sofia's Child has entered the room and is stating its case to the Critic. I do not want to announce the Child but would, rather, help Sofia 'see' the Child, if she can. Because I want her to 'see' this, mirroring in the usual verbal way of analysis does not seem apt. So, I ask Sofia if she would be willing to switch places with me, just for a moment, and watch as I sit on the couch and read back to her the words she has just spoken. I explain to her that I am stepping out of my usual role as analyst to do this and will do so only briefly. Sofia agrees. We slowly switch; she sits in my chair, and I sit on the couch. I read back to her what she has said, trying to catch some of her tone, body posture and feeling, but purposely not otherwise imitating her – because I lack the skill to do so and do not want to seem as if I am mocking her.

I then ask Sofia what she has experienced as I have read back her words to her. She says that she sees a child trying to speak up and having trouble doing so. She adds, 'I have the feeling the Critic is protecting that Child by not letting it out.' I reflect back to her my own sense that this may well be true. I ask her if she would like to speak again from the Critic's position and then continue the dialogue with the Child on the couch. She says she would. I resume my analytic chair as she moves to the Critic's position.)

128

CRITIC: (*sitting in Sofia's analytic chair*): I'm only taking care of you. You don't know about this world. So just stay deep down. You don't need to face the world. Just stay deep down there buried. Don't worry. I know how to protect you.

CHILD: (*sitting on edge of couch, head up, looking more at the Critic*): Oh, no you don't. I want to come out. I want to come out and breathe some fresh air. I don't feel sad any more. Just let me out. (Sofia begins to weep, and she speaks a few words so softly I cannot hear them. She then continues.) I am so tired. So tired of always doing what you tell me to do. Staying in my corner and shutting up!

CRITIC: (*sitting in Sofia's analytic chair and acting as if to take the upper hand completely*): Now, you see what happens if you come out. Do you feel better now? Do you?

CHILD: (*sitting on edge of couch*): Yes, I do! Yes, I do. At least I know I'm still here. Sometimes I have felt as if I am nothing.

(*Here, I suggest to Sofia that because the Child has come into focus, maybe it would be helpful if she used one of the many pillows in the room to stand in for the Child. This will permit her as her present self to address the Child directly, just as she does the Critic. Sofia readily accepts the idea. She chooses a small green pillow to be the Child. She places the pillow–child on the couch at the end near the chair–Critic. She sits in the middle of the couch and begins to soothe the Child.*)

SOFIA: (*speaking to the Child and stroking it*): I know that you're hurt, that you're sad, that you're lonely. But if you want to change, I can keep you company. You have a right to be sad and lonely. That right is not being honored right now. But we can change that. You can talk to me if you want to.

(*This scene is striking in several ways. The Child has appeared, embodied in the room, separate from Sofia. The Child lies between the Critic and Sofia, as if a child lying between its father and mother. I imagine both the positive – protective and realistic – aspects of the Critic, and his negative aspects – hypercritical, imprisoning, and possessive. Also, we see Sofia-as-mother reappear here and take care of Sofia-as-child. The scene is thus poignant and integrative. It spontaneously ties together earlier work in the analysis without any need for comment. Critic, Child and Sofia are together, and this time the Critic is not frightening or angry enough to destroy the drama, as happened almost a year earlier, in the 25th hour.*)

CHRIS (*asking very gently*): Can you switch to the Critic, Sofia?

(*Sofia sits in her analytic chair as the Critic. The Critic then speaks in a voice that alternates between a sophisticated, urbane, almost Cary Grant-like charm and the bullying of a tough, insensitive tyrant. I fail to note down most of what the Critic says, but I do recall these words of sarcasm.*)

CRITIC: Oh, gosh! What a great tragedy we have here! Come off it. That child's not starving. This is not some African famine.

129

(After going on like this for some time, the Critic pauses. Sofia has been working hard and looks tired. I don't want to suggest she return once more to either the Child or herself on the couch, but would rather she come to that idea on her own, if she thinks of it and wants to try it. Thus, I ask, 'Do you want to stop here, or . . . ?' Before I can finish, Sofia leaps out of the role of the Critic, takes two steps to the front of the couch, wheels around before the Critic, looks down on him and speaks directly at him for the first time.)

SOFIA: *(to the Critic)* FUCK OFF!!! *(Sofia then adds some choice words in Italian, turns to me, laughing, and says she has told him he is 'a piece of shit'.)*

Here, the enactment phase ends. Sofia looks visibly relieved. We discuss what has transpired. She says the Critic is like a 'Demon–Lover'. I am rather startled because we have never used this term in her analysis, yet, it is a concept I have been thinking of ever since hearing Donald Kalsched speak about it in a lecture more than a year before. She notes how this inner figure both imprisons her and protects her.[7]

I reflect back to her how her body posture in relation to the Critic/Demon–Lover has shifted over the drama: from lying low and avoiding him, through half-facing him but with the weakness of a child, to directly facing and standing above him. She seems more relaxed than at the start of the session, but she is also very realistic, noting that she has taken one step and still has a long way to go.

Over the ensuing months, Sofia becomes involved in a passionate but difficult relationship with another young man, Amos. In her analysis, she undertakes more mini-dramas, all involving the Child, the Critic/Demon–Lover, and herself. The relationship with Amos provides the subject around which these two inner figures and Sofia confront one another. Sofia renames the Critic/Demon–Lover yet again, referring to him as 'Mafia Godfather'.[8] She focuses on this figure's more positive qualities when she first names him, saying, 'He automatically protects you. He turns against you only if you dishonor the family.' Only after some discussion does her focus switch to Mafia Godfather's more negative qualities. As the enactments continue, Mafia Godfather typically acts like a possessive father or jealous Demon–Lover, who lists many reasons why Amos is no good for Sofia. The Child, meanwhile, favors Amos. Sofia notices that she occasionally identifies with the Child, but more often with Mafia–Godfather.

Gradually, Sofia begins to occupy a third position, separate from the Child and Mafia–Godfather. She begins using a chair other than her analytic armchair to represent Mafia–Godfather, and she places his chair far across the room from her own. Once, she 'enlists a good friend's help' (putting her friend's chair right next to her own) in the battle against Mafia Godfather. Thus, while his power continues, she stands apart from him and works to come to terms with him.

130

There is no mistaking the power of this Critic/Demon–Lover/Mafia–Godfather complex. In the 25th hour it arises and dissolves the initial enactment. In the 58th hour, it manifests as Ivan, whom Sofia confronts. Now, it appears as the sometimes charming, sometimes crude Demon–Lover/Mafia–Godfather. It has protected and imprisoned Sofia's Inner Child for decades. So, too, it has protected and stuffed Sofia. She and I reflect upon this key, complicated inner figure in its dark and light, frustrating and helpful, negative and positive aspects. Thus, while the psychodramatic enactments are unusual in the analytic setting, Sofia's analysis proceeds much like a classical analysis: connecting her inner and outer lives – moving from emotions, to complexes and the personification of underlying archetypal energies.

Sofia's inner confrontation is remarkably similar to active imagination. The figures arise from inside. They are spotted first in the 25th hour. The Critic is referred to thereafter sporadically. The Child reappears more clearly in the 58th hour when Sofia recalls herself at age 11 with her mother in the foreign hotel. The Child and Critic come together in the 63rd and 64th hours. Thereafter, they frequently join us in the analysis. As Sofia's inner aspects become more differentiated and personified in this way, she gains some ability to stand up to the forces within that pull her this way and that.

It is also worth noting that, except for my initial naming of one figure (the Critic), Sofia has had the freedom to let her inner figures arise spontaneously and to name them herself. The enactments take Sofia and me into her inner world, where we encounter and experience the forces that lie there. For example, the mini-dramas reveal the urbane sophistication that the Critic–Godfather often exudes. He reasons well and at times speaks with the most soothing British accent imaginable. When I hear this voice, I realize and reflect back to Sofia that it is no wonder he has held sway over her for so long. Without the capturing of nuance, tone, subtle emotions, facial expression, body posture and movement that the enactments permit, I might never have gotten the visceral and paradoxical qualities of this very complex figure.

Conclusion

Reviewing this work that Sofia and I did several years ago brings to mind a few concluding observations. First, I am reminded of how the psychodrama enactments within Sofia's analysis *both* significantly improved my understanding of her outer relationships and inner complexes *and* greatly helped Sofia to engage key people in her outer life, to access and honor her emotions and feelings and to de-identify from and come to better terms with both her Inner Critic and Inner Child.

Second, I am not recommending the use of psychodrama techniques with most analysands. I used the enactment processes seen herein as a key part of my early analytic practice with only two of my first eight analysands. In subsequent years, I have tended to use techniques and ideas from psychodrama that take less dramatic forms (partly because of the limitations of the analytic space in which I have practiced). For example, I regularly have analysands and dream group members bring the dream more alive by having them tell it twice, by having them 'set the scene' on the carpet in the middle of the room or sketch certain images, and by asking them to relate dialogue (whether from a dream or with an actual person) with as much exactness as they can remember. These and other techniques that require patience and attention to sensate detail help analysands and dream group members find greater meaning in their dreams, as well as identify and practice ways of improving their significant relationships.

Third, the guideline of *less is more* is critical. In the last enactment described here, Sofia worked for a very long time, but only because we had a double-hour session, she very much wanted to continue, and she chose to do so at each point when I offered her the chance to conclude the enactment. In most analytic sessions, such a long working through would not be possible or recommended. My hope is that this account shows the fine balance the analyst needs to strike *between* providing a safe space and way of working *and* an environment that encourages the analysand to stretch when she or he is ready to do so.

Fourth, related to the preceding point, I hope that Sofia's three enactments show *how* one can maintain a safe analytic container even as one works at times with psychodramatic techniques. Clearly, one needs to be trained in this way of working and to practice it, at least initially, under supervision or consultation. Also, the other safeguards already described need to be in place. If these requirements are met and the analysand's safety is put first, then using psychodrama in analysis offers possibilities for working that bring unique benefits.

Finally, I close by simply underlining that patient attention to the inner and outer *prima materia* has a way, all by itself, of showing analysand and analyst what life and psyche are calling the analysand toward. Psychodrama, more than anything else, has given me the patience and trust to do this careful work. It remains amazing to me how little acts of careful re-membering and re-imagining show analyst and analysand what they have been missing and need to attend to.

Notes

1 While a training candidate at the C. G. Jung Institute–Zurich, I also worked in psychodrama for three years with Analysts Helmut and Ellynor Barz. On several occasions, I co-directed psychodramas – twice with Helmut and at other times with training candidates in the Barz's psychodrama institute. At the same time, I used psychodrama techniques in analysis with some of my analysands. That work was done under supervision and led to my thesis on the use of psychodrama in analysis.

2 I wish to express my profound gratitude to the person who is represented here as Sofia, both for the opportunity to work with her and for her generous permission to allow me to share with the public those parts of her life and analysis that follow.

3 This initial 'exchange' between Sofia and Ivan shows why the analyst should take great care to 'warm up' the analysand, set the dramatic situation and explain the techniques to be used. Here, Sofia is switching between the play world and the analytic world and between herself and Ivan without changing her physical position in the room. If this were how she had worked in her first two enactments (not described here), it would have strongly contraindicated the use of psychodrama within her analysis: it would have suggested a sense of identity too weak to maintain her center as she changed between playing herself and other people. Here the problem arises much more because of my failure to warm up Sofia adequately and to explain to her how we will work. I thus intervene at this point to set about correcting a problem for which I was responsible.

4 I already know a great deal about Rachel from earlier sessions and decide there is no need for her to be introduced, especially since she is serving here only as a silent support person. In other circumstances it would be appropriate to ask Sofia to introduce Rachel, just as Ivan has been introduced. In such an instance, because Rachel is a positive figure, I would ask Sofia to introduce her before the more troublesome Ivan.

5 I fail to notice at this point that Sofia is diverging from her custom of choosing a straight-backed chair to play any figure other than herself. I usually ask Sofia (or any analysand) to reserve her usual analytic chair for herself. By this means, I try to help her maintain a clear sense of herself, as distinguished from the other figures. In essence, the analytic chair serves as the place of the ego or conscious self. The gift of my mistake in this instance is substantial, however: her placement of the Critic in her own chair shows how closely identified she is with that figure.

6 The chair is positioned in relation to the couch in such a way that I immediately picture Freud (in the Critic's position) sitting at the head of the couch, behind and unseen by the reclining Sofia in her bed. I do not share this image with Sofia, but I am smiling to myself at the image.

7 Donald Kalsched would soon publish these ideas in *The Inner World of Trauma: Archetypal Defenses of the Personal Spirit* (Kalsched 1996).

8 Here we see how the incarnation of the Inner Critic is shifting from the more archetypal Demon–Lover to the more personal Mafia-Godfather, Sofia, having been raised in Italy. This shift occurs within subsequent psychodramatic enactments and reflection and discussion in analysis.

References

Jung, C. G. (1964) 'Analytical Psychology and Education', in *Collected Works 17*, Princeton, NJ: Princeton University Press, 1981.

Kalsched, D. (1996) *The Inner World of Trauma: Archetypal Defenses of the Personal Spirit*, London and New York: Routledge.

9

PSYCHODRAMA AND THE RESOLUTION OF THE TRANSFERENCE AND COUNTER-TRANSFERENCE

Mariolina Graziosi

During my Jungian training in Zurich I took part in a series of psychodrama seminars with Doctor Helmut Barz and Ellynor Barz. It was my first experience of Moreno's psychodrama, and I was deeply touched. Since then I began to understand that psychodramatic techniques could contribute to Jungian analysis by deepening the experience of the psyche. A basic assumption in both approaches is that the psyche has a dramatic structure, and the healing process can occur only if the afflicted person can get in touch with it. The psychodrama technique is very powerful because it consists in the representation of the soul's theatre in external space, giving it a three-dimensional reality. This makes it possible to externalize the drama taking place within. To stage the inner struggle is very important not only because the person can confront his own ghosts, but also because he can share the inner experience with other members of the group. The advantage of both aspects is that the person can overcome the feeling of isolation and the deep shame that is often part of any psychic struggle. As in Greek theatre, the group witnesses the representation and becomes a container that receives and accepts it without judging. Thanks to the positive attitude of the group, the person feels once again reconciled with the community. This feeling of belonging plays a central role in the resolution of psychic conflicts.

Moreno makes an explicit reference to the links between psychodrama and Greek theatre, arguing that psychodrama is, at one and the same time, its heir and its development: its heir because, as in Greek theatre, it mirrors the group; its development because in psychodrama the psyche itself is put on stage, as Moreno emphasizes: 'The stage isn't conceived as it is in the theatre; it is a social stage, the actors aren't actors but real persons, and they do not perform but represent themselves' (Moreno 1946, p. 21). Staging the psychic struggle allows the person to get out of the grip of the unconscious since the ego plays a central role. The patient dramatizes his inner conflict with the help of auxiliary egos, reinforcing the role of the consciousness that confirms or resists the patient's experience (Moreno 1946, p. 49). To stage a conflict means to be able to experience both the wish and the defence mechanisms, as Moreno underlines: The psychodramatist thinks in the following way: 'Why not let the patient express these inner thoughts and efforts of his rather than aiming at the analysis of his resistance?' (Moreno 1946, p. 43)

The role of the psychodramatist is to stage everything the patient expresses, taking into consideration the various details so that all the different parts of the psyche are represented. Moreno's idea of the setting is linked to his theory of the self. He posits that the self emerges from the roles. He assumes the presence of different selves: the emotional self, the social self, the physiological self – all these partial selves gradually moving towards integration. Moreno rejects the idea of a metaphysical self that evolves to complete maturity. But the roles themselves do tend to combine and bind together. Should this process of combining roles become disturbed, then an integrated self cannot function, and the personality is stuck in a state of disequilibrium (Moreno 1946, pp. 36–7).

The participation of the group is also a crucial element in the dramatization. The members of the group participate both as spectators and during the discussion that follows in which they express what they have experienced during the representation. It is a moment of confrontation based prevalently on sharing the inner experience. This confrontation is very important because the person who has put his own conflicts on stage can listen to other possible ways of perceiving and understanding the problem and, most important, can learn how to take into consideration other points of view. As Moreno emphasizes in his narration of the first time he improvised psychodrama: '. . . even the Supreme Being depends on the other "Auxiliary egos" . . .' (Moreno 1946, p. 63).

Psychodrama and psychoanalysis

With respect to psychoanalysis, psychodrama replaces the dyadic relationship of analyst and patient with a group. Each member of the group functions both as spectator and as actor. No participant is totally confined to and isolated within the role of the patient who needs help. In this regard, Ottavio Rosati observes: 'Moreno invented an antithetical way of communication [to Freud's]: the stage of the psychodrama is open to the gaze of the group and can be changed with new choreography, with new light. To the ability of open ears, Moreno adds the ability of open eyes' (Rosati 1985, p. 17). As Rosario suggests, psychodrama goes beyond a dialogue between two persons: it opens up a three-dimensional space in which sensations, observations and words all participate together. The insight into the inner struggle emerges from action rather than through explanation.

In orthodox psychoanalytic practice the patient lies on the couch with the psychoanalyst behind, so that their eyes do not meet. The interaction between psychoanalyst and patient is based on two narrations. Moreno describes the innovation of psychodrama with respect to psychoanalytic technique in the following way:

> In 1914 in Vienna there were two antitheses to psychoanalysis: one was the rebellion with respect to the individual by the group that had been put aside: it was a first step beyond psychoanalysis, to 'the psychotherapy of the group'. I introduced this specific term in order to underline that I was dealing with group therapy and not only with sociological or psychological analysis. The other was the rebellion of the actor who had been displaced by the word. This was the second step beyond psychoanalysis, to 'psychodrama'. In the beginning was existence. In the beginning was the other.
>
> (Moreno 1946, p. 34)

Moreno considers that psychodrama brought a significant change, which the last sentence summarizes using two lapidary phrases: *in the beginning was existence; in the beginning was the other*. With the first phrase Moreno argues that psychodrama replaces the dialogue of patient and psychoanalyst with the countless interpersonal interactions between actors in which spontaneity plays a central role. He uses the term 'existence' because what is recreated is life in which the existential search for meaning plays a central role. One finds meaning in actions as much as in processes of reflection. And Moreno firmly believes that the psychic healing process requires spontaneity. In psychodrama every form of expression is used: interaction, dance, music, words, all characterized by their degree of spontaneity (Moreno 1946, p. 46), whereas in psychoanalysis spontaneity is confined to the practice of free association. All these spontaneous elements contribute to the experience of catharsis, to the abreaction of strong repressed feelings. Freud also considered abreaction crucial for the psychoanalytic cure (Freud 1893–95, p. xix), but Moreno points to psychodramatic abreaction as even stronger because there is more than one: catharsis occurs in the patient, in the auxiliary ego(s) and in the group or public. These are all co-existential parts of any psychodramatic representation.

With the second phrase, *in the beginning was the other*, Moreno emphasizes the extent to which psychodrama has a social matrix that the psychoanalytic setting lacks. The conflict is reproduced in a social setting that recreates the web of interpersonal interactions and the confrontation between different points of view, different sensibilities and different interpretations. As described by Moreno, psychodrama has the characteristics of a small human society in which the audience represents public opinion, the actors represent the protagonist, and the director is a leader in search of meanings. The director is the symbol of a well-balanced action that integrates, coordinates and finds a synthesis of all the participants. In psychodrama the revision of the reality function occurs within this social context. Since the aim of psychoanalysis is also to restore the reality function, in psychoanalytic treatment, the restoration of reality is the result of the confrontation between the narratives of the patient and the analyst, with the text of the analyst functioning as a *metatext* that interprets with psychoanalytic concepts the events narrated by the patient. However, in psychodrama the revisioning of the reality function is the result of the active representation of the events (Moreno 1946, pp. 318–19). Moreno argues for the necessity to recreate the dynamic of a small society rather than merely to explain a conflict, in much the same way that the social psychologists George Herbert Mead and Herbert Blumer argue that meanings are constructed through an interactive process and should not be reduced to a given set of concepts (Blumer 1986; Mead 1934). Of course, Jung also criticized the psychoanalytic use of a reductive method and privileged the need for a symbolic analysis that respects a plurality of meanings.

Psychodrama and analytical psychology

If in the Freudian setting there are two narrations – that of the patient and that of the analyst – then in the Jungian setting in which the patient and analyst sit facing each other, an additional narration based on the formation of a therapeutic third is forged within the *temenos*, the sacred space in which the patient explores and re-experiences his own inner conflicts. The analysis centres on inner figures, on inner images regarded as symbols of the psychic dynamic or drama. I think we can say that an inner theatre is evoked, and this theatre becomes an additional subject of the analysis.

In this sense, there is a compatibility between Jungian analysis and Moreno's psychodrama. Dreams offer the main psychic material in Jungian analysis. The interpretation of dreams consists in narrating the dream and evoking it in such a way that the dreamer enters into the spirit of the dream and re-experiences it. Of course, Jungian analysts differ in their approaches to dream interpretation, some tending to amplify the dream with mythological material while others stick to the images and emotions of the dream (Berry 1982; Whitmont and Brinton Perera 1989). For instance, James Hillman, in order to re-establish the connection between the dream image and its mythical roots, proposes the *epistrophe* that he defines as a re-tracing of the event to its imaginative background (Hillman 1979, p. 14). In spite of all the differences in Jungian psychotherapeutic practice, the need to experience the dream and respect its symbolic nature is always present. And in the Jungian setting, the analyst shares the inner experience of the patient so that the analyst can participate from within the images of the psychic struggle of the patient (Jung 1945). In a similar way, psychodrama not only uses dreams as psychic material but takes up as its *modus operandi* the same structure as a dream, as Moreno pointed out to Freud:

> The link between the psychodrama and the dream is evident from Moreno's famous answer given to Freud who asked him what he was doing: 'I start where you end, Professor. You teach people to understand their dreams, I try to give people the courage to continue to dream'.
>
> (Rosati 1985, p. 17)

Moreno identifies the extent to which the reductive analysis of a dream confines it to concepts, thereby diminishing its imaginative and therapeutic impact.

Psychodrama and analytical psychology both honour the dream because the imagination retains a central role in its interpretation. Psychodrama and Jungian analysis share this fundamental orientation: that the life of the psyche should not be reduced to abstract concepts. Because the psyche is inherently dramatic, it needs to dramatize wishes as conflicts, because in these representations the soul has its home. Images that function as symbols and metaphors are the language of the soul, and the psyche is the inner space where they take on life. Both psychodramatic and Jungian settings recreate that inner space, holding as a basic tenet that the healing process can be realized only by reconnecting consciously to these psychic experiences. Hillman expressed this view with the phrase: *similia similibus curantur* ('like cures like'; Hillman 1997, p. 306). Dramatization promotes the conscious experience of what is structured dramatically in the unconscious, giving space to difficult feelings rather than cutting off conflicts with reductive reasoning.

Transference and counter-transference

Freud discovered the transference during the early period of his pioneering work. He describes the psychological mechanism of transference in his last introductory lecture on psychoanalysis:

> the patient has transferred on to the doctor intense feelings of affection which are justified neither by the doctor's behavior nor by the situation that has developed during the treatment. . . . This new fact, which we thus recognize so unwillingly, is known by us as *transference*. We mean a transference of feelings on to the person of the doctor, since we do not believe that the situation in the treatment could justify the development of such feelings. We suspect, on the contrary, that the whole readiness for these feelings is derived from elsewhere, that they were already prepared in the patient and, upon

the opportunity offered by the analytic treatment, are transferred on the person of the doctor.

(Freud 1917, pp. 548–50)

For Freud, the transference is the central moment of the psychoanalytic treatment because the whole of the patient's illness is concentrated upon this single point, the relation to the analyst. At this moment a newly created and transformed neurosis confronts the analyst because all the patient's symptoms abandon their meanings as originally presented and take on a new sense expressed in the language of the transference. This allows the analyst to open mental compartments that have been closed and inaccessible, to explain to the patient how the feelings do not so much arise from the present situation in the analytic relationship as they repeat something that happened earlier. In this way, the analyst induces the patient to transform mere repetition into meaningful memory. Managing this new artificial neurosis coincides with the resolution of the illness that brought the patient to therapy.

Jung acknowledged the crucial importance of Freud's theory of transference. In *The Psychology of the Transference* (1946), Jung identified it as the Alpha and the Omega of the analytic method. Still, he didn't literalize the erotic feelings of transference, and he didn't regard the transference as only erotic in character: it can also express other drives, such as the will to power described by Adler, which coexist with sexuality and often make it difficult to discern which predominates. Nor did Jung consider the transference to be the only therapeutic tool at his disposal. For him the cause of transference is a loss of energy from the ego and a spontaneous activation of the patient's unconscious that is then transferred or projected:

All unconscious contents, once they are activated – i.e., have made themselves felt – possess as it were a specific energy which enables them to manifest themselves everywhere (like the incest motif, for instance). But this energy is normally not sufficient to thrust the content into the consciousness. For that there must be a certain predisposition on the part of the conscious mind, namely a deficit in the form of loss of energy. The energy so lost raises the psychic potency of certain compensating contents in the unconscious.

(Jung 1946, p. 180)

In some cases, a certain amount of energy, no longer finding a conscious outlet, streams off into the unconscious, where it activates other compensating contents, which in turn begin to exert a compulsive influence on the conscious mind. In other cases, a spontaneous activation of unconscious contents occurs, which produces a sudden change in personality. In the latter cases, during the incubation period the analyst can observe a loss of conscious energy: the new development has drawn off the energy it needs from consciousness. The potency of the unconscious contents always indicates a corresponding weakness in the conscious mind and its functions.

The fascination that the unconscious material has on the patient also has an impact on the unconscious of the analyst, who answers with a counter-transference; in other words, the analyst projects on the patient a content of his own of which he is unconscious (Jung 1948, p. 273). The occurrence of the transference and counter-transference forms an unconscious relationship between the analyst and the patient that is crucial for the analytical work. The counter-transference, Jung explains, is as useful and meaningful – or as much a hindrance – as the transference of the patient. Jung's idea of the counter-transference recognizes the presence of the analyst's unconscious next to that of the patient and how the two connect. As Jung says: 'Doctor and patient thus find themselves in a relationship founded on mutual unconsciousness' (Jung 1946, p. 176). Jung uses the metaphor of the wounded healer for describing the relationship between the two unconsciouses. The image suggests that the wounds of the analyst become a source of knowledge for the understanding of the patient's suffering:

> The doctor, by voluntarily and consciously taking over the psychic sufferings of the patient, exposes himself to the overpowering contents of the unconscious and also to their inductive action.
>
> (Jung 1946, p. 176)

The therapeutic possibility lies in the fact that the analyst, being in touch consciously with his own unconscious, has the tools to understand the content of the unconsciously constellated material and for this reason can help the patient to recognize it, establishing within a more cooperative attitude between the ego and the non-ego, between consciousness and the unconscious.

Jung distinguishes between knowledge and understanding: the first refers to objective knowledge, the second to subjective knowledge. It is thanks to subjectivation – in technical terms, the transference and counter-transference – that the doctor gives up general principles, which are the foundation of objective knowledge, and moves to understanding, a knowledge that comes from the unconscious relationship, that is to say, from the deep psychological experience (Jung 1958, p. 273). The unconscious relationship formed within the transference and counter-transference is also emotionally important for the patient because previously the patient was alone with his burden, isolated in a spiritual loneliness which neither he nor anybody else could understand and which was bound to be misinterpreted.

Jung's idea of the transference and counter-transference deepened the knowledge of the psychic process involved in the therapeutic relationship. Freud dismissed the role of the analyst's unconscious and in order to make it impartial introduced the therapeutic advice of impartiality and the distance of the analyst from the patient as a requirement of the therapeutic setting. Jung, instead, rightly recognized it and explained how it could be a valuable source.

Transference and *tele*

Jung expresses in images taken from alchemy his view of transference and counter-transference as the transfer of material from the unconscious of the patient to that of the therapist. Like the alchemists, Jung identifies a confusion of instinct and spiritual aspects as a cause of psychic imbalance that affects the neurotic person. Healing occurs through a process that differentiates these two aspects and, in so doing, transforms the *massa confusa* by bringing order where there was chaos, as a result transforming the personality. At the same time, the alchemists rejected the dichotomy within the Greek philosophical tradition between body and spirit, and between inanimate and animate objects. They perceived a continuum between the spiritual and the material, a united reality set in motion by a continuous dynamism that goes from the invisible to the visible and vice versa. The body-and-spirit continuum supersedes the classic distinction between physics, the world of bodies, and metaphysics, the world of principles. Alchemy postulates, instead, a reciprocal permeability. (Maria Prophetissa, the only woman alchemist known in history, developed an analogy between the human body and metals, based on the assumption of the continuum of body-soul-spirit and, in her well-known doctrine, countered the contradictory concept of the One versus the Many with a paradox of multiplicity within unity, expressed numerically as a progressive movement from 4 to 3, to 2, to 1; see Von Franz 1980.) Alchemy describes a process such as a distillation in three stages: *nigredo, albedo, rubedo* (Edinger 1995). In *The Psychology of the Transference*, Jung uses images from the alchemical text, *Rosarium Philosophorum*, to describe three stages in the process of psychic transformation. The first manifestation of the transference coincides with a *disiunctio* that, in alchemical language, is called *nigredo*. In this phase a shared unconscious identity forms between analyst and patient but outside consciousness: this bond is recognized only later and indirectly by its effects. Occasionally, dreams occur announcing the appearance of the transference. Common motifs, Jung says, that symbolize the beginning of the transference include a fire that has started in the cellar, or a burglar who has broken in, or an erotic situation.

The unconscious content that is projected onto the analyst forms a third, something in addition to the patient and the analyst themselves. This element has been described as a field present between the analyst and the patient. The Gestalt therapist Kurt Lewin was the first to speak of a field area. He maintained that the behaviour of a person is due to the interdependence of two factors: personality and environment. Field is defined as 'the totality of coexisting facts which are conceived of as mutually interdependent' (Lewin 1951, p. 240). Lewin's field theory has inspired a group of Jungian analysts who have applied the notion of interactive field to analysis. In the Jungian view the field is a third area with its own objectivity that affects the rapport between the patient and the doctor. Being aware of it means that experienced feelings are seen as a quality field and not something to own or identify with. Nathan Schwartz-Salant defines the third area as an interactive field that partakes of the objective properties of the collective unconscious as well as of the combined subjectivities of analyst and patient (Schwartz-Salant 1998, p. 33). The alchemists personified this third as Hermes or Mercurius, the duplicitous god of revelation who possesses both the highest spiritual qualities and a shady character. To deal with unconscious contents demands endless patience, perseverance, equanimity, knowledge, and ability on the part of the analyst. On the part of the patient, a capacity for suffering is required. The analyst can propose only to accept and endure the conflict just as it is. Jung describes the resolution of such conflict as the restoration of an equilibrium between the ego and the non-ego, a *religo*. This goal can be accomplished if the unconscious forces are taken into consideration so that the status of *disiunctio* transforms into a *coniunctio*. The process of transformation occurs both in conscious and unconscious ways. This opus is experienced as a miracle – what the alchemists called *Deo Concedente*, which expresses not a platitude but a precise orientation of respectful humility towards a process that the participants can only know partially. In his late work, *Mysterium coniunctioni*s, Jung emphasizes that the work of conjoining is not only the accomplishment of the analyst and the patient together but also the result of an autonomous process of the psyche.

Moreno writes in similar way when he differentiates the transference, which he considers a secondary structure, from the primary psychic connection, which he defines with the Greek term *tele*. He writes:

> Transference is the development of (unconscious) fantasy that the patient projects on the therapist, surrounding him in a kind of spell. But there is another process that takes place in the patient, in that part of his ego that isn't charmed by autosuggestion. This process appraises the therapist and values intuitively what kind of person he is. This sensation addressed to the immediate behavior of the therapist, physical, mental or of any other kind, makes up the relation of *tele*. *Tele* (from the Greek, meaning 'far away, influence from a distance') means sensation between one individual and another, the cement that keeps a group united. It is *Zweifühlung* in opposition to *Einfühlung*. Like a telephone, it has two ends, and it facilitates two-way communication. *Tele* is a primary structure, while transference is a secondary structure. After the transfer has been worked out, some conditions of *tele* keep working. *Tele* stimulates a stable association and a permanent relationship. It is believed that in the genetic development of the newborn, *tele* comes to the surface before the

transference. The relationships of *tele* between the protagonist, the therapist, the auxiliary ego and the significant dramatis personae of the world that they portray have a fundamental importance for the therapeutic process.

(Moreno 1946, pp. 45–6)

Moreno's concept of *tele* resembles Jung's view of the transference and counter-transference. Like the concept of transference and counter-transference for Jung, Moreno's notion of *tele* posits a primary structure whose manifestations are unconscious. Moreno considers the concept of a personal unconscious inadequate to explain the formation of *tele*. For him it is necessary to recognize a reality that is even deeper, where the unconsciouses of two or more people are linked through a system of co-unconscious states: 'For instance, the psychotherapy of a married couple or of a family must be realized in a way that the interpersonal psyche of the group is also acted out, so that all their relations based on the *tele*, their co-conscious and co-unconscious states, are put on stage' (Moreno 1946, p. 41). So while Jung confines himself to the connection between the unconscious of the analyst and that of the patient, Moreno examines all the possible connections between the different psyches that form the group, and he wants to facilitate the element that connects them. But both Jung and Moreno speak of the communication between co-unconscious states as the basis for the empathic relation between two or more people. From my point of view, Moreno overlooks the fact that, in Jung's theory, alienating complexes situated in the realm of the personal unconscious, which are experienced as fragmentary and dissociative, are still, at their core, the expression of archetypes that carry possibilities for shared meaning and connection. Nevertheless, from a Jungian perspective, on Moreno's stage both the personal and the collective unconscious are represented. Jungian analyst and psychodramatist Wilma Scategni notes Moreno's inability to see the connection between the personal and the collective unconscious and the fact that *tele* in psychodrama is a positive manifestation of the collective unconscious (Scategni 1996, p. 70).

Although coming from two different points of views, both Jung and Moreno see a deeper layer beyond the personal unconscious. The main difference between their perspectives is that, for Jung, the deeper layer contains archetypes, and he defines it as collective unconscious. Moreno speaks of the interpersonal psyche and does not recognize the presence of archetypes and connected complexes; instead, he envisions co-conscious and co-unconscious states as the result of *tele*. The psyche can be represented only in interconnectedness, because it cannot belong just to a single individual in isolation. The interpersonal psyche belongs to a group and must be reproduced in such a context (Moreno 1946, p. 41). While Jung recognizes a latent structure from which psychic life develops, Moreno refuses the idea of a latent structure that pre-exists the performance of roles. The self emerges from roles.

This difference between Jung and Moreno carries implications for how they resolve the transference and counter-transference. For Jung it is a natural process that occurs partly in the unconscious. Like the process described by the alchemists, it is the result of a psychic transformation that accomplishes the unity of opposites of which the psyche is made and thereby transforms the personality. For Moreno the resolution of the conflict occurs at the level of interpersonal psyche where the cathartic process takes place and strong abreactions occur, given that the psychodrama is made up of the relationships of *tele* between all the participants. Once the conflict is overcome, the integration between the different selves takes place, and as a result the personality is transformed. In spite of these differences, Jung and Moreno share the notion that the resolution takes place in a primary structure where the relationship with the other is central, where emotions and symbols originate, as well as complexes caused by the family and the social environment of the person involved, and where something surpasses the conscious life. It can be called either collective unconscious or *tele*. Both express a dimension in which existence has its roots.

Conclusion

Psychodrama and analytical psychology both recognize that the language of the psyche is symbolic and that dramatization is the best way to get in touch with and resolve the inner conflicts manifest in the psyche. Clearly, the Jungian view of the transference and counter-transference enriches psychodrama. Moreno's idea of *tele* enriches Jungian theory as well. As practitioners, both recognize the existence of a layer beyond the personal unconscious, and they describe healing as a potentiality sparked in the encounter with the unconscious – for Jung, between the analyst and the patient, for Moreno, between the group members. Jungian analysts now often employ the concept of an interactive field in which emotions play a central role in describing a third area constellated in the analysis when the transference and counter-transference is present (Kast 1995, pp. 38–9). This idea of an interactive field closely resembles Moreno's idea of the interpersonal psyche as defined by the interaction between different psyches.

Jung and Moreno both replace a reductive approach with the creation of a space for soul, wherein imagination is the main vehicle and the inner conflict is experienced dramatically rather than explained. Order does not signify finding the answer so much as re-connecting with meanings – with the multiplicity of meanings that reside in a polytheistic psyche. For this reason, to solve a psychic conflict does not mean to find an existential model but, rather, to reconnect with the roots of being from which meanings derive. Jung strongly believed that the main psychic problems of modernity derive from the loss of roots, and to reconnect must be the goal of psychotherapy. Psychodrama shares much the same aim, even though it speaks of the need to restore the equilibrium between different selves in order to form an integrated self.

In spite of all the differences, as practitioners Jung and Moreno recognized the importance of living out a psychic problem. This means that feelings, besides words, have a central place. Furthermore, this means going back to the roots of the problem, to that deeper layer where the individual psyche is connected to other psyches. The collective roots are present in both approaches, even though for Jung the collective roots are made up of cultural patterns inherited philogenetically and corresponding to a universal dimension that unites all humankind, while for Moreno they correspond to a social matrix. Furthermore, both thinkers have contributed to the recognition of a collective dimension that cannot be separated from the individual unconscious, and both have given a therapeutic method for reconnecting the personal to the collective. For the assumption of an isolated psyche they have substituted the centrality of relationship, of the interpersonal, and they have recognized healing as a process based on interaction rather than on explanation. The psyche is a laboratory, and the healing process takes place not in the aseptic realm of intellectualizing, but in the forge of action and active imagination. Healing can assume the traits of an alchemical process, as Jung believes, or that of a drama, as Moreno thinks, but both recognize the importance of the spontaneous process in which life reproduces life and, in the act of reproduction, transforms itself. Such a transformation is less like a definitive achievement and more a web of new possibilities emerging from the experience of an inner unity.

References

Berry, P. (1982) 'An Approach to the Dream', in *Echo's Subtle Body*, Dallas, TX: Spring Publication.

Blumer, H. (1986) *Symbolic Interactionism*, Berkeley, CA: University of California Press.

Edinger, E. F. (1995) *The Mysterium Lectures*, Toronto: Inner City Books.

Freud, S. (1893–95) *Studies on Hysteria*, New York: Basic Books, 1957.

Freud, S. (1917) *Introductory Lectures on Psycho-Analysis*, New York: W.W. Norton & Company, 1966.

Hillman, J. (1979) *The Dream and the Underworld*, New York: Harper and Row; *Il Sogno e il Mondo Infero*, trans. A. Bottini, Milan: Adelphi, 2003.

Hillman, J. (1997) *The Soul's Code*, New York: Warner Books; *Il Codice dell'Anima*, trans. A. Bottini, Milan: Adelphi, 2009.

Jung, C. G. (1945) 'On the Nature of Dreams', in *The Structure and Dynamics of the Psyche, Collected Works 8,* Princeton, NJ: Princeton University Press, 1969.

Jung, C. G. (1946) 'The Psychology of the Transference', in *The Practice of Psychotherapy, Collected Works 16,* Princeton, NJ: Princeton University Press, 1966.

Jung, C. G. (1948) 'General Aspects of Dream Psychology', in *The Structure and Dynamics of the Psyche, Collected Works 8,* Princeton, NJ: Princeton University Press, 1969.

Jung, C. G. (1958) 'The Undiscovered Self', in *Civilization in Transition, Collected Works 10*, Princeton, NJ: Princeton University Press, 1964.

Kast, V. (1995) 'A Concept of Participation', in M. Stein (ed.), *The Interactive Field in Analysis*, Wilmette, IL: Chiron Publication, pp. 37–61.

Lewin, K. (1951) *Field Theory in Social Science: Selected Theoretical Papers*, ed. D. Cartwright, New York: Harper & Row.

Mead, G. H. (1934) *Mind, Self, and Society*, Chicago, IL: University of Chicago Press.

Moreno, J. L. (1946) *Manuale di Psicodramma*, trans. O. Rosati, Rome: Astrolabio, 1985.

Rosati, O. (1985) 'Introduzione', in J. L. Moreno, *Manuale di Psicodramma*, trans. O. Rosati, Roma: Astrolabio.

Scategni, W. (1996) *Psicodramma e Terapia di Gruppo*, Como: Red edizioni.

Schwartz-Salant, N. (1998) *The Mystery of Human Relationship: Alchemy and the Transformation of the Self*, London: Routledge.

Von Franz, M. (1980) *Alchemy*, Toronto: Inner City Books.

Whitmont, E. C. and Brinton Perera, S. (1989) *Dreams, A Portal to the Source*, London: Routledge.

10

THE LOSS AND GAIN
OF TIMING
Active imagination in
performance

Barbara Helen Miller

Considering performance, the old adage holds: 'timing is of the essence.' In the sport of high-jumping, for example, the jumper could be in excellent condition, well prepared for the competition, but should the timing be *off*, perhaps through hesitation or eagerness, then the jump is not successful. In the theatre, the comic line is experienced as comic when the performer has *the* timing right, and the death throes of the hero are truly tragic when concisely timed. My experience of performance is in the field of music, as a cellist, and I know these failures in my own field: of being well prepared but then having a moment of hesitation or eagerness and missing the *jump*, of speeding up when one should be slowing down to communicate a funny moment that is then not funny, of expressing pathos that is so overstated that no one is moved.

I would posit (which is another not uncommon observation) that the great disrupter of the desired timing in a performance of a seasoned performer is due to an interruption in the performer's concentration. When we can rule out deficiencies in concentration due to various physiological causes, such as fatigue or illness, a diagnosis from analytical psychology for a disruption of attention might hypothesize that an autonomous complex has been constellated, and that the complex has momentarily eclipsed the otherwise directed attention. Such a break in attention is demonstrated by C. G. Jung's word association experiments (Jung 1904–7, 1910). There he showed that certain stimulus words disrupt the attention of the test taker, noted by the test giver as delayed responses. Constellated complexes produce directly observable stereotypical complex-driven behaviours and, for the test taker, a subjective feeling tone. In daily life the complex, when operating without the subject's awareness, has an impinging influence, so that, subjectively, one does not feel free.

147

Rather than a thorough exposition of Jung's complex theory, I hope to give the reader a more experiential account of the complex, and to use 'relationship' as my principal example. In any relationship we – normally – experience the change from being close, connected, and loving to being separate, rejected, and unloved, and then back again to being close. A complex can form around either of these directions: in such cases the ego has identified with only one side of a more complete relationship. For example, we have identified with being loving and do not consciously negotiate being rejecting. The unplanned outcome of this construction, however, is that we experience rejection in its many guises during our transactions as *done to* us. This movement is intrapersonal as well as interpersonal.

Jung notes the intrapersonal connections and sense of relating (Jung 1929, para 125–7); however, similar conclusions arise when examining the external field of interrelatedness. Jacob L. Moreno's observations offer corroborating conclusions. Moreno assessed the degree of spontaneity and creativity operating in the interpersonal relation (see Stephenson 2009, p. 138). The models for psychopathology proposed by Jung and Moreno are not identical, but the models do share similarities that can be noted by the actual therapeutics employed by Jung and Moreno. Jung therapeutically employs active imagination for the problem defined as the eclipsing of the ego by an autonomous complex. Active imagination involves imagining and encountering a personification of that function of relationship (or impulse) that is out of view and held by the complex. The praxis is dialogical, imaginational, spontaneous, inspired, and creative of the transcendent function that communicates to both of the dialogic partners. In an effective psychodrama, Moreno's praxis, the role-playing in a psychodrama allows for an expression of both the entrenched and the missing part of the relationship. Moreno's group psychotherapy provides a safe container for exploration; the stuck, predictable, stereotypical behaviours when played as a role facilitate authentic here-and-now exchanges between people. Moreno writes: 'The here (this place) and now (this moment) of existence is a *dialectic* concept' (Moreno and Moreno 1959, p. 226). In the daily life of an individual, the *taking* on of a role as a finished product is called by Moreno a role conserve, which can be stuck and predictable; in psychodrama the act of role-*playing* is a spontaneous play and dialectic. With successful group psychotherapy there is a 'flow' between the participants, visible in the group cohesiveness, in the reciprocity of relationships, communication, and shared experiences. These creative moments Moreno called experiences of *tele*, and *tele* speaks to 'the emergent cohesion of a social configuration' (Moreno 1960, p. 17). Are Jung's transcendent function and Moreno's *tele* similar? They are both the outcome of engagement in dialogue. Given Moreno's greater emphasis on the social, it would be taking the comparison too far to say they are identical; however, they both speak to problems of timing and seek solutions in the re-gaining or re-establishing of relationships in time.

My deliberations include anthropological studies, and I am struck by the similarity of *tele* and anthropologist Victor Turner's description of *communitas*. Turner built on Arnold van Gennep's tripartite model of rites of passage – the three phases of separation, margin/*limen*, and aggregation. In the liminal phase, the structured social bonds (political-legal-economic positions with types of evaluation/hierarchy) are not operative – that is, *not* operative during the phase of liminality is the model of human interrelatedness that is structured and often hierarchical. The phase of liminality privileges *communitas*, the bonding among equal participants. Turner writes of the spontaneous, immediate, concrete nature of *communitas* – that it involves the whole man in his relation to other whole men. There is an aspect of the potential in *communitas*, the mood is for what is possible and is creative. 'Relations between total beings are generative of symbols and metaphors and comparisons; art and religion are their products rather than legal and political structures' (Turner 1969, p. 372). Turner argues that the experiencing of a generic bond between human beings is not some kind of herd instinct, but is a product of 'men in their wholeness wholly attending' (Turner 1969, p. 373). And the cultural forms that facilitate *communitas* provide a set of templates or models for the periodical reclassifications of reality and man's relationship to society, nature, and culture.

Moreno and Turner were perhaps unaware of each other's work, but they both acknowledged incorporating Henri Bergson's principle of *élan vital*. Bergson (1946) saw intuition as a mode of reflection and a method of thinking in duration (Bergson 1946, p. 88). For Bergson, intuition directly perceives and experiences the continuous flow of reality. Moreno considered that spontaneity – spontaneity that propels the speaker to associate – was required for mental healing processes; however, the presence of spontaneity in itself is not the 'cure' (Moreno 1946, p. xii), play is the positive factor linked with spontaneity and creativity. Moreno gave Bergson credit for having brought the principle of spontaneity into philosophy (Moreno 1946, p. 8) but critically commented that Bergson having made his *élan vital* so creative, 'a category of the moment could not develop a significance of its own' (Moreno 1946, p. 103). Turner considered that Bergson saw in the words and writings of prophets and great artists an expression of the *élan vital*, or evolutionary 'life-force' (Turner 1969, p. 372).

Among analytical psychologists, 'duration' could be understood in terms of the numinous experience of archetypal expressions. An interesting resonance can be noted between the analytical psychological observation that 'Deeply integrative numinous experiences can feel both utterly new and as though they had always been somehow known' (Hunt 2012, p. 78) and Bergson's defining of duration, which equals memory plus the absolutely new. In the terms of analytical psychology, echoing Jung, integrative experiences speak of the transcendent function.

Turning our attention now to music, we can make several observations. Music's capacity to communicate is proverbial. Keeping in mind the importance of communication and shared experience from Moreno's group therapy, we can compare the outcome of *tele* in psychodrama to what is emerging in the listening audience or players of a successful performance – for example, of Beethoven's Fifth Symphony. Not every performance evokes the emergent experience of *tele*, but when it is palpable in the concert hall, the performer knows that he or she is, together with the other musicians, in a flow. Music can give expression (as if one were taking on a role) to the different impulses of a relationship (imagine love and rejection). When one hears or plays the opening four notes of Beethoven's Fifth Symphony, there is often a tingling at the back of the neck (I even had it while *thinking* about writing this example). What are those four notes? What role do I feel into? There will never be one answer, but one experience says 'this is fate' – 'you are *here*'. We need not stay in classical music for our examples. Consider the Portuguese music genre of Fado (destiny, fate) that is linked to the Portuguese word *saudade,* which betokens the feeling of loss, a permanent, irreparable loss and its consequent lifelong damage. On the other side of experience and returning to Beethoven, there is a military trumpet call in the third act of his opera *Fidelio* (Leonore No. 3 Overture). The call is muted, by being played off-stage, and one's listening is intensified. In the opera the situation has been hopeless, and the trumpet call signals that release is on its way. We could say of this trumpet call, 'this is redemption'. To express fate and redemption adequately, we need to have these expressions in our repertoires, and timing is of the essence.

The failures – when the timing is *off* and there is no *tele* as an outcome of a musical performance – can also be revealing for an understanding of what is happening during a performance. For this investigation I use information that I gathered during conservatory experiences, which continue to inform my questioning. Some of these questions concern the conflicts of a violinist, a friend of mine at the conservatory. At the time, I was struck by the violinist's dream:

> I am on the stage and playing the violin; the stage is otherwise empty. I look into the hall and see, to my horror, that occupying all of the seats is my father.

Having this dream facilitated a decision for the dreamer. He decided not to try to become a professional violinist, but to become a musicologist. This he did, and he was very successful and respected. He continued to play violin, but then for 'fun'.

The associations of the dreamer are also helpful for viewing the inner dynamics. He said that one of the things that bothered him most about his father was that after a performance his father asked *other* people what they thought of the performance and did not respond to his son from out of his own experience. The experiences of 'not responding' and 'not using one's own ears' were, we can conjecture, aspects or schema of his father complex. And then (just as the 'rejecting' in the example above is felt as being done to me, rather than that I also reject) 'not responding' and 'not using one's own ears' characterized his unsuccessful performances, but now they were his own shortcomings as a violinist, not his father's. A major necessity for a performing musician: always use *your* ears. One can be dying of nerves, but be an active listener. Of course, this is not easy. With fear there is an inclination to close down the senses, rather than being open and continuing to register every small nuance. We move almost automatically into flight, fight, or freeze mode. The 'closing down' that can happen during a performance would, I think, be adequately diagnosed as the eclipsing of the ego by a complex. We might ask, who is listening then? I would offer that the autonomously complexed performer has a fantasy of the best-representation-of-his-complex as listener. However, this representation of another's ears, not being the ears of the performer, results in a performance where all of the valuable information is lost. As it was for my violinist: his father's ears were of no use to him.

If the complexed performer were asked, 'Who did you fantasize as listening?', he might be able to tell you, but only if it were very safe to do so. Usually, however, the whole question is so surrounded by shame that no reflection seems possible. But, as the discussion above shows, we can have a representation of our complex in a dream. The complex, working autonomously, closes down the senses; however, consciousness of the complex can change this automatism. Therefore the question can be asked, can we use the dream to open up the senses? The working hypothesis, introduced above, is that when actively engaging with more aspects of a relationship, there is often an emergent experience of *tele*.

For some years now I have applied what I will now be calling 'active imagination' during my cello practice sessions. This application was occasioned by what had become a semi-regular occurrence during my practice sessions: a dream scene from a dream the night before would suddenly appear during an otherwise focused practice session. The dream fragment was often emotionally charged, and I had no reason that I could discover why it should appear just then: I had not remembered it upon waking, and I was not calling it up. However, holding the dream scene in my mind's eye did not distract from my motor coordination and often added expressiveness to the passage I was at that moment playing. I experimented with actively calling up a dream scene during technically demanding moments: the surprisingly successful result was my application during the bow changes. An opportunity presented itself in 2009 to give a demonstration and test the applicability. The Fourth International Conference of Analytical Psychology and Chinese Culture, Shanghai, April 2009, was the venue and opportunity for giving a workshop that was, in essence, an exercise in active imagination with two cellists from the Shanghai Conservatory. The following is my account of this work.

151

Case study

The two cellists who so graciously accepted my invitation, Miss Chen and Mr Geng, were accomplished musicians with a large repertoire. They brought, of course, their instruments, but they were also asked to bring a recent dream. The workshop was held on the campus of Fudan University, in a hall with a capacity of one hundred people. The hall was full to capacity with students. Miss Chen played, beautifully and from memory, the prelude to the sixth Bach cello suite. I then asked her her dream. Miss Chen related, 'I am in my room, and two angels enter through the open window. I stand looking at them in amazement. Then they depart through the window.' I asked Miss Chen to select a moment in the dream that she would hold in her mind's eye during the exercise. She chose the moment when the angels departed. I explained to Miss Chen that we were now going to find in her performance a place to apply this 'vision'. She proceeded to play Tchaikovsky's Rocco Variations, very well. I was looking for a place in her performance where an increase of concentration would be an improvement, and she was not making my search easy. After the first variation I asked her to play the third variation, which is slow and melodic: this was because a slow movement presents particular difficulties where an increase of concentration is often very rewarding. I needed now to go into minute detail, and I asked her to play only the first four bars. Then I found where extra concentration would be useful, in her bow changes. We call these changes 'down bow' and 'up bow', and they take place at the tip of the bow and at the 'frog' of the bow. I instructed Miss Chen to call up her dream vision a fraction prior to the bow change, hold during the change and then to release the vision a fraction after the change. During those four bars, she had five bow changes. This was, so to speak, the moment of truth: would she do it, and would there be an appreciable difference? To the infinite delight of Miss Chen, Mr Geng, and myself, she did it, and the difference was that now there was a magnificent musical expression. She repeated the exercise, with the same good result.

Mr Geng took his place as performer and told his dream: 'I am running away, those pursuing me will kill me. I wake before they catch me.' I asked which moment he would hold in his mind's eye. He said the last moment, where they are almost on him. He played the opening of Shostakovich's first cello concerto, very well, and I thought, 'I am not going to find a place where increased concentration would improve the performance'. So I asked if he would play a different piece. He chose Dvorak's cello concerto and it was only in the slow, melodic second theme that I finally found what I was looking for.

For Mr Geng the improvement would not be found during the bow changes, but during the last 1/3rd of the down bow, before changing to the up bow. On the F# of two-and-a-half beats. We settled on the six bars of this melody, and in those six bars the F# is played twice. I pointed out the exact place on the bow where he should call up his vision: the last 2/3rd of the down bow, hold, and release the vision prior to the up bow change. Again, it was a moment of truth, and Miss Chen was now sharing my earnest interest in what would happen. The magic happened – a totally convincing, mature musical expression, beautiful, rich and voluptuous, as is needed for this melody. And the same happened with the repeat of the exercise.

Miss Chen, Mr Geng, and I could recognize the difference, the before and after, in the performances. For us, it was very clear that a remarkable improvement had occurred by the holding of the vision at the desired location. Our public was attentive, but I sincerely doubt that they grasped what had taken place, or even really noted that something *had* happened. But they showed their appreciation by asking Mr Geng to play a dream. He promptly played *Aprés un Rêve* by Faure. So ended our adventure.

What happened and how? Through having had the experience in question myself, I can first introduce the subjective components: At the moment of holding the dream vision, while executing a technical movement, kinesthetic awareness multiplies. And at the same moment the expressiveness of the musical phrase so produced increases. The feeling is: 'I am engaged to tell *this* story; it feels to be an important story. It should be carefully executed, no cutting corners, no inner voice that says, "Oh, well, tomorrow we can get it right": no, it is *now*.' My understanding is that communication happens on many levels at once, considering that every execution of a movement involves feelings of kinesthetic flow, and communication is involved to register, as well as, to execute. The *how* to perform as well as *what* (musical intent) to perform are ingredients of this communication. So I postulate that improving communication is the handmaiden for improved concentration.

What role did Mr Geng's dream play? To all appearances the dream ('I am being chased, they will kill me') was very different in what it expressed from what the Dvorak phrase expressed, which is akin to 'I love you'. However, what did Mr Geng's performance of the two F#s lack initially? They lacked *tension*. Miss Chen's dream had two angels arriving, being present, and departing. Her concentration during the bow changes was improved by calling up the moment of the angels' departure. A relationship between the turnaround at the bow change and her dream, with the aspects of arrival, being, and departing, was perhaps felt. With my own practice of active imagination, each time the dream vision was held while executing a chosen technical movement, I had the sense of the question, 'Are you a part of this communication?' And the answer came, 'Yes, I am a part.' The effectiveness of using the dream came in part because the dreamer carried the sense of the dream being uniquely *their* dream, and with employment of the dream the sense of *me* resonated. When working with a dream, there can be an experience of embodiment.

Exploring embodiment and the
psychology of musical performance

Embodiment, or the embodied mind, reflects the idea that the motor system influences our cognition, just as the mind influences bodily action. Performance, and in particular timing in performance, includes the registration, perception, gathering of information and decision making that works together with a physical movement. The results of the above experiments, the performers' increased awareness and their use of kinesthetic flow, can be examined in the light of two inquiries: entrainment and vitality forms.[1]

Entrainment is a phenomenon in which two or more independent rhythmic processes synchronize with each other. Synonyms for entrainment include 'coupling', 'phase locking', and 'attunement.' Attunement is the preferred term in developmental psychology. Recently, ethnomusicologists (Clayton, Sager, and Will 2005) considered the significance of entrainment for various directions of music research, including self-synchrony and interpersonal synchrony in musical performance. In the following I set out findings presented in their article 'In Time with the Music: The Concept of Entrainment and Its Significance for Ethnomusicology.'

Entrainment, first identified in 1665 by the Dutch physicist Christian Huygens, was a result of his invention of the pendulum clock. Two such clocks, when placed on a common support, would synchronize with each other. Much of the succeeding work on entrainment has been carried out within the fields of mathematics and physics with non-linear systems. Entrainment of physiological rhythms shows that it has importance in the world of living organisms.

Entrainment processes are largely constrained by non-conscious and procedural factors. Endogenous or naturally occurring rhythms within the body include the heartbeat, blood circulation, respiration, locomotion, blinking, secretion of hormones, the basic rest and activity cycle, and many others. These endogenous rhythmic processes interact within a single person in many different ways, and they interact between individuals. We entrain to environmental cues, such as the day and night pattern of light and dark, as well as to other individuals, and we engage in self-entrainment. There appear to be healthier and less healthy ways in which to be entrained. Should the healthy functioning of a system require a certain degree of entrainment, a lack, a weakening or an excessive strengthening of entrainment would then be associated with an unhealthy state. The disruption of 'normal' entrainment can be found in conditions such as epilepsy, Parkinson's, and autism.

Self-entrainment by humans and animals, where two or more of the body's oscillatory systems become synchronized, is exhibited in physical activity. A gesture by one part of the body, such as arm movement in walking, tends to entrain gestures by other parts of the body. There is not a rigid mechanical coupling, in that arms and legs remain independent. The rhythms displayed

by two or more oscillating systems become entrained, but the rhythmic patterns do not coincide or overlap exactly: they maintain a 'consistent relationship' with each other. There is a fascinating difference between animal and
human entrainment: both the animal and the human move rhythmically, but
humans can entrain their movements to an external timekeeper. We dance;
(strictly speaking) animals do not.[2] Looking at entrainment and brain waves,
even as the study of electroencephalogram (EEG) waves are incomplete records
of neuronal activities in the brain, the frequency bands appear to reflect certain
mental states. Some of the alpha and beta waves can be synchronized –
entrained – to the frequency of an external stimulus, and subjects enter trance-
like states, experiencing dream-like visions or deep peacefulness. Music, an
external oscillator, can entrain our internal oscillators. However, people will
have different entrainment experiences, even though participating in the same
musical performance.

Entrainment research includes the interaction and communication between
human individuals and points to the rhythmic organization of both verbal and
gestural communication. Speech and gestures become strongly coupled in
adults (having been loosely coupled from birth), the strong synchronization of
speech and manual gestures being used for communicative purposes in adults.
The effectiveness of this coupling can be seen in cases where speech and
gesture are mirrored: for instance, when speakers stutter, gestures (also) tend
to stop during the stuttering episode. A positive social experience is associated
with a degree of mutual rhythmic entrainment during communication (speech
rhythms can match those of the dialogic partner). It is interesting to note that
the entrainment should not be too 'perfect' for a positive experience: too
tightly coordinated or totally uncoordinated entrainment are both assessed as
less positive. Social music-making, with its bodily resonance and profound
aesthetic experiences, can increase fellow feeling and motivate a person's
identification with the social group in which the musical experience was made
possible.

Entrainment in human cognition includes, it is theorized, three primary
stages. There is, first, perception, the priming of the listener to form expectations; when these are met, there is synchronization; and if the expectations are
not met, there is the third option of adjustment. The priming is used to focus
attention to 'catch' upcoming events. So, synchronizing follows priming and
happens when our expectations are met. Synchronization is then a verification
of the correctness of our expectations, and when our expectations do not match
what happens next, synchronizing has not occurred. Entrainment in music is
seen to be a highly flexible process that can accommodate complexity, and
when there is disparity, an adaptive response is triggered. In music we are following the highly coherent patterns of rhythm, melody, and harmony, the
steady beat, in particular, functioning as a centring. Perception is primed by
schemata (learned knowledge structures), which were learned from previous
musical experiences. The response to musical cues shows that there is

attention and entrainment that matches external oscillators *and* oscillators influenced by our own cognitive capacities. A music-making human can be seen as embodying multiple oscillators. There is a process of self-synchrony as well as entraining to external stimuli.

With an understanding of entrainment in place, I would like to return to Jung's theory of complexes and the relationship with musical performance and active imagination. Entrainment answers, to some extent, one of our riddles for performance failures: the body has many rhythms that may, at times, be at odds with each other, and a performer's kinesthetic action may be out of rhythm with that of another performer. The performer's expectations have not primed him/her to 'catch' what will happen next. The ego in Jung's theory is also a complex, but it serves life relatively well because this complex is built up based on the individual's physical existence. We could speculate that the ego complex has received multiple experiences of entrainment, via both external oscillations and self-entrainment, and therefore knows pretty well where it is in the world and has therefore also a rich repertoire of entrainment options and can gain even more entrainment experiences through knowing what to expect. An autonomous, non-ego-oriented complex disrupts the attention of the ego complex. This activated complex tells the individual what to expect but is only partially correct – not correct enough to experience satisfying entrainment with an external oscillator, or to self-entrain. The impulses from the complex speak about expectations that tend to be self-fulfilling prophecies and play havoc with the healthier self-entraining impulses. Due to an over-active ego-eclipsing complex, priming that has failed does not encourage the third option of searching or taking the next creative step of adjustment.

Fortunately, the disruptive complex is represented in dreams. I say fortunately, because we have then, via the dream, an entrainment option that will resonate with the dreamer's body. The dialogue between ego and the imaged complex/dream facilitates an embodied experience. The attending to the dream image at a specific chosen moment, while executing a technical movement that produces music, has this element of dialogue.

With regard to vitality forms, Daniel Stern (2010) uses 'dynamic forms of vitality' in his concern about the dynamic aspects of human experience, that of 'force', 'movement', 'space', 'directionality', 'aliveness', 'time' and 'intensity'. As with entrainment, applying vitality forms to our understanding of performance brings to the foreground the additional important view of mutual regulation – that is, we build up a repertoire of vitality forms, the representation of which can, in turn, trigger vitality forms. Therefore, presented in the following are some of Stern's tenants from *Forms of Vitality*.

There appears to be a basic Gestalt in our observations and experiences of the inanimate world, interpersonal relationships and the products of culture, which is informed by movement, time, force, space, and intention, just as in recognizing a familiar face, though the face is composed of separate elements, our experience is holistic. Each individual has a movement signature that we recognize, among others, in their walk and hand gestures, which is the other's 'dynamic movement signature.' Dynamic vitality forms give emotions their final expression: for example, anger can 'explode', 'ooze out', 'sneak up', or be 'cold.' Vitality forms have no specific sense (vision, audition, touch) organ, but appear to arise from many parts of the brain simultaneously. Dynamic forms are intrinsic to an actor, dancer or musician's performance. The great performers communicate well the dynamic experience of the story.

Movement may be our most fundamental experience; from out of 'approach' and 'withdrawal' a whole host of meanings and their representations are developed. Dynamic information is needed to recognize interpersonal happenings. Already from infancy there is building up an implicit knowing of how the relationship moves along, answering the important questions: Is mother fully there? When is her anger cresting? Included in mother–infant interactions is the sharing of vitality forms. The vitality form matching is an attempt by mother to share the infant's subjective experience. The mother does not imitate the movements of the infant exactly but puts them into her 'own words', so to speak; by using her voice and/or gestures she resonates. This assures the baby that mother understood what it felt like doing what the baby did. It is a frequently employed attunement, which establishes and re-establishes the intersubjective field. Affect attunement (matching vitality forms) is best seen in spontaneous interactions, where there is richness in dynamic features, aliveness, and vitality. They create a running dialogue and, perhaps most importantly for the attachment process, relatively prolonged moments of mutual regard, which Stern and the Boston Change Process Study Group (of which he is a member) have called 'neonatal moments of meeting.'

They have proposed that a 'moment of meeting' is the *transactional* event that rearranges the patient's implicit relational knowing by rearranging the intersubjective field between patient and therapist (BCPSG 2010, p. 33). This is also the case for the transition to a more inclusive and coherent mutual regulatory system between parent and child, which hinges on a moment of meeting changing the intersubjective recognition and creating an opening for new initiatives (p. 34).

Movement therapies rely on vitality forms, as do role-playing techniques. Music-making, with its musical interplay, offers mutual recognition in shared moments of entering the same dynamic flow. When a shared common experience is realized between the players, this can move (as do 'moments of meeting') the relationship to a deeper intersubjective level.

Discussion

Stern shows that an ongoing dialogue, where vitality forms have been confirmed and answered, can result in an experience of deep connectedness – a 'moment of meeting'. Moreno's psychodrama praxis fosters here-and-now exchanges between people, which are dialogic and constitutive of *tele*. Jung's practice of active imagination moves dialogically and is creative of a third, the unifying activity of the transcendent function. Spontaneity has been cited in these therapies as helpful and can be used as a measurement; this is congruent with the lack of spontaneity of the 'role conserve' and the autonomous complex. These are therapeutics that can facilitate in (re)-establishing the effective timing in performance, by encouraging a transactional event that rearranges the intersubjective field, creating an opening for new initiatives.

The concept of three primary stages from entrainment research is helpful for picturing when timing is 'off'. There is, first, perception, the priming of the listener to form expectations; when these are met, there is synchronization; and if the expectations are not met, there is the third option of adjustment. Perception is primed by schemata (learned knowledge structures), which were learned from previous musical experiences. We synchronize, in part, through having our expectations met. We are creative when we adjust our expectations and can then, in turn, find our match and synchronize. The priming is used to focus attention to 'catch' upcoming events, and when the timing is not optimal in a performance, I suggest that the problem is with our expectations, which are falling short or inadequate to the task.

Active imagination in practice has similar stages. A visual image is engaged that expresses a relatively unknown impulse. Such engagement or dialogue can reveal one's expectations so that the impulse is no longer unconscious, and one thereby achieves a coherent state of consciousness, where there is flow, a unity with self and world. It should be emphasized that there is real work involved; active imagination is not a free-floating fantasy.

That active imagination is quite different from fantasizing can be brought into focus by returning to the example of my Conservatory violinist. With this example, there is both a recurring fantasy that is disruptive for the performance and a dream of this disruption. Should the violinist recognize that he has such a negative fantasy, which plays up while he performs (that of his judgmental father), the solution is not to have a positive fantasy, as in 'Well, then, I fantasize myself into being successful.' Such a positive fantasy (employed like a cognitive strategy) is used in order *not* to have the negative fantasy – that is, it is used defensively – and this actually brings a splitting in his concentration. The proof can come swiftly: the next performance is as poor as the last. What offers a solution is to include the realities of the violinist's experience during his performance as much as possible. One impulse or reality, as we have seen in Mr Geng's case, is, 'I am afraid', with its accompanying tension, but which, when engaged with, increased his concentration.

Tension is a vitality form. In my assessment of Mr Geng and Miss Chen's 2009 active imagination, the vitality form in the dream appeared to relate/match/dialogue with the physical technical application. For Miss Chen, the turnaround of the angels in the dream matched the turnaround of the bow change. For Mr Geng, the tension of being pursued in the dream dialogued with the tension (or feeling of extension) in the down-bow. On the one hand, we could say the dream is but an approximation of a vitality form expression; but, on the other hand, as we see in the mother's dialogue with her infant, it *should* be an approximation, just enough to let the infant know there is attunement. A repertoire of vitality forms is built up that can be used to trigger vitality forms. And there are similar conclusions from entrainment research: that the entrainment should not be too 'perfect' for a positive experience. Attunement is happening in the dialogue. Viewing the dialogue (in terms of vitality forms mirrored between mother and infant that leads to moments of meeting or as in active imagination and psychodrama) allows us to grasp (a vitality form!) the change it facilitates in performance. How do we maintain the flow of kinesthetic information? There is priming, using expectations with which we can 'catch' upcoming events. We dialogue, we engage, and thereby entrain, we are then synchronizing our actions to the rhythms that are music.

An autonomous complex, with its faulty expectations, can take us out of engagement with others and with ourselves. A similarity, that of a structure that primes expectations, is suggested by the functioning of the autonomous complex and Moreno's 'role conserve'. I would like to build on this similarity and include Turner's exposé of the two models for human interrelatedness. There are (1) structured social bonds (political–legal–economic positions with types of evaluation) often based on hierarchy, and (2) the bonding found in rites of initiation, *communitas*, which is an outcome of whole human beings wholly attending. During an initiation rite, the candidates have been stripped of any hierarchy they had. They are each other's equals during the *liminal* phase. They, so to speak, resonate together. Their experience of entrainment builds up a repertoire of *communitas* that can be used again, so that in future, human interrelatedness is not exclusively by social hierarchies. In psychodrama and active imagination, the 'role conserve' or 'personification of the complex' is taken into consideration. It is momentarily in a position of equality with its dialogic partner, and the interaction is creative of a third experience. This also builds up a repertoire that can be used again; these are expectations that allow us to 'catch' what will happen next, which can be the musical expressions of excluding or including, of rejecting or loving.

In conclusion, the timing of the performer resonates with multiple oscillators: *optimal* timing in musical performance resonates *and* communicates with multiple oscillators. We can, after all, dance!

Notes

1 This exploration does not do justice to the literature that could also clarify the results. Such an overview can be found in Mitchell Kossak (2007) and his research into the experience of the jazz musician in their method of improvisation. He has called attention to the practice of psychotherapy in general and expressive arts

therapies specifically in their utilization of 'the kind of free playing found in free jazz in order to achieve a state of attunement . . .' (Kossak 2007, p. 33). He includes Jung's idea of active imagination as perhaps being the most closely aligned with free jazz in its stated goals, which is the creation of a third; there is a negotiated collaboration between conscious and unconscious impulses, emerging to a new unitive state of consciousness (p. 33). Special mention should be made of psychoanalyst D. W. Winnicott (1971), known in particular for his observations of play in children and alertness to the fact that the therapist and patient need to find a way to play before interactivity and responsiveness can occur. In the field of anthropology, special mention should also be given to Thomas J. Csordas (1996), in his considerations of embodiment and efficacy in performance. Also see Miller (2010) for an exploration of the embodied countertransference. Coming to my attention too late to integrate into this chapter, but corroborating how in mother–infant communication there exist noticeable patterns of timing, vocal timbre, and melodic gesture, see *Communicative Musicality*, edited by Malloch and Trevarthen (2009).

2 'The human ability to keep time should be distinguished from the ability of most animals (including humans) to move in a metric, alternating fashion. What is special about humans is not their capacity to move rhythmically but their ability to *entrain* their movements to an external timekeeper, such as a beating drum' (Brown, Merker and Wallin 2000, p. 12 – as quoted in Clayton, Sager and Will 2005, p. 17).

References

Bergson, H. (1946) *The Creative Mind: An Introduction to Metaphysics*. New York: Kensington Publishing Corp.

BCPSG (2010) *Change in Psychotherapy, a Unifying Paradigm*. Boston Change Process Study Group. New York–London: Norton.

Brown, S., Merker, B. and Wallin, N. L. (2000) 'An Introduction to Evolutionary Musicology', in N. L. Wallin, B. Merker, and S. Brown (eds.), *The Origins of Music*, Cambridge, MA: MIT Press, pp. 3–24.

Clayton, M., Sager, R. and Will, U. (2005) 'In Time with the Music: The Concept of Entrainment and Its Significance for Ethnomusicology', in *European Meetings in Ethnomusicology* 11 (*ESEM* CounterPoint 1), pp. 3–75.

Csordas, T. J. (1996) 'Imaginal Performance and Memory in Ritual Healing', in C. Laderman, M. Roseman (eds.) *The Performance of Healing*, London: Routledge, pp. 91–113.

Hunt, H. T. (2012) 'A Collective Unconscious Reconsidered', *The Journal of Analytical Psychology*, 57 (No. 1), pp. 76–98.

Jung, C.G. (1904–7, 1910) 'Studies in Word Association' in *Experimental Researches*, Collected Works 2, Princeton, NJ: Princeton University Press, 1973.

Jung, C. G. (1929) 'Problems of Modern Psychotherapy', in *The Practice of Psychotherapy, Collected Works 16*, Princeton, NJ: Princeton University Press, 1966, pp. 53–75.

Kossak, M. (2007) *Attunement: Embodied Transcendent Experience Explored through Sound and Rhythmic Improvisation*. Ph.D. dissertation, Cincinnati, Ohio: Union Institute & University.

Malloch, S. and Trevarthen, C. (2009) *Communicative Musicality: Exploring the Basis of Human Companionship*. Oxford: Oxford University Press.

Miller, B. H. (2010) 'A Sami Healer's Diagnosis: A Case of Embodied Counter-transference?', in R. Jones (ed.), *Body, Mind and Healing after Jung*, London: Routledge.

Moreno, J. L. (1946) *Psychodrama*, Vol. 1, Beacon, NY: Beacon House.

Moreno, J. L. (1960) *The Sociometry Reader*, Glencoe, IL: Free Press.

Moreno, J. L. and Moreno, Z. T. (1959) *Psychodrama*, Vol. 2, Beacon, NY: Beacon House.

Stern, D. (2010) *Forms of Vitality: Exploring Dynamic Experience in Psychology, the Arts, Psychotherapy, and Development*. Oxford: Oxford University Press.

Stephenson, C. (2009) *Possession, Jung's Comparative Anatomy of the Psyche*: Routledge.

Turner, V. (1969) 'Liminality and Communitas', in M. Lambek (ed.), *A Reader in the Anthropology of Religion*. Oxford: Blackwell, 2002, pp. 358–74.

Winnicott, D. W. (1971) *Playing and Reality*, London: Tavistock Publications.

11

ENCOUNTERS WITH JUNG AND MORENO ON THE ROAD OF BRICKS AND MOSS

Emilija Kiehl

> Chance is always powerful. Let your hook be always cast; in the pool where you least expect it, there will be a fish.
>
> (Ovid, 2 AD, p. 315)

I was surprised and glad to receive Craig Stephenson's invitation to contribute to this book about Jung and Moreno but also of two minds about it because, what can I say about Moreno? I attended a course in psychodrama almost a couple of decades ago and have not used it in my clinical practice, nor kept in touch with developments in the field, ever since. However, it was during that psychodrama course, which I joined out of curiosity and with no conscious anticipation of the profound changes it was to bring my way that I went into Jungian analysis and on to Jungian training. Unbeknownst to me, my unconscious was working out a plan that goes back to a more distant past, and psychodrama presented an opportunity for its realization.

Craig was one of the fellow students in the course. A conversation with him was particularly significant in this turn of events, and I will say more about it later. His invitation, many years later, to write a chapter for this book felt like a call for me to revisit the realm where past and present experiences merge into one enfolding narrative. So, I thought, my offering could be an exploration of the connection between Jung and Moreno in my own life. What, at the time, seemed like chance encounters with their thinking was interconnected with times and places, people and events and circumstances that led to and created this present moment. Following the stream of events that make up this autobiographical essay, I might evoke a theme or a principle that links them together. I already know that one of the elements that make up such a connection will be synchronicity.

162

The warming-up process

So, where does this narrative begin? A memory pops up from the early 1970s in the now ex-Yugoslavia, my country of origin: a sentence from a very popular book of children's answers collected by two psychologists, entitled: *Pencil Writes with the Heart* (the title was taken from the colloquial children's word for the graphite in the pencil as the pencil's 'heart' – Rupnik and Nešić 1972). To a question about the notions of beginning and end, one little boy answered: 'The beginning was when I was born, and there is no end.' Another child added: 'But there is also when there is no beginning and no end!'

I was introduced to the study of psychology in the third year of grammar school and also discovered that I was interested in psychiatry. Psychoanalysis was on the curriculum, and although Jung was mentioned, he was seen as somewhat of a mystic, and his work was not given as much attention in the mainstream as the work of Freud, Adler and Fromm (although Freud was also criticized for not taking into consideration the social aspect of psychic life). In a society firmly grounded on the principles of Dialectic Materialism, the philosophy of the 'Leftist Hegelians' Feuerbach, Marx and Lenin and the belief that scientific rationalism was the holder of all truth, there was little space for any form of 'mysticism'. Nevertheless, interest in Jung from the time before the socialist revolution continued to grow, and works by Jung and about Jung continued to be written and translated into Serbian (then called Serbo-Croat: apparently, these were the first translations of Jung into an East European language). Five volumes of Jung's *Collected Works* were translated in the 1970s, and my father bought them for me as soon as they were published. This was a surprise present, as my father was an admirer of Adler and Fromm: 'I thought you might be interested in Jung', he explained. By then, I had already acquired *Man and his Symbols* (Jung 1964) and James Legge's translation of the *I Ching* (1899), but I had yet to discover Jung's involvement with Taoist thought: Richard Wilhelm's translations of the *I Ching* (1951) and *The Secret of the Golden Flower* (1931) came into my life a little later and have remained my companions ever since.

Man and his Symbols and the *I Ching* made a tremendous impression on my young mind. They seemed to be talking about a realm of existence I had sensed since early childhood – the realm that encompasses both the 'real world' and the timeless world I knew in dreams. This childhood sense of an invisible interconnectedness, the awe at the vicissitudes of life and the experience of being in the world would return again and again in my future involvement with the practice of meditation and movement, encounters with people, with certain ideas and works of art, all the way to psychodrama, Jungian analysis, Jungian training, and up to the present day.

Meaningful encounters and meaningful coincidences

Among the ideas that have made the most profound influence on my understanding of the human condition is Jung's concept of the Self – Self as an
archetype, and personal self. Coming across this concept at once opened a new
dimension in my search for understanding and confirmed what I intuitively
seemed to have already 'known'. Self is for Jung 'the principle and archetype
of orientation and meaning' (Jung 1963, p. 224); it is the centre and the circumference of the psyche, encompassing both its conscious and unconscious
aspects. The individual self is 'connected to all other human (and perhaps also
non-human) selves' (Clark 2006, p. 20). Self is interconnected with the realm
of the collective unconscious and 'the most profound patterns in mind, culture
and nature, what [Jung] called "archetypes"' (Cambray 2009, p. 2). Ego is
born out of the self and functions as the centre of the field of consciousness;
ego's concerns are personal identity, maintenance of the personality, continuity over time and mediation between conscious and unconscious realms.
Ego is responsive to the demands of the self, which is the ordering principle of
the entire personality (Samuels, Shorter and Plaut 1986, p. 50). Ego can never
fully comprehend the self but perceives it through symbolic representations
and symbolic events that carry a particular resonance. The encounters between
ego and self can generate creativity and have a numinous quality. The goal of
these encounters is the development of the personality through the growing
capacity for creative self-expression. In psychodrama, this process is facilitated
by *meaningful encounters* among the participants in the session. Meaningful
encounters present an opportunity for emergence of a new point of view that
can affect psychological transformation.

Encounter as an archetypal force is very present in the political and cultural
history of the countries on the Balkan Peninsula, where both Moreno and I
were born. Throughout this turbulent history, the creative and destructive
aspects of the archetype have expressed themselves in the collective psyche
renowned for altruism, warmth and hospitality as well as passionate hatred
and bloody wars. The motif of encounter is woven into the fabric of life of my
first home city, Belgrade. Belgrade is an ancient city built on the foundations
of one of the greatest Neolithic cultures, Vincha, that goes back to 2300–
2000 BCE, on the confluence of two rivers, Sava and Danube (according to
legend, the Danube is one of the four rivers that spring from Paradise). The
Argonauts, Celts, Huns, Romans, Turks, Byzantines and Crusaders all passed
through Belgrade, 'leaving behind traces of their power, their rage and their
cultures' (Pavić 1998). Because of its geopolitical position, on the threshold
between the East and the West, Belgrade has stood on the way – and in the
way – of the imperial powers of all ages. At one time, the Turks called Belgrade
'the Portal of Wars', and Christians called it 'the Bastion of Christianity'. In
the thirteenth century Belgrade became the capital of the medieval kingdom
of Serbia. In the twentieth century it became the capital of Yugoslavia, and,

following the civil war and the break-up of Yugoslavia in the 1990s, it is once again the capital of Serbia. Centuries of political and cultural pressure from the West and the East alike might explain the sometimes fierce resolve of the people from the region to preserve a degree of authenticity and continuity of their cultural individuation within the mixture of Eastern and Western influences. In the accounts of Jung's and Moreno's lives I was particularly moved by their courage and determination to differentiate and develop their own thinking against the predominant trends of the time: a deeply valued archetypal need that permeates the culture of my ancestors.

The intimations of the intricate fabric of Belgrade's rich history and diverse culture were present in all spheres of life, and the sense that everything was more than it seemed goes back to my earliest memories. Our secluded children's playground looked at a slightly raised green lawn with a small walled garden at the back of a church. This view was in sharp contrast to the urban façade of the front entrance into the church, which blended seamlessly into the cityscape. I remember finding the oppositeness of these two views, and the fact that together they formed a whole picture, fascinating. My family were atheists, and we never went to church. Nevertheless, for me, the church garden was full of wonders. I liked to gaze at the trees and plants and the moss growing between the bricks on the garden wall, wondering how it got there. The deep green colour of the moss against the terracotta bricks was beautiful and somehow timeless.

The timeless moss also grew around an ancient citadel built by the Romans, on the cliff overlooking the juncture of the two rivers in the heart of the city. The fortress still bears the name it was given during the Ottoman Empire: Kalemegdan. Apart from wars against the various invading forces from near and far, Kalemegdan was also a scene of duels between local gentlemen of different epochs defending their honour, and even today the Turkish word *megdan* is sometimes used poetically to denote a battle in defence of honour.

A large park encircles the fortress and its many gates. In the 1930s, Belgrade Zoo joined the museums, churches, art galleries, sports terrains and restaurants scattered around the park. Families with small children, lovers, tourists, sports enthusiasts and pensioners playing chess on the benches can be seen in Kalemegdan at all times of day or night. Homesick country folk meet there to dance to the music from their regions. The flow of stories and legends about the historical and personal dramas set in Kalemegdan since time immemorial (according to one, Attila's grave lies beneath the fortress) continues today, creating new narratives. The two rivers meeting, the lush flora, the mossy ancient Roman well in the centre of the park (leading to a still largely unexplored subterranean system of passages out of the city), the roaring of tigers and bears from the zoo; the promenading people of all ages – all this makes Kalemegdan a stage where the story of the wonders and tragedies of life is played out continuously. I walked there countless times, with my parents and friends, on my own. Moreno was in Belgrade in the late 1960s. I have wondered whether he ever walked in Kalemegdan.

Theatre of spontaneity

During my student years, a group of friends often got together in my apartment and discussed philosophy and literature, read plays and made music. One day five of us decided to form a theatre company. We named it 'The Theatre of Mystery'. We began to meet early every morning in the Student Cultural Centre's large hall with a piano, and through music, movement and discussion arrived at an idea for a play, which we then collectively wrote, directed and performed on the Centre's main stage. The Centre was renowned for its annual international student cultural festival, called 'April Encounters', and the now famous performing artist, Marina Abramović, began her career there. We entitled our play 'Life is a Strange Thing'. Unbeknownst to us, the concept of theatre that emerged from our rehearsals contained many elements of Moreno's Immediate Theatre (which he later referred to as Impromptu Theatre in the United States). His biographer, René Marineau, explains Moreno's thinking about theatre and therapy as a formulation of four types of 'revolutionary theatre', of which the Immediate Theatre was one:

> [The] immediate theatre is based on spontaneity: theatre is what is happening in the here and now, what is being created as life unfolds. It is the theatre without spectators, theatre that presents *das Ding an Sich,* the thing in itself. This is the theatre that leads to creativity through the use of imagination and a spontaneous event. It is total drama: everyone is part of it as an actor and protagonist. It evolved from Moreno's experience with children and his impromptu group.
>
> (Marineau 1989, p. 79)

Some elements of what Moreno called *axiodrama*, which 'aims at the purging of *cultural conserves* and stereotypes within the individual' (Marineau 1989, p. 71), were also present in our enterprise. This idea was certainly a part of our burgeoning social consciousness, and there was also an aspect of what Jung would have termed individuation:

> . . . becoming an 'in-dividual', and, in so far as 'individuality' embraces our innermost, last and incomparable uniqueness, it also implies becoming one's own self. We could therefore translate individuation as 'coming to selfhood' or 'self realisation'.
>
> (Jung 1953, p. 173)

Looking back at our performance, I can see many archetypal themes, among them a scene of rebirth, that emerged from this collective encounter with the unconscious – an individual archetypal need finding its realisation in a collective search for self-expression.

In his autobiography Moreno describes his own encounter with the creative unconscious, which he shared with his wife at the time, as a discovery of 'a language that is understood by all men, [that] gives us hope, gives us direction, gives our cosmos direction and meaning' (Moreno, quoted in Marineau 1989, p. 62). He discovered that

> The universe is not just a jungle or a bundle of wild forces. . . . It is basically, infinite creativity. And this infinite creativity which is true on all levels of existence, whether on the physical, social or biological . . . whether it is in the past or in the present or in the future, ties us together. We are all bound to one another by responsibility for all things.
>
> (Moreno, quoted in Marineau 1989, p. 62)

For Moreno, this vision of *unus mundus* was his rebirth that brought forth his philosophy of spontaneity and creativity. The experience culminated in 'a voice of God' speaking in verse, which Moreno transposed into his poem, *The Valley of May,* a vivid depiction of a lush realm of creative inspiration, bursting with emotion. Moreno passionately believed in the unconscious potential for psychological transformation through creativity. He was to pursue his vision in many forms throughout his life.

At an earlier time, he had an experience that may be thought of as a precursor to the images that found more mature poetic expression in *The Valley of May*. In his autobiography he gives an account of a moment that determined the course he was to follow and, later, realize in psychodrama. One night, in his youth, he found himself wondering through the dark empty streets of the provincial German town of Chemnitz where he was living with his parents, unable to make sense of his thoughts and feelings about the approaching life changes:

> . . . Looking up, I found myself in a little park standing in front of a statue of Jesus Christ illuminated by the moon's faint light. It drew my gaze and I stood transfixed. In the intensity of this strange moment I tried with all my will to have that statue come alive, to speak to me. I wanted Jesus to move out of the stone and act out his life there in the park for the people of Chemnitz. . . . From then on, there was a surplus of meaning in everything I did and in everything which was done around me.
>
> (Moreno, quoted in Marineau 1989, pp. 24–25)

Moreno goes on to describe the choice he felt this numinous encounter placed in front of him: to follow the way of the family he was born into, or 'to follow the universe, as Jesus had'. He chose to follow the universe. His desire to see Jesus act out his life for the people of Chemnitz pointed towards and paved the way for Moreno's future creative self-expression in psychodrama.

Warren Colman might say Moreno's ego chose to follow the self. Colman (1999) looks at individuation as a co-creative relationship between ego and self, whereby the ego is that which individuates, and in the process, the potential of the self is realised through their relationship and mutual becoming. The self is the ordering principle of the process whose goal is an increasing ego consciousness, an increasing capacity to witness and effect the transformation they both undergo. In this process we may participate in many situations whose meaning is, at the time, incomprehensible to the ego. The combination of the external and the internal elements involved and a maturation within the passage of time can produce a phenomenon that reveals underlying patterns of events that have preceded and resulted in an observed moment. Jung called this synchronicity, a powerful experience that opens the mind to new possibilities, 'offering a glimpse of the interconnected fabric of the universe' (Cambray 2009, p. 31).

Moreno's experience in the park in Chemnitz may be seen as a synchronistic event. The unexpected encounter with the statue of Christ in the heat of the moment in his search for answers to deep existential questions offered him a glimpse of his future personal, professional and socio-political orientation. According to his biographer, Moreno had a tendency towards megalomania, and in this and other meaningful events in his life he saw the confirmation of his childhood sense of being a special person with a special mission. Moreno was aware of this tendency, but for him megalomania is a natural state: 'It has, like any other natural state, normal and pathological forms' (Marineau, 1989, p. 24). That is to say, the inflation of the ego in response to the different order of psychological power contained in the self may be a natural response in as much as that energy can overwhelm the inspired ego. Moreno was able to use this energy creatively: many years later, it produced psychodrama. According to Marineau, there were occasions throughout Moreno's life when megalomania would seize his creative vision, disrupting his relationships and altering the course he was striving to follow, but he remained faithful to his quest for continuous self-expression in challenging circumstances, new cultures, different languages. In this pursuit, Moreno did not always act from an ethical position. Perhaps he saw these actions as offerings to his Muse, as if in a realm free from the considerations of ordinary human relationships. In his passionate belief in the transforming power of artistic expression, he followed his Muse, in her different guises, where she took him.

In *Modern Man in Search of a Soul*, Jung says about the two realms in an artist's life:

> The secret of artistic creation and of the effectiveness of art is to be found in a return to the state of *participation mystique* – to that level of

experience at which it is man who lives, and not the individual, and at which the weal or woe of the single human being does not count, but only human existence. This is why every great work of art is objective and impersonal, but none the less profoundly moves us each and all. And this is also why the personal life of a poet cannot be held essential to his art – but at most a help or a hindrance to his creative task. He may go the way of a Philistine, a good citizen, a neurotic, a fool or a criminal. His personal career may be inevitable and interesting, but it does not explain the poet.

(Jung 1933, p. 176)

On the path of his own individuation, Jung was faced with a crucial decision whether to follow the voice of the self or stay in the fold of the psychoanalytic movement, where he was the favourite son. His quest for understanding psychic life brought him to a realm that psychoanalytic thinking could not reach – indeed, one that psychoanalytic thinking wanted to reduce to a reachable realm. For Jung, accepting a reductive interpretation of the power of the psyche to transcend the boundaries of rational thinking would have been a betrayal of his own experience. In 1911, he made the decision to publish *Wandlungen und Symbole der Libido* (in English, *The Psychology of the Unconscious*, later revised as *Symbols of Transformation*), in which Jung anticipates the development of a non-reductive view of psychic processes that laid the foundation for his system of thought. It also marked his parting with Freud. In his Foreword to the fourth edition, 37 years later, Jung describes how the ideas that had been fermenting in his mind broke through and took shape in this book:

The whole thing came upon me like a landslide that could not be stopped. The urgency that lay behind it became clear to me only later: it was the explosion of all those psychic contents which could find no room, no breathing-space, in the constricting atmosphere of Freudian psychology and its narrow outlook.

(Jung 1956, p. xxiii)

Jung hastens to add that he 'has no wish to denigrate Freud'; however, the conceptual framework into which Freud fitted the psychic phenomenon seemed, to Jung, 'unendurably narrow'.

Liberating his psychological model from the confines of 'the outmoded rationalism and scientific materialism of the late nineteenth century', Jung created a space for a non-reductive approach to the cultural, religious and spiritual realms of psychic life. The break-up with Freud opened a way into this space and a deeper involvement with the unconscious, which Jung entered on his own. From the years of his courageous empirical exploration of this realm emerged a work of tremendous creativity, the *Red Book*.

Thus every experience contains an indefinite number of unknown factors . . .

(Jung 1964, p. 23)

When the ego that seeks to know and the self that wants to be known meet, they each carry to the other a sense of urgency, and such times provide a sense of living connection and meaning. For our small group of students, the creation of 'The Theatre of Mystery' was such a time. Moreno believed that groups have a capacity for transcendent interconnectedness, and we certainly felt a powerful synergy in the group. Our collective exploration of the unconscious and the shared creative expression of that experience on the stage found a way to our audience, and, although none of us was trained in the dramatic arts, our performance was received with quite unexpected praise and enthusiasm. Here Jung's concept of individuation, his model of the self and the creativity in the ego–self relationship would have been an invaluable resource for making sense of our experience. We could have understood our endeavour as a dialogue between ego and self in a collective active imagination, as Margaret Clark describes:

> The ego is deliberately set aside temporarily, and images from the unconscious arise and develop; the ego watches the story unfold as in a theatre, noting the plot, characters, setting, dialogue. It is important that the unconscious psyche expresses itself as fully as possible, before the ego intervenes to try to understand and interpret.
>
> (Clark 2006, p. 93)

However, such understanding was not available to us at the time. Growing up in the confluence of the religious and philosophical influences from the East and the West, we had a sense of the spiritual significance of what we were experiencing, but a deeper understanding of the psychological processes involved could have strengthened the vessel of shared creativity that our play had formed for us and for our audience. An activation of a collective transcendent function (a dynamic internal space where the conscious and the unconscious can have a dialogue) sustained by our collective ego would have facilitated a transition into a more mature level of creativity. However, the transforming power of what was 'cooking' in the vessel was difficult to manage. As a consequence, following our success, our complexes sought to take control over the creative process and shape it according to the expectations of the audience. The spontaneous spirit of the group was constrained, and we began to disagree about our next project – or, as Colman would put it, we mistook the value of our creative capacity that this experience was showing us for the glamorous surface of what it had produced. The group's creative inter-relationships no longer provided a space for our individual self-realization, but only for the expression of the persona (Colman

170

1999, p. 24). Interestingly, we took to wearing masks in the play that emerged at that time.

I now think of that collective creation as the potential space where each of us was able to bring an individual experience of being in the world, both witnessing it and creating it on the stage. In the words of the Sufi teacher, Inyat Khan, we were in a 'mirror-land with a living phenomenon'. In this mirror:

> It is not only projecting and reflecting that takes place . . . but the phenomena of creation: that all that is projected and reflected is created at the same time, and materialized sooner or later.
>
> (Khan, 1976, p. 21)

After the play with masks, the group dissolved, but the process that had brought us together continued, in different ways, through different times and with different people, while our connection with each other moved to the invisible realm of memory. In the liminal space of the 'mirror land' we felt it was time for change. I decided to move abroad.

Synchronicity in the undercurrent

London was renowned for its many schools of spiritual development, and I wanted to explore the different philosophical systems these schools were offering. A friend jokingly commented that neurotic Belgrade intellectuals would have nowhere to go after I left (it had not occurred to me that our gatherings in my apartment might have been healing for some). Two young women, working at the Student Cultural Centre café, turned up to say goodbye with a parting gift: the *I Ching*, translated by Richard Wilhelm. 'We thought you might like to take this book with you', they said. I opened the book and discovered Jung's Foreword. For a moment, everything felt new and old at the same time. The sense of interconnectedness of the elements that brought about that moment gave me the feeling that my decision to leave my hitherto protected life was granted 'from above'. I was ready for a new chapter.

What followed were years of exploring the London 'spiritual scene', and many meaningful events and encounters. One such encounter came by chance, via a bottle of plum brandy brought to our house by a friend from Belgrade, who asked if a psychiatrist living in London could come to pick it up. It had been sent by his mother. At the time I was working on the translation of the play *Broken Glass* by Arthur Miller, whose heroine suffers from a mysterious psychosomatic condition. The combination of the work I was doing and the psychiatrist's visit rekindled my interest in psychiatry. I found myself wanting to know the details of his work. I discovered that, apart from psychiatry, he was also a psychodrama therapist and teacher. I had not heard of psychodrama before and was intrigued by the combination of theatre and psychology. I told him about my interest in both fields, and a couple of months later I had a phone call. The psychiatrist was starting an introductory course in psychodrama in a local London hospital, and, although the course was aimed primarily at mental health professionals, he thought that I might be interested in coming to the initial session.

The psychodrama group was in some ways similar but also quite different from the groups I was familiar with, as this group was made up of people who sought primarily professional, as well as personal development, and the leader of this group was not a teacher of a spiritual discipline or a philosophical system, but a psychiatrist and a psychotherapist.

We began with a warm-up that brought back vivid memories of my theatre rehearsals. The improvisation on a theme, suggested by the director, created a space where the group members could explore ways of relating to each other. Within that space and the developing dynamics, an aspect of a group member's life emerged as living material for exploration in a psychodrama. The stage was thus set for creating an opportunity for 'the protagonist' to arrive at a new understanding of his or her material. Looking at the psychodrama process in the context of the transcendent function, Jungian analyst and psychodrama therapist Helmut Barz describes this process in which:

> All previously-known possibilities of shaping unconscious contents can be brought together in psychodrama, where thinking and feeling, perception and intuition are brought to play as much as are body and soul, individual and group, outer and inner world, subject and object, Apollonian and Dionysian emotional involvement.
>
> (Barz 1993, p. 184)

Closely following the dialogue between the protagonist and a role-player, an attuned psychodrama director is able to sense the right moment for a role reversal. In the symbolic representation of the situation that the protagonist wants to make sense of, role reversal can activate the transcendent function and bring about a change of attitude. The director must also have a talent for theatre. Pointing at further links between Moreno's and Jung's thinking, Barz goes on to say:

> . . . the leader will always seek a scene that contains an archetypal constellation, with or without having heard of the concept of 'archetype'. Good theatre is always archetypal and every psychodrama strives to be a good theatre.
>
> (Barz 1993, p. 185)

Introducing Moreno's thinking in the first session, the director said that one of the main aims of psychodrama is getting in touch with one's creativity. I became curious. I did not expect this to be anything more than a new but

172

short-term cultural experience. How would I be affected by this process if I stayed on, I wondered. Although I had some idea that 'getting in touch with my creativity' through psychodrama – or any other psychotherapy – meant making conscious something that was unconscious, I could not imagine where this new self-exploration might take me. However, I felt hopeful that from the point of view of creativity, the process might have a beneficial effect on my work as a literary translator and also on my overall personal development. I was mindful of the Taoist thought that the slightest wave of the hand moves molecules all the way to the end of the universe. Everything we do affects everything and everyone else. So I decided to come to a few more sessions.

A new member soon joined the group: Craig Stephenson. In a conversation during a break I discovered that Craig was about to complete his training in Jungian analysis and would be leaving for Zurich soon. Again I was curious and also impressed. I told Craig that I had been thinking about going into Jungian analysis ever since I discovered Jung's writings. Craig assured me that I would have no difficulties finding a suitable analyst in London. He told me about the London training institutions and about the differences in their thinking. I wanted to know about his training, and at one point he said: 'you seem very interested in Jung. Have you thought about training yourself?' 'But my background is philology and literature', I said. 'So is mine', said Craig.

This conversation took place at the time when my Tai Chi teacher asked if I would like to train in Chinese medicine or perhaps become a teacher of Chi Kung. I found it interesting that two unconnected people came up with ideas for my change of profession at the same time; moreover, with no conscious thought about it on my part. However, I had no plans to change my career and saw this as just a coincidence. The emerging theme persisted nevertheless, and I found myself often almost having to convince my psychodrama group colleagues that I was not a psychotherapist, nor planning to become one; 'but you *feel* like a psychotherapist, or a healer!' commented one. Sufis believe that things people say in passing may contain a message from God. I eventually remembered this and began to wonder if something important was going on that I needed to become aware of. I decided to stay on when the group was closed to newcomers and the course moved to a new level.

About a year later, I became the – somewhat reluctant and shy – first student to direct a piece: the colleague who had said that I felt like a therapist or a healer wanted me to direct a piece on something she was concerned about. For reasons of confidentiality, I cannot say more about this, except that as the director I relied on a combination of what I had learned in psychodrama, on my past experience on the stage, and my intuition. At times I felt at a loss, but in the sharing part of the session, I heard that the production did create something of value for the protagonist and the role-players. Their experience of the piece revealed to me a level of connection in the group that I had not been aware of.

In my subsequent work as an analyst, I have not consciously used Moreno's thinking. However, writing this essay has shown me the way psychodrama did indeed put me in touch with my creativity: during the course I learned how to use a very particular level of self-awareness with empathic attention to another's internal world – the essential ingredient for the formation of the therapeutic vessel where psychological transformation becomes possible. In order to be able to receive what was on offer in this learning process, I had to go back to the place in myself where some prior learning was stored. The experiences in meditation, the *I Ching*, Tai Chi, the studies in esoteric psychology, all became components of the new skill I was learning. But the link did not stop there. I needed to go all the way back to the curious child gazing at the moss and bricks on the church garden wall, waiting for their truth to be unveiled. This was the source from which I drew the inspiration for what was in store next. I needed to learn a new language and find a way to transfer the skills I acquired in the schools of spiritual development into the field of psychology. Although for some time I continued to imagine myself to be on the margins of the group, unbeknownst to my conscious ego, I had been in training. The vicissitudes of the interior of the psyche, the interplay of archetypal forces and figures, they were all present on the psychodrama stage, and the fact of their existence entered my experience during the course.

Towards the end of the following year, I left psychodrama to begin preparations for Jungian analytic training. Grounded in the therapeutic stance that was formed in me in psychodrama, I was able to translate many of the notions I had learned there into the language of analytical psychology. I left psychodrama when the group reached the stage leading to qualification, and a deeper commitment needed to be made. The question of whether or not I wanted a different or an additional profession came up again, and I remembered my conversation with Craig. I realized that among all the options that chance and circumstances had laid out in front of me, this one resonated most deeply. By that time, Craig had left the group to prepare for his final exams in Zurich. I telephoned him, and, as a result of our conversation, I was soon in Jungian analysis. From then on the doors towards Jungian training began to open. Once again, the interconnectedness of all the elements involved generated a sense of meaning and purpose, and, so equipped, I entered a new phase in life. Craig and I had no further contact with each other for almost two decades.

There's a surprise at the end. Everything should connect to everything.

(Okri, 2012, p. 51)

I saw Craig again in 2010, this time in Montreal, at the XVIII Congress of the International Association for Analytical Psychology (IAAP). He presented a paper on Jung and Moreno, which I made sure not to miss. That paper led to the creation of this book. The long cycle of events leading to this moment is closing, as a new one emerges.

In this essay, I set out to find a connection between Jung and Moreno in my own individuation. The sequence of events that had led to my discovery of their legacy and the effect of those discoveries on my subsequent choices reveal a direction – a process of accumulation of experiences that ferment in the unconscious until the right mixture of the internal and external conditions produces a moment of change. Jung has created a philosophical system that, like Moreno's theatre of spontaneity, can open the way into a psychic space where the encounter of ego and self can take place in a form observable to the ego and therefore in service to a particular stage in the goal of individuation. As Jung writes,

> Individuation appears on the one hand as a synthesis of a new unity which previously consisted of scattered particles, and on the other hand, as the revelation of something which existed before the ego and is in fact its father or creator and also its totality.
>
> (Jung 1942/1954, quoted in Clark 2006 p. 81)

> However, the goal of individuation . . . is important only as an idea; the essential thing is the *opus* which leads to the goal: *that* is the goal of a lifetime. In its attainment "left and right" are united and conscious and unconscious work in harmony.
>
> (Jung 1946, p. 200; original italics)

This narrative suggests the presence in childhood of the intimations of the enfolding goal of individuation from the timeless zone of the Self. In my clinical work, I strive to hear that voice in the context of my patients' own unique paths. The pointers on the winding road that has brought me to this moment were already present in my childhood fascination with nature and culture coexisting in the bricks and moss of the church garden wall; in the later thirst for knowledge beyond my conventional education; in the resolve to follow the direction that emerged from what I was learning and feeling: to leave the fold of my country of birth and make my home in a foreign land. Jung's model of the psyche, as I understand it, provides a theoretical framework that encompasses all levels of my experience. Psychodrama created an empirical vessel where the different strands of my past experiences could come together, ferment, cook and in time produce a new pointer on my path. What at the time seemed like chance turned out to have been meaningful events within 'a system of cooperation where things are both themselves and symbols, and correspondences' (Okri; 2012, p. 51).

Epilogue

As I was writing the closing paragraphs of this essay, I unexpectedly received an invitation from 'The London Psychodrama Network' (whose existence I was unaware of) to join a session in a nearby venue. The theme was 'Mirroring in Life, Mirroring in Groups'. The director was the psychiatrist who had introduced me to psychodrama all those years ago. I confirmed my attendance straight away. This will be a new encounter with Moreno's life's work – my understanding of psychological processes now rooted in Jung's model. Will there be a connection? Moreno and Jung shared the belief in the validity of subjective reality and the importance of living one's truth. Moreno was critical of Jung's model of psychological growth as too intrapsychic. Perhaps he was not aware that Jung did acknowledge and wrote about the importance of relationships with others:

> Without the conscious acknowledgement and acceptance of our fel-lowship with those around us there can be no synthesis of personality. ... The inner consolidation of the individual ... emphatically includes our fellow man.
>
> (Jung 1946, p. 233)

In other words, an essential element of what makes up the path of individuation is the quality of one's relationships with others. According to Miller (2004), towards the end of his life Jung expanded his original understanding of the transcendent function to include the interpsychic sphere, stating that although the transcendent function results in psychic shifting, '. . . an alteration is possible only if the existence of the "other" is admitted' (Jung 1954, quoted in Miller 2004, p. 79). Or, as John Beebe puts it:

> The transcendent function is realized synchronistically when there is a shift away from a desire to know and control towards a desire to relate and understand.
>
> (Beebe 1993, p. 118)

In this view, the transcendent function becomes a space for and an instrument of mediation, not only between consciousness and the unconscious, but also between 'I' and 'other', 'me' and 'not-me' (Miller 2004, p. 80).

This was on my mind as the psychodrama session unfolded. There was a rhythm in the movements of the protagonists and role players in and out of their roles; in the role reversals and in the mirroring in pairs – 'the shuttling to and fro of arguments and affects' (Jung 1916/1957, p. 90). In the fluidity of the psychological phenomena oscillating between polarised states: conscious/unconscious, subjective/objective, personal/impersonal, inner/outer, differentiated/unified, separated/merged (Miller 2004, p. 112), I felt Jung and Moreno connecting in my experience of this new encounter with psychodrama. I promised to stay in touch with the group.

References

Barz, H. (1993) 'The Transcendent Function and Psychodrama', in *Proceedings of the XII Congress of the International Association for Analytical Psychology Chicago 1992*, Einsiedeln, Switzerland: Daimon Verlag.

Beebe, J. (1993) 'Response to "Another Degree of Complexity" by Aime Agnel' in *Proceedings of the XII Congress of the International Association for Analytical Psychology Chicago 1992*, Einsiedeln, Switzerland: Daimon Verlag.

Cambray, J. (2009) *Synchronicity; Nature & Psyche in an Interconnected Universe*, College Station, Texas: Texas A&M University Press.

Clark, M. (2006) *Understanding the Self-Ego Relationship in Clinical Practice: Towards Individuation*, London: Karnac Books.

Colman, W. (1999) 'Creation and Discovery: Finding and Making the Self', *Harvest*, 45 (1), pp. 52–69.

Jung, C. G. (1933) *Modern Man in Search of a Soul*, London: Routledge Classics/Kegan Paul, Trench, Trubner & Co, 2001.

Jung, C. G. (1942/1954) 'Transformation Symbolism in the Mass', in *Psychology and Religion: West and East, Collected Works 11*, London, Routledge & Kegan Paul, 1958, pp. 201–298.

Jung, C. G. (1946) 'Psychology of the Transference', in *The Practice of Psychotherapy, Collected Works 16*, London: Routledge, pp. 163–326.

Jung, C. G. (1953) *Two Essays on Analytical Psychology, Collected Works 7*, London: Routledge, 1966.

Jung, C. G. (1954) 'Letter to Père Lachat, March 27, 1954', in *The Symbolic Life, Collected Works 18*, Princeton: Princeton University Press, pp. 679–691.

Jung, C. G. (1956) *Symbols of Transformation, Collected Works 5*, Princeton: Princeton University Press, 1956.

Jung, C. G. (1916/1957) 'The Transcendent Function', in *The Structure and Dynamics of the Psyche, Collected Works 8*, Princeton, Princeton University Press, 1960, pp. 67–91.

Jung, C. G. (1963) *Memories, Dreams, Reflections*, London: Collins and Routledge & Kegan Paul, Fontana Press, 1995.

Jung, C. G. (1964) *Man and His Symbols*, London: Aldus Books Limited, 1969.

Jung, C. G. (2009) *The Red Book: Liber Novus*, London and New York: W. W. Norton & Company.

Khan, I. (1976) *The Palace of Mirrors*, Geneva: International Headquarters of the Sufi Movement.

Legge, J. (1899) *The I Ching*, New York: Dover Publications Inc., 1963.

Marineau, R. (1989) *Jacob Levy Moreno 1889–1974: Father of Psychodrama, Sociometry and Group Psychotherapy*, London: Routledge

Miller, J. C. (2004) *The Transcendent Function; Jung's Model of Psychological Growth through Dialogue with the Unconscious*, Albany, N.Y.: State University of New York Press.

Moreno, J. L. (1985) *The Autobiography of J. L. Moreno*, Boston: Moreno Archives, Harvard University.

Okri, B. (2012) 'Wild' in *Wild*, London: Rider for Ebury Publishing, Random House Group Company, 51.

Ovid, (2 A.D.) *Ars Amatoria*, Book III, Part IX, in *The Wordsworth Dictionary of Quotations*, Ware: Wordsworth Editions Limited, 1998.

Samuels, A., Shorter, B. and Plaut, F. (1986) *A Critical Dictionary of Jungian Analysis,* London and New York: Routledge & Kegan Paul.

Rupnik, V. and Nešić, B. (1972) *Olovka piše srcem (Pencil Writes with the Heart)*, Belgrade: Beogradski Izdavaćko-Grafićki Zavod.

Pavić, M. (1998) *A Short History of Belgrade*, Belgrade: Dereta.

Wilhelm, R. trans. (1931) *The Secret of the Golden Flower*, London: Routledge & Kegan Paul, Henley: Kegan Paul, Trench & Trubner, 1962/1979.

Wilhelm, R. trans. (1951) *The I Ching, or Book of Changes*, London: Routledge & Kegan Paul.

INDEX

group psychotherapy 5–6, 9, 18, 21, 22, 66, 148; Jung on 8, 83
Grüninger, J. 13

Hancox, J. 13
healing, performativity of 12
Hermes 78, 142
Hildegard von Bingen 77
Hill, J. 11, 101–113
Hillman, J. 98, 103, 137, 138
hole, working of, in psychodrama, clinical example 69–80
Hunt, H. T. 149
Huygens, C. 154
hysteria as theatricality without play (N. Micklem)13

I Ching 163, 171, 174
I–Thou relationship 23
Ibsen, H. 22
imagination, active, see active imagination
Immediate Theatre, based on spontaneity 166
Impromptu Theatre, New York 20, 166
individual psyche, self defined in terms of 7
individuation 45, 64, 83, 113, 165, 166, 169, 176; as co-creative relationship between ego and self 168; goal of 175; and groups 92 [move towards, in psychodrama 89]; Jung's concept of 83, 170, 175
infinite creativity 167
Inner Child 131
Inner Critic 131, 133
inner theatre: dream as 84–88; in Jungian setting 137
insight, moments of, in psychodrama 88
Institute for Psychodrama, Zumikon, Switzerland 9, 68, 69
institution(s), unconscious of 84
intellectual analysis, inadmissible in psychodrama 35
interactive field 142; concept of, in Jungian analysis 144
interpersonal psyche 143, 144
interpersonal relatedness, selfhood in 4
interpersonal relations, spontaneity and creativity in 148
interpsychic sphere, and transcendent function 176

intrapsychic model of self 14
intuition as mode of reflection 149
Irish National Theatre, Abbey Theatre, Dublin 18

Jung, C. G. (*passim*): active imagination, *see* active imagination; collective unconscious, concept of 7, 22, 69, 83, 142, 143, 144, 164; complex(es) [at centre of theory of 3; empirical investigations of 3; theory of 156]; on countertransference 140; creativity 168–169; cultural patterns of society 107; defining self in terms of individual psyche 7; depth psychology of 83; dream work of, vs. Moreno's 98; ego as complex 156; Eros principle 2; four psychological functions of 98; and Freud [break-up with 169; relationship of 1]; individuation 166; concept of 170; goal of 175; inner theatre 20; interest in Taoist thought 163; intrapsychic map of self 8; intrapsychic model of self 14; knowledge and understanding, distinction between 140; *mana*, concept of 88; and Moreno [differences in resolution of transference and countertransference 144; fundamental differences between 2; practices of psychotherapy of, as creatively oppositional 14]; mutual unconsciousness of analyst and patient 140; *Mysterium Coniunctionis* 72, 75, 142; non-reductive view of psychic processes 169; participation mystique 168–169; personifying, concept of 3, 4, 11, 14; psyche, model of 175; psychic problems of modernity 144; psychic transformation, stages in process of 141; psychopathology, models for 148; *religo* 142; synchronicity 168; transference, theoretical concepts of 12, 139; use of images from alchemy 141; word association experiments 147
Jung Institute (Zurich) 68, 81, 101; training at 69–70
Jungian analytical psychology 84
Jungian psychodrama 11, 25–42, 43–66, 68; and dream enactment 83–99; five 'media' in 25; intellectual